Schriften zum europäischen Management

Reihe Herausgegeben von
Roland Berger, München, Deutschland

Die Reihe wendet sich an Studenten sowie Praktiker und leistet wissenschaftliche Beiträge zur ökonomischen Forschung im europäischen Kontext.

This series is aimed at students and practitioners. It represents our academic contributions to economic research in a European context.

Weitere Bände in der Reihe http://www.springer.com/series/12472

Alexander Rhode

Public Procurement in the European Union

How Contracting Authorities Can Improve Their Procurement Performance in Tenders

Springer Gabler

Alexander Rhode
Berlin, Germany

Dissertation Universität Potsdam, 2019

Schriften zum europäischen Management
ISBN 978-3-658-28072-7 ISBN 978-3-658-28073-4 (eBook)
https://doi.org/10.1007/978-3-658-28073-4

Springer Gabler

This Springer Gabler imprint is published by the registered company Springer Fachmedien Wiesbaden GmbH part of Springer Nature.
The registered company address is: Abraham-Lincoln-Str. 46, 65189 Wiesbaden, Germany

Table of contents

Table of figures

Table of tables

1. Introduction

1.1 Scope of the present work

In the European Union (EU), public procurement is a substantial economic factor: Public procurement spending accounts for about 13% of the EU's overall GDP (European Commission, 2016).[1] In absolute terms, the European public expenditures on works, supplies, or services accounted for approximately € 2015.3 billion in 2015. Comparable to the levels of other OECD countries, EU governments spent, on average, about 30% of their total budget on public tenders (OECD, 2017). Global public procurement spending accounts for up to 20% of global GDP (World Bank Group, 2016). Public procurement is not only economically significant with respect to expenditures but also with respect to the income of potential suppliers. For example, government demand profoundly affects companies in the construction industry; in the defense industry, public authorities are typically the only available customers.

Due to its economic scale, public procurement spending significantly influences the financial stability of public budgets within the EU. Likewise, more cost-effective public procurement may increase welfare by easing fiscal consolidation and helping to maintain government service offerings (Thai, 2017b). In the wake of the European sovereign debt crisis of 2009, EU governments have faced increased pressure on their budgets. As a reaction to their tight budgetary situations and to cut their expenditures, most EU member states have implemented austerity measures, among other policies, by focusing on improving public procurement outcomes.

Due to these financial challenges, the public sector needs to increase its focus on its core areas of responsibility (Schedler & Proeller, 2011). The associated outsourcing and contracting out of public service tasks has

---

[1] This figure excludes spending in the utilities and defense sector by Contracting Authorities.

A. Rhode, *Public Procurement in the European Union*, Schriften zum europäischen Management, https://doi.org/10.1007/978-3-658-28073-4_1

further increased the need for successful performance management in public tenders. Coincidently, the attitudes of citizens toward the public sector have changed. Taxpayers increasingly think of themselves as the public sector's clients: They demand that public authorities manage their tax revenues carefully (Schapper, Malta, & Gilbert, 2006). Because public authorities spend a substantial portion of their budget on tenders, they ought to spend taxpayers' money frugally when sourcing from private-sector suppliers. Accordingly, procurement officials increasingly face legitimation pressure and demand for more economic efficiency – like the performance standards of the private sector.

As a reaction to the obligation to do more with less, EU regulators have implemented various reforms to enable higher public procurement performance. To counteract the absence of competitive market pressure in the public sector, the European Commission has released a set of Directives that strictly control and significantly standardize tenders across EU member states.[2] The Directives are primarily aimed toward increasing "the efficiency of public spending to ensure the best possible procurement outcomes in terms of value for money" (Dimitri, 2013). To achieve this goal, the Directives strongly emphasize the compliance, standardization, and predictability of tenders.

As a result, Contracting Authorities must comply with a detailed set of regulations that severely limit their discretion in designing and conducting tenders (Chong, Klien, & Saussier, 2016). Researchers and practitioners alike have criticized the Directives for having increased the rigidity on tenders (Coviello, Guglielmo, & Spagnolo, 2018). The Directives have transformed procurement regulation in the EU from a framework that gave the member states and Contracting Authorities significant degrees of freedom into a system of highly standardized rules (Arrowsmith, 2006).

Public procurement regulation faces the primary challenge of balancing the tension between allowing discretion to improve economic efficiency and maintaining control against mismanagement (McCue, Prier, & Swanson,

[2] The European Commission has at least partly achieved this goal of increased performance: Previous studies have estimated that the introduction of the Directives has led to a 2.5% to 10% increase in the monetary value of EU tenders between 1992 and 2003 (Molander, 2014).

2015). Typically, regulators pronounce the predictability of tenders to enforce the avoidance of collusion, favoritism, or corruption. Thereby, they make it impossible for Contracting Authorities to react to the heterogeneous requirements of their tenders flexibly.

The stronger emphasis on predictability and the imperative for legal compliance distinguishes public procurement from private-sector purchasing. These particularities (at least partly) explain why the acquisition prices that the Contracting Authorities achieve are inferior to those from private-sector organizations (Afonso, Schuknecht, & Tanzi, 2005). Whereas public procurement officials may sacrifice efficiency for the sake of regulatory compliance, their private-sector counterparts strive to lower their costs (Telgen, Harland, & Knight, 2007).[3] Due to omnipresent profitability pressures, private-sector purchasers naturally act in more strategic and market-oriented ways in comparison with Contracting Authorities. Thus, purchasers in the private sector have gained years of advanced experience in identifying, developing, and implementing performance-oriented measures.

Researchers have argued that Contracting Authorities should learn to apply the best practices from the private sector to improve the outcomes of their tenders (Tadelis, 2012). In the public sector, procurement officials use a specific set of regulated mechanisms to determine the tender results based on offers from potential suppliers. Designing these rules based on private-sector experiences might improve performance levels while still allowing compliance with the regulatory stipulations of the Directives. For example, Contracting Authorities may draw inspiration from the private sector to increase the simplicity, flexibility, and freedom of choice in tenders.[4] Both

---

[3] The "Public Procurement Guidance for Practitioners" published by the European Commission (2018) nicely exemplifies the risk-averse preferences in public procurement: This guide possesses the subtitle "on avoiding the most common errors in projects funded by the European Structural and Investment Funds." Its content mirrors this subtitle by focusing on legal and processual recommendations while remaining completely silent about any performance-oriented measures.

[4] The idea to adopt the best managerial practices from the private sector has gained long-term practical popularity in the public sector – also outside of tenders. The concept of New Public Management (NPM) popularized the idea to improve public-sector performance by applying private-sector insights (Christensen & Lægreid, 2002). In recent decades, inspired by NPM, EU governments have privatized parts of their services, adopted a

empirical research and practical examples have argued that the public sector can improve its efficiency by sensibly adopting practices from the private sector (Minchuk & Mizrahi, 2016). Prior studies have estimated that Contracting Authorities may achieve procurement cost savings of 15% to 20% by implementing the managerial best practices from the private sector (Eßig, 2013).

However, a successful transfer of the managerial best practices requires procurement officials to possess the necessary scope of action to implement them effectively. The regulatory restrictions set by the Directives may prevent Contracting Authorities from reverse-engineering performance-oriented measures from the private sector (McCue et al., 2015). In every tender stage, a wide range of regulations severely affect interactions with potential suppliers. As the most prominent example, the Directives strongly favor the use of auctioned procedures, even though private-sector purchasers regularly prefer negotiations over procurement auctions (Bajari, McMillan, & Tadelis, 2009).

Even if Contracting Authorities possess the scope of action needed to implement performance-oriented measures, such measures do not necessarily lead to the same outcomes as in the private sector. Despite the many commonalities within the roles, processes, obligation, requirements, and goals, management in public procurement profoundly differs from private purchasing in many dimensions (Murray, 1999). The Directives' general principles of non-discrimination, transparency, and equal treatment restrict the extent to which procurement officials can engage with potential suppliers. Thereby, regulations do not only restrict buyers' scope of actions but also any buyer-supplier relationships (Wang & Bunn, 2004). In public tenders, the interaction between parties focusses on the price and the submission of offers. Typically, the procurement officials cannot enter private talks with suppliers to explore options for mutual benefits. In private purchasing, buyers and suppliers meet face-to-face and exchange information verbally. But at the other side of the information-richness spectrum, parties impersonally exchange written messages within public procurement. Because the human factor plays only a minor role in tenders, the perceptions of

---

more client-oriented approach, began to measure their efficiency, and changed their personnel incentive structure (Schedler & Proeller, 2011).

satisfaction, fairness, and ethics likely may become much less relevant within the buyer-supplier relationship.

These behavioral, informational, and structural particularities of public procurement bear the risk that private-sector best practices might backfire for Contracting Authorities. Suppliers might react differently to the same performance-oriented measures – in particular, when they aim to affect interpersonal processes or buyer-supplier relationships.

1.2 Research questions

In conducting the present research, we acknowledge that both the application and the impact of performance-oriented measures heavily depend on the particularities of public procurement. Hence, we have chosen a multistage research approach to adjust for this critical codependence: By answering various interrelated and cumulative research questions, we aim to explain how Contracting Authorities can improve their procurement performance in public tenders.

1. Research question: What scope of action do Contracting Authorities have in the design of tenders?

From a Contracting Authority's perspective, performance management primarily concerns increased efficiency, or synonymously: better value for money (Schapper et al., 2006). Efficiency describes the relation between inputs and outputs. In performance management, the balance within this relation gives rise to the question of whether an organization does things in the right way. To assess managerial discretion in tenders, we must first define the actual scope of actions of Contracting Authorities (i.e., identify the things to do). The present work employs a standard processual procurement model discussed, among others, by Van Weele and Eßig (2017) to identify in a step-by-step manner the tender design options provided by the Directives. This identification allows us to locate and detail the performance-oriented measures for Contracting Authorities (i.e., define the right way to do things).

2. Research question: Given their scope of action, how can Contracting Authorities improve their procurement performance in tenders?

Because previous studies have thus far failed to holistically investigate how Contracting Authorities can improve their procurement performance in tenders, the present work considers findings of adjacent research fields to provide insights for identifying performance-oriented measures. Particularly within the sphere of negotiations, past academic research has identified a plethora of performance-boosting measures (Malhotra & Bazerman, 2008). We supplemented these findings with further insights from research on purchasing, demand auctions, housing transactions, and (whenever possible) public procurement. We combined these insights to establish several working hypotheses on how Contracting Authorities can improve their performance in tenders.

3. Research question: How have empirical studies focused on public tenders evaluated the impact of the identified measures on procurement performance?

As previously argued, the findings from adjacent research areas can merely provide ideas about how to develop measures that will allow Contracting Authorities to boost their performance. The manifold behavioral, informational, and structural particularities of public procurement entail the risk that a direct and straightforward transfer of insights from other kinds of economic transactions might backfire. Therefore, we turn to the existing scattered empirical studies on public tenders that may have reported supporting evidence for the previously proposed working hypotheses.

At this point in the present work, we will carefully assess whether the previous empirical evidence is sufficient to provide procurement officials with research-based recommendations about how to use their scope of actions to influence tender outcomes positively. Figure 1 summarizes the research design and results of the present work concerning the first three research questions. It shows that previous empirical studies have supported most of the working hypotheses. However, Figure 1 demonstrates that past empirical research did not provide sufficient insight to reliably assess the performance impact of the release (of different kinds) of starting prices in public tenders.

Figure 1: Identified scope of action and working hypotheses in the different tender phases

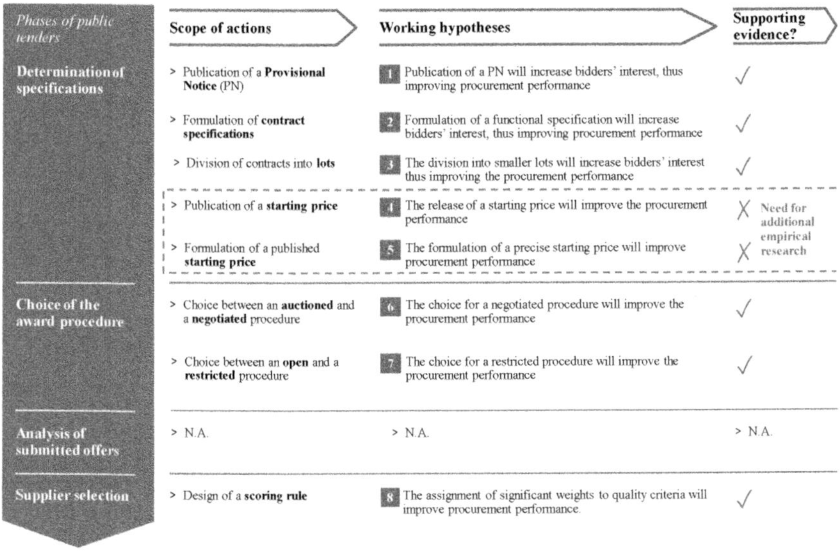

Source: Own illustration

The identified research gaps come as a surprise because first-movers in private purchasing regularly employ starting prices in order to anchor potential suppliers and influence outcomes (Voeth & Herbst, 2015).[5] Previous research has continuously implied that buyers can gain a first-mover advantage by formulating starting prices (Galinsky & Mussweiler, 2001). In public procurement, Contracting Authorities always act as first movers and can thus decide whether to release or conceal a starting price. The Directives allow but do not require the publication of the starting price at the beginning of a tender. Because procurement officials must estimate the contract costs before the tender begins, publishing this estimate as a

[5] The term "first offer" might be more common than "starting price" in the sphere of private purchasing where parties typically settle acquisitions via negotiations. However, to avoid confusion, the present work will use the term "starting prices" to refer to all reference prices supplied by first movers at the beginning of acquisitions. Past studies have demonstrated that different kinds of starting prices cause anchoring effects (that are similar to first offers in negotiations) in several economic transactions (Bucchianeri & Minson, 2013; Lucking-Reiley, Bryan, Prasad, & Reeves, 2007; Northcraft & Neale, 1987).

starting price would not result in additional transaction costs. Because a first-mover advantage (like in negotiations) can arise in tenders, it is a mystery why Contracting Authorities would decide not to release a starting price. This apparent research gap provided us with the opportunity to formulate two additional research questions as a basis for our empirical investigation.

To answer the research questions, we used data on actual public tenders published by the European Commission (EC). The data set consisted of standard forms filled out by Contracting Authorities in the EU. The Directives demand that Contracting Authorities publish both the announcement (Contract Notices) and the results (Contract Award Notices) of tenders in the Official Journal of the EU (OJEU). To empirically investigate the following research questions, we extracted the published standard public procurement forms from the OJEU. In sum, we compiled a data set of more than 20,000 tenders conducted from 2012 to 2015.

4. Research question: Can Contracting Authorities improve their procurement performance by publishing a starting price at the beginning of a tender?

We investigated the Contracting Authorities' decision to disclose a starting price and its impact on procurement performance. Although the Directives require Contracting Authorities to assess the value of contracts before the tender starts, many transactions (about 30% in the final data set) concealed their starting prices. Because this nondisclosure (which might forgo exploiting a potential first-mover advantage) was puzzling, we aimed to examine the determinants of the releasing or concealing of a starting price. We speculated that starting prices in public procurement might not always yield a first-mover advantage but could backfire by lowering the number of submitted offers and preventing lower than expected bids.

5. Research question: How should Contracting Authorities formulate a starting price at the beginning of a tender to improve their procurement performance?

We ascertained that not only can Contracting Authorities decide whether to publish a starting price, but they also have the first-mover freedom to define its numerical form and its precision. The Directives allow procurement officials to choose between starting price points and starting price ranges. If procurement officials opt for a starting price point, they can freely define their precision. For example, a Contracting Authority can call for a tender by estimating the monetary value of a contract at "1,000,000 EUR" (a round starting price point), "999,999 EUR" (a precise starting price point), or "900,000 EUR to 1,100,000 EUR" (a starting price range). Inspired by somewhat contradictory insights of past anchoring studies on the performance advantages of using precise starting price points (Loschelder, Stuppi, & Trötschel, 2014), imprecise starting price points (Lee, Loschelder, Schweinsberg, Mason, & Galinsky, 2018; Loschelder, Friese, Schaerer, & Galinsky, 2016), and starting price ranges (Ames & Mason, 2015), we hypothesized that the different kinds of starting prices would influence procurement performance in tenders. The different kinds of starting prices may impact tender results by distinctively influencing the cognitive decision-making processes of bidders, even though from a strictly rational point of view, they provide almost the same information.

Figure 2 details the 4th and 5th research questions and summarizes the investigation of the identified research gaps. The figure covers the research hypotheses that we derived from said research gaps and briefly outlines the results of the econometric investigations that were based on the tender transaction data.

Figure 2: The present work's empirical investigations

		Research gap	Research hypotheses	Empirical results
Publication of a starting price	1	Why are some Contracting Authorities **more likely than others** to **release starting prices**?	Buyer, market, and contract **conditions** affect the **likelihood of starting price** disclosure	**Starting price release** depended on procurement officials' levels of **professionalism** and **market norms**
	2	Why do **not all auctions release starting prices** given their potential positive impact on outcomes?	The **release** of starting prices improves **procurement performance**	The release of starting prices correlated with **higher performance levels** and did not truncate bids
	3	Does the **performance impact** of a starting price arise independent of **anchor-disconfirming evidence**?	Salience of **similar contracts** procured at different prices decreases the **potency of starting prices**	Increased **price heterogeneity** of similar contracts significantly **decreased the performance impact**
	4	Do starting prices create **barriers to entry** for potential suppliers?	The **release** of starting prices lowers the **number of bids** that are submitted	Starting prices **increased bidders' interest** by **lowering information asymmetries**
Formulation of a published starting price	1	How does the **precision of a starting price** affect procurement performance?	Increased **precision** of starting point prices improves **procurement performance**	Higher **precision increased the potency** of starting point prices
	2	Do **overly precise** starting prices backfire by signaling of **low** procurement officials' **competence?**	The **relation** between starting price precision and performance is **inverse U-shape**	Increased **precision linearly correlated** with **better performance** levels
	3	Does increased starting price **precision backfire** by signaling higher procurement officials' inflexibility ?	**Increased precision** reduces the number of **submitted offers** by signaling procurement officials' inflexibility	Precise starting prices **attracted more bidders** as their increased credibility **lowered entry risks**
	4	Do **starting price ranges** yield informational and relational **benefits** that improve performance?	**Starting price ranges** improve **procurement performance** by being less aggressive and inducing politeness	Starting price ranges did **not shape suppliers' beliefs** about possible outcomes and did **not induce politeness** in the form of lower bids

Source: Own illustration

1.3 Scientific approach and empirical methods

When discussing scientific approaches, researchers usually distinguish between the inductive and deductive approaches (Keuth, 2013). In the inductive approach, researchers develop general propositions, theories, or hypotheses based on observations. Due to the ever-limited number of observations, researchers can formulate only probability statements regarding the validity of their discoveries. By contrast, the falsifying approach leads researchers to draw logical conclusions based on existing theories. They examine such conclusions by applying empirical methods. Thus, their results show whether the examined theory remains valid. However, a theory always holds only preliminary validity. If researchers falsify a theory, it loses its universality. A falsifiable conclusion can never be correct with absolute certainty but only for the time being. Researchers may classify a theory as the best currently available theory if it is based on empirical findings from previous studies on similar matters (Chalmers & Bergemann, 2007).

The present work attempts to live up to the claim made by Chalmers and Bergemann (2007). Our aim was to consider all theoretical and empirical work relevant to the research questions defined above. All these research questions refer to the overarching research objective of the present work: How can Contracting Authorities improve their performance in tenders? Therefore, we aimed to identify and analyze their scope of actions and the existing managerial measures that will allow Contracting Authorities to achieve higher performance levels. Consequently, with the present work, we concentrated on the standard business administration objective of optimizing outcomes. We formulated the (working) hypotheses from the perspective of the procurement officials who manage the tender processes in Contracting Authorities.

As a result, with the present work, we primarily derived practical recommendations instead of developing a theoretical model that holds general validity. Consequently, the present work corresponds to the application-oriented nature of business administration research (Berndt & Fantapié Altobelli, 1998). Because procurement officials (responsible for awarding contracts) can use the recommendations when carrying out actual tenders, we aimed to fulfill the objective of business research to yield insights that enjoy relevance for managerial decision-making in practice.

However, the theoretical foundations of the present work did not rely on economic models developed in business administration research. Instead, we combined insights from different research streams such as economics, psychology, game theory, as well as behavioral and linguistic sciences. A significant part of the present work relied on the assumption of a rationally acting homo economicus. We will mainly refer to this assumption when developing the working hypotheses regarding the impact of performance-oriented measures. Particularly in the (later) empirical parts of this paper, however, we regularly used sociopsychological models as a supplement to classical economic theory (e.g., when examining the effects of starting prices in tenders).[6]

---

[6] A central assumption of classical auction research best exemplifies the need to include noneconomic considerations: As its name suggests, the Revenue Equivalence Theorem

Hence, we assume that rationality governs the informational exchange and social interaction between Contracting Authorities and potential suppliers in tenders. However, rationality fails to capture all phenomena that might arise in public procurement entirely. Instead, bounded rationality causes systematic deviations from rational behavior. To capture these deviations, we integrated behavioral models to explain the observed decision patterns that may deviate from predictions of classical economic theory. In summary, in the present work, we relied on both classical economic and behavioral models to answer our application-oriented research questions. Given that earlier empirical studies on public procurement have overlooked mainly how procurement officials can improve procurement performance in tenders, the interdisciplinary scientific approach of the present work seemed appropriate for analyzing how procurement officials' managerial decisions may improve tender outcomes.

The present work was aimed at fulfilling the structural and procedural requirements of a deductive research approach to develop research-based recommendations that procurement officials can use for performance management in practice. Figure 3 outlines the distinct stages of this scientific approach.

(RET) implies that all standard auction designs lead to identical results (Krishna, 2010). If the various assumptions of the RET were to apply to tenders in practice, the relevance of the present work's research questions would significantly decrease. Because regulation typically demands that buyers conduct public tenders as procurement auctions, the RET would imply that the design choices of procurement officials may only marginally influence outcomes. However, the behavior of real human beings in actual auctions typically refutes the assumptions of the RET (Hossain & Morgan, 2005). Past research has accordingly implied that different tender designs are correlated with different performance levels (Tadelis, 2012).

Figure 3: The present work's scientific approach

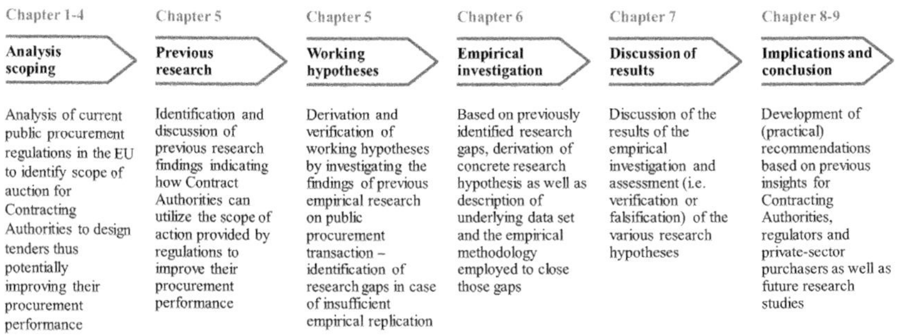

Source: Own illustration

1.4 Structure of the present work

In structuring the present work, we followed the scientific approach discussed above. Thus, we relied on an archetypical deductive research design consisting of hypothesis generation, hypothesis review, and discussion of results, which we supplemented by deriving comprehensive recommendations for practitioners.

As shown in Figure 3, we began by scoping the scientific analyses. The first chapter is introductory in nature—in it, we present the research questions, describe the scientific approach, and define the structure of the present work.

The second chapter describes and analyzes the foundation of public procurement in the EU. It thereby provides a frame of reference for the subsequent generation of hypotheses. First, the chapter establishes the general nomenclature by defining the key terms used in public tenders. Second, it identifies the scope of public procurement by comparing public procurement to private-sector purchasing. Finally, the chapter introduces EU regulation and the managerial demands for Contract Authorities to deepen their understanding of the particularities of public procurement.

Based on such particularities, the third chapter discusses performance management in tenders. It begins by identifying the goals of Contracting Authorities. It discusses the managerial goal of increasing procurement performance in tenders. Because Contracting Authorities must cope with different objectives and potentially the conflicting interests of stakeholders, performance in public procurement is less clear-cut and straightforward than in private-sector purchasing.

The fourth chapter focuses on the role of Contracting Authorities, given the previously discussed public procurement particularities and the definition of performance in tenders. The chapter aims to answer the question of how Contracting Authorities in the EU can pursue their performance objectives within the given regulatory framework conditions. We investigate the regulatory consequences of the Directives to identify the scope of actions that Contracting Authorities may exploit to improve their performance levels. In other words, we exclude all the tender design elements where strict regulations do not provide Contracting Authorities with any managerial discretion. To achieve this goal, we analyze the tender process in three consecutive stages. First, we describe the general course of action. Second, we examine the applicable regulations within the Directives. Third, we identify which scope of actions (i.e., tender design options) procurement officials possess despite (or because of) these regulations.

Based on the identified scope of actions, the fifth chapter discusses the performance-oriented measures that Contracting Authorities may employ in tenders. In order to comply with the notions of the deductive approach, we developed empirically falsifiable or verifiable working hypotheses on the basis of existing theoretical research (Chalmers & Bergemann, 2007). To test these hypotheses, we aimed to include all relevant findings of the scattered empirical studies on public tenders. The research questions require an empirical investigation because the particularities of public procurement may profoundly moderate the impact of any performance-oriented measures. When we did not find enough empirical evidence to support the working hypotheses, we drew on the thus identified research gaps as a basis for the empirical investigation.

We present this empirical investigation in the sixth chapter. In the beginning, we briefly summarize the gathered insights and the identified research gaps to derive concrete research hypotheses. These research hypotheses provide the foundation for the empirical investigation. To validate them, we employed a comprehensive data set of actual tenders conducted in the EU that we describe in the subsequent section. Besides describing the chosen approach to select, clean, and prepare the data set, this section discusses the methodology of the applied econometric models and contains their empirical results.

The detailed discussion and evaluation of the empirical results take place in the following Chapter 7, which consists of two distinct sections. On the one hand, the chapter examines the relation between the publication of a starting price and procurement outcomes. On the other hand, the chapter investigates how procurement officials should formulate published starting prices to increase their performance.

Based on the results from the previous chapters, the 8th chapter develops practical recommendations. The chapter begins with the development of a practice-oriented classification for the different kinds of public tenders to provide concrete managerial recommendations. Next, we discuss the applicability of the developed performance-oriented measures in accordance with this classification. The chapter provides procurement officials with a guide that offers a set of recommended measures for each kind of tender. The chapter complements these managerial recommendations by discussing further implications for public procurement regulators and private-sector purchasers.

The concluding Chapter 9 summarizes the answers that the present work provided for the initially formulated research questions. Based on this summary, we assess the scientific contributions of the present work and outline the perspectives for further empirical studies in the hitherto sparsely researched field of public procurement

2. Tenders in the EU

2.1 Definitions

2.1.1 Public procurement

Previous literature has often used the terms procurement and purchasing interchangeably (Caldwell & Bakker, 2008). However, in the present work, we employ more practice-oriented definitions: Procurement refers to acquisitions within the public sector, whereas purchasing applies to the private sector. Prior studies have typically followed the same approach by denoting purchasing as the process of acquisition in the private sector and procurement as a term for government acquisitions (Arlbjørn & Freytag, 2012).

Public procurement refers to when public sector organizations purchase works, supplies, or services (Uyarra & Flanagan, 2010). Public sector organizations require specific items to fulfill their political, economic, and social tasks. They can meet the demands for these items in three different ways. First, they can try to produce the required works, supplies, or services themselves. Second, they can try to implement the means of expropriation (i.e., transfer the ownership of the demanded item based on their sovereign powers). Third, they can engage in public procurement as the most frequent option. In this case, the public sector satisfies its demand in an economic transaction with external suppliers utilizing private-law contracts.

The present work defines public procurement as the sum of all the private-law economic transactions in which a public-sector organization engages in the acquisition of items to fulfill its consumption needs. Because public authorities usually engage in public procurement whenever they cannot provide the necessary items themselves, they source a diverse variety of works, supplies, or services (Erridge & McIlroy, 2002): The spectrum ranges from essential supplies such as stationery to complex construction

A. Rhode, *Public Procurement in the European Union*, Schriften zum europäischen Management, https://doi.org/10.1007/978-3-658-28073-4_2

works such as airports. The diversity within public procurement reflects the heterogeneity of public tasks that include areas such as education, culture, media, science, health, sport, and social affairs, as well as financial, judicial, police, and military services (Eßig, 2013).

2.1.2 Tenders

Tenders act as the standard public procurement vehicle (Saussier & Tirole, 2015). Tenders are economic transactions in which a public-sector organization aims to award a contract to the best potential supplier. In most cases, tenders follow a non-negotiable selection process based on a set of specific award criteria known to all suppliers. In such open procedures, all potential suppliers can submit offers.

Prior research has often defined open procedures as first-price procurement auctions in which suppliers submit a single bid. The lowest bid always wins, and the auctioneer pays the price of the lowest bid (Bajari et al., 2009; Hong & Shum, 2002).[7] Such a definition only applies if procurement officials award the contract to the lowest bidder and when no further price negotiations take place. However, since the 2014 reform, procurement regulation within the EU has required awarding the contract to the most economically advantageous offer, considering criteria other than price. Under these conditions, a tender does not represent a first-price procurement auction but a scoring auction (Asker & Cantillon, 2008). Sometimes, the regulation allows for further negotiations with suitable bidders after the end of an auctioned procedure. This also contradicts the first-price principle.

However, the current versions of the Directives still define the open procedures as the standard mechanism. Procurement officials can use negotiations only under specific circumstances defined by the Directives. Thus, when not explicitly stated otherwise, the present work assumes that procurement officials conduct a tender as a procurement auction.

[7] This operationalization differs from most private-sector procurement auctions in which sellers can usually submit multiple bids in a real-time environment with at least some degree of visibility among suppliers (Carter et al., 2004).

2.1.3 *Procurement auction*

A procurement auction acts as an allocation mechanism for a single buyer of a specific item facing a group of potential suppliers; the buyer uses a specific set of rules to determine purchasing outcomes on the basis of bids by potential suppliers (McAfee & McMillan, 1987). Goldberg (1977) interpreted procurement auctions as both a substitute and a complement for price negotiations. In principle, procurement auctions are a specific form of a price negotiation: Buyers and potential suppliers come together to find a joint agreement on the purchasing terms for works, supplies, or services. Compared with the price negotiations, where parties meet in separate and successive negotiations, potential suppliers submit their bids simultaneously in procurement auctions.

Procurement auctions may possess two significant advantages (Carter et al., 2004). First, they help to enforce favorable final prices as they increase the competition among buyers. Second, due to the shortened lead times, buyers can handle more procurement processes or use the time gained for other activities such as searching for new suppliers or more intensive negotiations in other areas. However, the second advantage only applies to private-sector procurement auctions that usually run for only a short period. In EU public procurement, the regulation demands that tenders possess more extended deadlines (usually several weeks).

Most previous research has used the term auction to describe both demand auctions and procurement auctions. From an economic point of view, sellers employ demand auctions as an allocation mechanism when they face a group of potential buyers – corresponding to a monopoly situation. In the reverse case of a monopsony, a buyer who is interested in a specific item faces a group of potential suppliers in a procurement auction (McAfee & McMillan, 1987). Conversely to a demand auction, the auctioneer aims to minimize the price in a procurement auction. In a demand auction, the auctioned item usually initially physically exists, and the auctioneer can describe it in detail. In procurement auctions, the winning supplier still must produce or render the auctioned item. Therefore, the auctioneers must define the item as precisely as possible through rather abstract contract specifications.[8]

Figure 4 identifies the different kinds of procurement auctions along two dimensions (the number of bids per suppliers and the degree of visibility between suppliers). Under the regime of the Directives, suppliers can only submit a single offer and do not know the offers that the other suppliers are making. Hence, the present work will refer to sealed-bid procurement auctions when talking about tenders if not explicitly stated otherwise.

Figure 4: Different kinds of procurement auctions

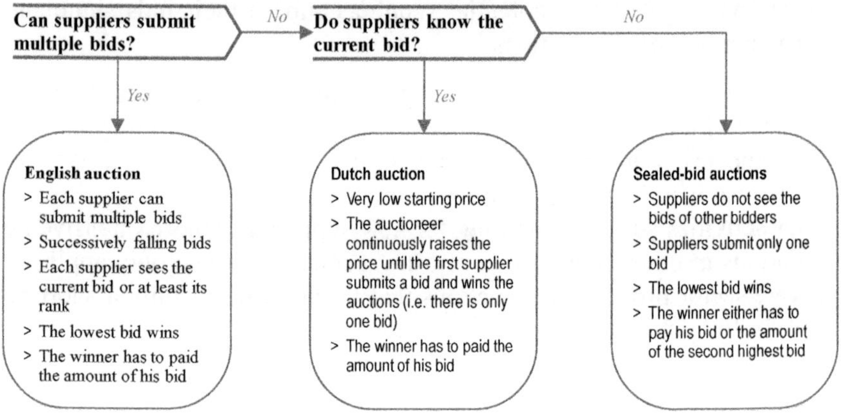

Source: Own illustration based on Engelbrecht-Wiggans, Shubik, and Stark (1983)

2.1.4 Private purchasing

We define private purchasing as an activity that provides a private-sector organization with the services, supplies, and works with the services, supplies, and works it needs to perform its (economic or social) tasks but cannot produce itself (van Weele, 2014). Therefore, managers in purchasing

[8] For reasons of simplification, most previous literature has focused on demand auctions. Authors have usually argued that a monopsony is essentially the same as a monopoly apart from the reversal of the signs of the variables (Carter et al., 2004). Whereas this assumption holds in most cases, the present work argues that, due to relational and informational particularities, one cannot transfer performance-oriented measures from demand to procurement auctions by merely adjusting the signs of the corresponding variables.

aim to source the necessary external resources under the most favorable conditions to allow their organization to improve or maintain its performance: Purchasing is a managerial task that not only has a strategic character but also contributes to the performance of the overall organization.

2.1.5 *Procurement performance*

In accordance with Section 3.2, we define performance as the efficiency goal to ensure the best value for money in a tender. However, to avoid redundancies, Chapter 3 will discuss discusses the nature of performance in public procurement in more detail. The same applies to the term performance management, which we will define based on the notions of New Public Management.

2.1.6 *Procurement regulation*

Prior studies have reported several similarities between public procurement and private purchasing as well as numerous features that differentiate the two sectors Murray (1999). Most importantly, differences exist in legislation, regulation, and compliance. Inspired by (McCue et al., 2015), we define procurement regulation as governments' control systems and accountability standards that are aimed at ensuring a necessary degree of oversight in the procurement process.

Procurement regulations represent the corresponding and fundamental legal guidelines that public authorities must obey when carrying out their tenders. Procurement regulation needs to allow Contracting Authorities to acquire the items required to achieve their organizational goals while preventing procurement officials from wasting taxpayers' money (Gragan, 2005). Likewise, regulation faces an inherent tradeoff between the economic efficiency of tenders and the need to maintain control over fraud and mismanagement (Schwartz, 2010).

2.1.7 *EU Directives*

In the EU, the Directives act as the primary system of the rules that regulate tenders. European procurement regulation contains both (a) general clauses that describe, for example, its general legal principles and (b) a plethora of specific rules (Bovis, 2012). Hence, depending on the type of Contracting

Authorities, procured contract, employed procedure, and contract values, a diverse set of procurement regulations apply:

> Directive 2004/18/EC and its successor Directive 2014/24/EU apply to Contracting Authorities defined as classical public administrations: Government agencies (at all levels of government), regional or local authorities, and bodies of public law (e.g., university clinics, educational institutions, and law enforcement agencies).
> By contrast, Directive 2004/17/EC and its successor Directive 2014/25/EU apply to public utilities (active in water supply, sanitation, energy supply, public transport, postal services, airports, seaports, inland ports, and other maritime, land, or air transport facilities).

Because organizations in the utility sector often face higher market pressure and (private sector) competition, the latter Directives allow for more flexibility. Because the demands for classical public administrations surpass those of public utilities, in the present work, we focus on procurement regulations for the first group of buyers. Thus, the term Directives in the present work refers to either Directive 2004/18/EC or Directive 2014/24/EU.[9] Section 2.3 will further discuss the differences between both Directives.[10]

2.1.8 Contracting Authorities

The Directives only apply to the so-called Contracting Authorities (Topp-Blatt, 2008). In tenders, organizations fall under the scope of the Directives only if they fit the legal definition of a Contracting Authority. Thus, the question of whether a buyer as a potential Contracting Authority has to comply with the Directives represents one of the most prominent issues of

---

[9] In the present work, we refer not only to the 2014 version of the Directives but also (whenever necessary) to the 2004 version. The empirical investigations of the present work employ field data from tenders conducted in the EU from 2012 to 2015. Because the member states could transpose the Directives into national regulations until 2016, Contracting Authorities conducted the tenders analyzed in the current empirical investigations under the regulatory umbrella of the Directives before the 2014 reform.

[10] An additional Directive "on the coordination of procedures for the award of certain works contracts, supply contracts, and service contracts by contracting authorities or entities in the fields of defense and security" covers defense contracts. However, the present work does not distinctively address this Directive because it follows the same principles as the other two while aiming to suit the specificities of defense contracts (Eßig, 2013).

public procurement law in the EU (Glas, 2012). In general, the term Contracting Authority refers to both public institutions and public utilities. However, the term public is not precise or free from overlaps.

Instead, the term may cover both purely governmental and administrative institutions and (partly or wholly private) enterprises that fulfill public tasks (e.g., road construction, inpatient healthcare). Therefore, regulators often draw the demarcation line based on whether a buyer carries out public tasks (i.e., followed to an institutional definition). However, within the EU, public tasks can vary from country to country and according to the administrative, legislative, or cultural background of a country (Eichhorn, 2001).

As a reaction, the EU Directives follow the definition of a functional Contracting Authority (Janssen, 2014). The European Court of Justice defines an organization as a Contracting Authority if one of the following characteristics applies:

> Public law regulates their composition and tasks
> A public body appoints its members
> A government guarantees the financial obligations

Still, national regulations might still follow the institutional definition. Due to the dichotomous nature of EU regulations, this distinction matters: Only if the value of a contract exceeds the respective monetary thresholds, the functional definition concerns the Contracting Authority; otherwise, an institutional definition may apply. The present work focuses on tenders published in the Supplement to OJEU (and on TED, the online version of the Supplement to the OJEU). Independent of their monetary value (i.e., whether they do or do not exceed the respective thresholds), all tenders published on TED need to comply with the Directives. Hence, the functional definition of a Contracting Authority applies to all tenders as discussed in the following.

2.1.9 Contracts

Procurement regulation in the EU needs to cover a contract to become active (Eßig, 2013). In public tenders, contracts are written cash-settled agreements between at least one Contracting Authority and at least one supplier. This definition does not require a long and complicated document; instead, a simple order by e-mail or an accepted invoice is sufficient. Also, the contract regulates the actual transaction between the involved parties. The supplier delivers the specified works, supplies, or services for which the Contracting Authority compensates him or her. The payment does not necessarily have to happen in monetary terms; it can also consist of economic exchange (e.g., licensing). In general, three different types of contracts for supplies, works, and services exist.

- Supply contracts refer to the procurement of goods. The EU Directives define supplies as materials covering a wide range of goods: from computers and office furniture to helicopters and trucks. The Directives consider leasing to be a supply rather than a service. Therefore, the leasing of a fleet by a Contracting Authority constitutes a supply contract. Such supply contracts must include all services directly related to the purchase (e.g., installation services). The value of these services adds to the total monetary value of the underlying contract.
- A work contract contains the execution and the planning of specific activities carried out by an architect or engineer. Therefore, the work itself must fulfill an independent economic or technical function.
- Service contracts act as residuals in legal terms and include all contracts that are not classified as a supply or work. One must distinguish between A and B services (e.g., provision of accommodation in a hotel, eating in a restaurant, advice in a law firm). Whereas the EU Directives thoroughly cover A services, a simplified set of rules apply to B services. The regulation does not need to standardize the acquisition of B services because the cross-border provision of B services takes place to a lesser extent.

2.2 Particularities of public procurement

Academic research and teaching alike have for a long time treated public procurement as a pure subset of private-sector purchasing (Wang & Bunn, 2004). Hence, some researchers have argued that practices in public procurement and private purchasing significantly overlap (Kolchin, 1990). The assumed similarities might to some extent explain the relative scarcity of studies on public procurement: Researchers have for a long time failed to analyze the particularities of public procurement and to compare them with private purchasing (Larson, 2009).

However, some studies have tried to identify the particular conditions under which Contracting Authorities operate in public procurement (Murray, 1999; Thai, 2001). Such particularities likely influence the behavior of Contracting Authorities and suppliers at all stages of a tender (Hertwig, 2014). These particularities may also affect performance management for procurement officials. Before analyzing these particularities, we first look at the similarities of public procurement and private-sector purchasing because this analysis eases the later identification of differentiating points.

2.2.1 Commonalities between public procurement and private-sector purchasing

In general, procurement in the public sector and purchasing in the private sector share many commonalities (Johnson, Leenders, & McCue, 2003). First, buyers pass through similar core phases during the acquisition of works, supplies, or services (Caldwell & Bakker, 2008). For example, the acquisition process always begins with the demand for specific resources that the buyer cannot provide on its own. This demand establishes the basis for engaging in a relationship with the supplier. Second, buyers procure similar items (Tadelis, 2012). Around 80% of public procurement projects resemble those in private sector purchasing (Murray, 1999).

Third, Contracting Authorities and private-sector purchasers pursue similar economic goals (Caldwell & Bakker, 2008). Buyers in both sectors engage with potential suppliers to acquire the items needed to reach their organizational goals. Whereas Contracting Authorities face more diverse goals in the public sector, they also pursue cost-efficiency (typically expressed and operationalized in financial terms). As argued in Section 1.1, Contracting Authorities must increasingly care about the value for money of their award decisions as well. Responsible officials and managers in both sectors pursue efficiency either by procuring a given solution at the lowest costs (minimum principle) or by buying the best available solution within a given budget (maximum principle) (Manso & Nikas, 2015). Both will always prefer a better commercial offer to a worse one when awarding a supplier. Similarly, they share the same process-related interests: Buyers in both sectors want to minimize the transaction costs that arise during the acquisition process (Telgen et al., 2007).

2.2.2 *Differences between public procurement and private purchasing*

Regulation differentiates public procurement from private purchasing (Thai, 2008). In principle, regulation reacts to many of the managerial, transactional, and processual particularities of public procurement. Regulation is aimed at supporting taxpayers' interest in the efficient, effective, and sustainable provision of public services. Regulators intend to enforce managerial discipline by increasing the predictability of tenders to counteract abuse, corruption, and general waste (Chong et al., 2016). Thereby, they want to ensure at least a certain level of efficiency: an economic, equitable, and comprehensible spending of public funds.

In both sectors, procurement goals heavily depend on overarching organizational interests. The goals of private-sector purchasers usually revolve around improving the company's profits (Larson, 2009; Murray, 1999). Thus, purchasers in the private sector predominantly strive for cost-efficiency. In public procurement, not only primary interests (e.g., achieving a certain level of performance) but also secondary interests (i.e., issues beyond the contract itself) can influence tenders (Eßig, 2013). Whereas the primary interests of the purchasing organization often overlap between the private and public sectors, secondary interests play a more significant role in public procurement. For example, Contracting Authorities may use tenders as a lever to implement government policy. If procurement officials are motivated to concentrate on secondary (social and political) interests, they might neglect the realization of primary (economic) interests.

Due to a lack of market discipline and a guarantee of steady tax income, procurement officials can, at least to some extent, neglect the efficiency of tenders to achieve the implementation of political goals (Erridge & McIlroy, 2002). In practice, Contracting Authorities may have access to nearly unlimited public funding sources. Thus, they can seek effectiveness rather than efficiency: In other words, they can aim at the best possible fulfillment of a public goal and care less about the resources they consume to fulfill that task. Likewise, public funds might allow Contracting Authorities to expand their efforts beyond socially optimum levels to maximize size, status, and influence.

The risk that Contracting Authorities will lose sight of cost-effectiveness requires processual regulation as a substitute for missing market pressures. In the EU, the Directives impose strict and substantial burdens on Contracting Authorities. Thereby, they increase the transaction costs for both buyers and suppliers (McCue et al., 2015).[11] Likewise, the Directives aim to control the incentives for corruption created by the interface of the public and private sectors (Coppier & Piga, 2006). Since the separation of ownership and control in tenders increases the risk of corruption, regulators have strongly emphasized predictability and transparency (Lundberg & Bergman, 2017).[12] They have deliberately sacrificed at least some procurement efficiency for the implementation of rules that catalyze routine tender actions.

The various scope and (sometimes) exceptionally high value of contracts provide another distinctive feature of public procurement (Erridge, 2007). Exceptional or unique quantity and quality requirements may characterize tenders. In such cases, no existing markets can meet acquisition demands by failing to provide a comparable price or a group of potential suppliers. Due to such an inadequate market overview, Contracting Authorities may struggle to tender a contract in a cost-effective way. Thus, Directives enforce award procedures that help to obtain an overview of the market to select the best available supplier.

2.3 Procurement law

In the EU, politicians and regulators have responded to the particularities of public procurement by installing an extensive and detailed regulatory

---

[11] The Directives are also aimed at ensuring fairness in public tenders: Without restrictive rules, suppliers could not interact at eye level with Contracting Authorities that possess more favorable financing options and can hardly go bankrupt. Moreover, regulating fairness includes placing limitations on political influence that may interfere in tenders (Murray, 2009).

[12] By contrast, the increased predictability of tenders might enable collusion (Dini, Pacini, & Valletti, 2006). Likewise, transparent processes may make cartels more sustainable. Standardized and published rules may allow for the prediction of a tender outcome, thus enabling a cartel to observe its members' actions and punish deviating behavior.

system. This system is designed to allow procurement officials to perform the juggling act of satisfying different interests at the same time. The regulatory framework in the EU comprises primary rules contained in the EC Treaty and secondary rules in the form of Directives adopted by the EU. The Treaty defines the general guidelines for the conduct of Contracting Authorities. It prohibits any form of discrimination (of suppliers) on the grounds of nationality (Article 12) and guarantees the free movement of goods (28), the freedom of establishment (Article 43), and the free movement of services (Article 49). By contrast, as a comprehensive control system, the Directives rely on a detailed set of rules to monitor the behavior of procurement officials in each stage of a tender.

2.3.1 Procurement regulation in the EU

2.3.1.1 Historical development

The regime of public procurement regulation in the EU is one of the oldest and most comprehensive trade regimes worldwide (Arrowsmith, 2008). The European Economic Community (the predecessor of the European Community) has regulated public procurement since the 1970s (Arlbjørn & Freytag, 2012). The European Community (the predecessor of the EU) adopted the first direct control Directives in 1989. In 1992, the Maastricht Treaty not only founded the EU but also established the basis for a unified procurement market. Since then, the degree of regulatory standardization across the EU has steadily increased (Arrowsmith, 2006). The Directives have significantly reduced the discretion of procurement officials and increased the comparability of tenders (Bergman & Lundberg, 2013).

In the 1990s, three different Directives covered the procedures for the awarding of public service contracts, public supply contracts, and public works contracts independently. The reform of 2004 replaced those Directives with two more pragmatic and coherent ones:

> Directive 2004/18/EC of the European Parliament and of the Council of 31 March 2004 on the coordination of procedures for the award of public works contracts, public supply contracts and public service contracts

> Directive 2004/17/EC of the European Parliament and of the Council of 31 March 2004 coordinating the procurement procedures of entities operating in the water, energy, transport and postal services sectors

Both Directives aimed to simplify public procurement: They increased the flexibility of procurement procedures to improve efficiency. To achieve this goal, both Directives have, among other things, created the opportunities to conclude longer-term framework contracts, to build central purchasing authorities, to conduct electronic tenders, and to conduct competitive dialogues.

In 2014, the EU adopted new Directives, which member states had to transpose into national law by 2016:

> Directive 2014/24/EU of the European Parliament and of the Council of 26 February 2014 on public procurement and repealing Directive 2004/18/EC

> Directive 2014/25/EU on procurement by entities operating in the water, energy, transport, and postal services sectors and repealing Directive 2004/17/EC

Primarily, the new Directives gave Contracting Authorities more flexibility in negotiating with suppliers during the selection phase. In addition to this fundamental reform regarding the award procedures (before the reform, the Directives placed substantial restrictions on negotiations), the new Directives brought about several procedural changes (Saussier & Tirole, 2015):

> Simplify procurement processes by reducing the administrative burden on Contracting Authorities: Member states must introduce e-notification and e-submission systems. Procurement officials should not require all participating tenderers, but only the winning supplier, to submit certain administrative documents.

> Mandatory inclusion of quality award criteria: Whereas the old Directives provided the choice between two award criteria (lowest price and MEAT), the new Directives force procurement officials to include quality criteria. They do not allow a contract to be awarded solely based on the lowest price.

> Ex-post contract adjustments: The new Directives describe situations in which parties may modify contract specifications after the tender. This extension authorizes previously prohibited renegotiations (previously, contractual changes always led to new tenders). After the reform, parties can now modify less than 10% (15%) of the original contract for supplies and services (works) without the need to retender. However, parties may only agree on non-substantial changes. Parties may also renegotiate a contract if unforeseen events occur or if they require additional services, while changing the supplier may result in significant disadvantages. The amendment must not change the general nature of the contract or increase the contract value by more than 50%.

> Encourage the participation of small and medium-sized enterprises (SMEs): In the past, strict requirements and administrative burdens have limited their participation. The new Directives make it easier to divide contracts into smaller lots and reduce the requirements for participation.

> Newly introduced structured innovation partnerships: Within the framework of partnerships, customers can develop new works, supplies, or services along with suppliers. Besides, the Directives have simplified the competitive dialogue as a procurement procedure to facilitate the awarding of complex projects and projects that are challenging to define.

> New life-cycle cost approach: This should encourage procurement officials to consider the full cost of their purchases to improve the competitiveness of environmentally friendly production processes.

> Publication of tenders: The Directives lay down strict rules for contracts awarded directly to a contractor without prior publication in the OJEU.

> Exclusion of untrustworthy bidders: Contracting Authorities may deliberately exclude from competition tenderers who have fallen behind in fulfilling their previous contracts. This possibility should promote contract obligations and prevent the submission of strategically undervalued bids – particularly in the changing regulatory environment. Otherwise, increases in renegotiation opportunities incentivize bidders to submit unrealistically low bids to win a contract and renegotiate it in the later phase of the projects.

2.3.1.2 *Legal Set-Up*

Public procurement legislation in the EU is dichotomous (Chong et al., 2016). Federal authorities remain responsible for the formulation and application of public procurement law. The EU has, however, harmonized the legal requirements for tenders across its Member States. The Member States must transpose the rules that were previously standardized at the EU level into national law. In other words, a unified framework standardizes the conditions within the EU, but national legislators implement them via detailed regulatory rules. Hence, the Member States have some discretion in how to transpose the Directives into national law.[13] National legislators do not have to implement Directives immediately. Instead, the EU Directives usually allow for a time of span of two years for their full implementation.

2.3.1.3 *Threshold values*

Monetary threshold levels determine whether a tender falls under the scope of the Directives. The Directives only apply to tenders above those thresholds. The Directives define them and adjust their monetary value every two years. The appropriate thresholds vary and depend on the kind of tender and Contracting Authority. Due to the higher average values, the threshold for works contracts exceeds the thresholds for service and supply contracts. Whereas similar thresholds apply to works across all parameters, additional factors determine the thresholds for services and supplies. Genuinely, government institutions have lower thresholds than other public organizations because they also fall under the legal umbrella of the Government Procurement Agreement (GPA), which defines lower thresholds.[14] Table 1 summarizes the threshold values from the year 2014.

---

[13] In Germany, for example, a range of different regulations (e.g., Gesetz gegen Wettbewerbsbeschränkungen, GWB; Vergabeverordnung, VgV; and several state-level laws) promulgated the Directives.

[14] The World Trade Organization (WTO) applies the GPA as a legal framework. In their primary objectives, the Directives and the GPA are similar. Both frameworks demand procurement officials to ensure competitive, efficient, standardized, open, and transparent tenders. Since comparable regulations apply in GPA countries and the EU, suppliers from the GPA countries have open access to EU tenders. Conversely, European suppliers can bid for tenders in the GPA countries. Because GPA and EU regulations legally overlap to

Table 1: Threshold values from the 2014 Directives

Type of authority / contract	**€**
Contracting authorities	
Works contracts	5,186,000
Supply contracts: government departments	134,000
Supply contracts: other public bodies	207,000
Service contracts: government agencies	134,000
Service contracts: other public bodies	207,000
Sector contracting authorities	
Work contracts	5,186,000
Supply contracts	414,000
Service contracts	414,000
Defense sector	
Work contracts	5,186,000
Supply contracts	414,000
Service contracts	414,000

Source: Directive 2014/24/EU (2014); Directive 2014/25/EU (2014)

The implementation of thresholds has divided procurement law in the EU into a two-tier system: Below certain monetary thresholds, tenders only need to comply with national regulations.[15] To avoid the stricter procurement regulations that exist on the EU level, Contracting Authorities may underestimate the contract values. As a reaction, the Directives provide specific rules for the estimation of contract values to prevent such behavior. When procurement officials estimate the contract value, they must include all the costs that might occur during the entire lifetime of the contract – comprising all related supporting activities.

The Directives typically forbid the splitting of the contract into different parts to circumvent procurement regulation. However, they allow and sometimes even require the splitting of high-value contracts. For example,

a large extent, the present work only discusses the principles of the Directives and their regulatory impact on procurement officials.

[15] Regarding their economic scale and scope, tenders above thresholds are significantly more critical (PwC, London Economics, & Ecorys, 2011). Thus, the present work focuses on tenders above the threshold value. We mainly cover the implications of the Directives while mostly neglecting potential differences on the national legislative level.

work contracts allow the outsourcing of subcontracts when they account for less than EUR 1 million and a maximum of 20% of the overall contract value. These stipulations want to foster the inclusion of SMEs—particularly into large (infrastructure) projects.

2.3.1.4 Scope

Procurement regulation in the EU provides for several exceptions on the contract level. The Directives define certain types of contracts that they do not apply to:

> The purchasing and leasing of already existing property – unless the supplier has technically (re-) designed the property following the requirements of the Contracting Authority.

> A different set of legislative rules cover military orders from the Ministry of Defense (e.g., aircraft, ammunition, or weapons). However, regular European public procurement legislation applies to orders by armed forces relating to non-military activities.

> Secret Service Orders or Mandates Serving National Security (e.g., systems to oversee criminal activity): The Directives do not cover these contract awards.

> Contracts awarded under the umbrella of international agreements and treaties (i.e., contracts where another international regulation applies) – projects from the World Bank provide an example where procurement officials need to adhere to special procurement rules.

> Contracts within the public sector (i.e., transactions between two public organizations) – although the Directives do not directly affect these transactions, the European Treaties cover them. Thus, procurement officials must consider regular market offers as well, e.g., a Contracting Authority can only carry out healthcare activities for another one if the latter has already considered offers from private-sector suppliers.

2.3.2 General principles of public procurement

Regulation always follows exogenously given economic, political, and social goals (Chong et al., 2016). Political objectives might influence the regulation more than economic goals. The Maastricht Treaty embodied different political goals that defined the general principles of public procurement in the EU. These general principles left their marks in the Directives and may provide regulators with a yardstick for solving some of the inherent tensions of public procurement. Accordingly, the Directives aim at helping Contracting Authorities select the best supplier while ensuring compliance with the general principles (Glas, 2012).[16]

Likewise, the principles have a considerable impact on the tenders because the European Court of Justice (ECJ) regularly bases its rulings on them (Arrowsmith, 2008). Contracting Authorities need to understand the consequences of the principles not only to deepen their understanding of the Directives but also to avoid legal uproars.

2.3.2.1 Equal treatment

The principle of equal treatment ensures that a Contracting Authority does not discriminate against suppliers (Arrowsmith, 2008). A Contracting Authority must treat all potential suppliers equally and provide them with the same information at all stages of a tender. The principle demands that fair, competitive conditions be created for all interested suppliers: They must apply the same competitive conditions to all potential bidders.

The impacts of this principle begin with the preparation and publication of the tender documents (the CN in most transactions). First, the Contracting Authority must ensure that all potential suppliers have access to the information necessary to participate in the tender. Second, the information on the contract specifications, eligibility criteria, and award criteria published in the tender documents must deal with all suppliers equally. Thus, procurement officials must consider how the benefits of certain suppliers may

[16] Regulators face a fundamental tradeoff between standardizing control and improving performance in public procurement. As the regulations become more numerous and stricter, both the predictability of outcomes and transaction costs increase. High transaction costs impede the goal of economic efficiency. Thus, regulators need to balance the demand for higher performance with the prevention of corruption and mismanagement. While a comprehensive set of rules lowers the risk of corruption, more discretionary rules allow Contracting Authorities to make more flexible and efficient decisions about awarding contracts (Tadelis, 2012). This tradeoff especially matters for tenders where the quality dimensions are hard to determine and are possibly non-verifiable. In such cases, strict and detailed rules may increase the risk of quality degradation (Lundberg & Bergman, 2017).

affect the tender outcome; some suppliers may have private information about Contracting Authority's intentions and expectations. Because such information would provide them with a competitive advantage, the Directives prohibit the participation of these suppliers.

2.3.2.2 Non-discrimination

The principle of non-discrimination closely corresponds with the principle of equal treatment.[17] Non-discrimination requires that all potential suppliers can openly access tenders, regardless of their origin or nationality (Arrowsmith, 2008). Therefore, Contracting Authorities must not discriminate (directly or indirectly) against suppliers based on their origins. The Directives established a set of requirements for contract specifications to avoid such discrimination. For example, a German contracting authority might not require a supplier to be registered in Germany or to have already done business with a German authority. Since procurement officials must not hinder the free movement of goods and services within the EU, they must formulate the specifications as neutral and as independent as possible from national market standards.[18] Likewise, the contract specifications may archetypally not refer to a specific product name or brand.

Given its economic significance, the public sector plays a crucial role in the development of the EU internal market and can promote intra-European trade. Before the implementation of the Directives, many governments introduced protectionist practices that gave preference to domestic suppliers, although both practices sharply contradicted the concept of a single European market (Arrowsmith, 2008).

Even if a Contracting Authority assumes that no foreign suppliers will participate in the tender, it must inform all potential suppliers in the EU. The legal obligation to publish all tenders in the Supplement to the OJEU and on TED ensures such public dissemination of information because anyone can freely access all published notices. Contracting Authorities must

---

[17] Both principles are distinctive factors in public procurement. While regulation forbids any form of discrimination, private law is fond of the discretion to allow buyers and sellers to agree on optimal solutions based on their economic needs.

[18] If it is necessary for the success of the tender, Contracting Authorities may discriminate against suppliers by demanding that they can speak and write in their official language.

publish not only a Contract Notice (CN), which provides information about forthcoming tenders but also a Contract Award Notice (CAN), which contains information about the results.

2.3.2.3 *Transparency*

The principle of transparency requires a clear supplier selection process. Therefore, procurement officials must use one of the standard procedures foreseen and approved by the Directives. In line with the principle of non-discrimination, transparency legally obliges Contracting Authorities to publish all relevant tender documents openly.

The principle of transparency acts as an excellent example of the far-reaching legal effects of EU regulation in practice. Since it shapes both European and national law, the principle also concerns below-threshold tenders. If Contracting Authorities do not publish those on TED as well, they must inform suppliers of their calls for tenders through other media such as their websites or in a European newspaper. This legal obligation explains why Contracting Authorities sometimes publish TED contracts below their thresholds – a publication ensures compliance with legal transparency requirements.

The principle of transparency regulates not only the publication of CNs but also their content. At the beginning of a tender, procurement officials must define all the supplier selection rules: They must define the eligibility criteria for the participation of interested suppliers and the award criteria for choosing the winning bidder. After awarding the contract, procurement officials must not only publish the tender results but must also (in advance) inform all unsuccessful bidders of the decision to award the contract to someone else and the reasons for rejection.

2.3.2.4 *Proportionality*

The principle of proportionality enforces the idea that procurement officials can only impose requirements and conditions on potential suppliers that suit the circumstances, i.e., the scope and size of the underlying contract (Arrowsmith, 2008). The contract specifications must not only comply with the principles of non-discrimination and equal treatment but must refer to the subject matter of the contract. All other kinds of available information must also fit the nature of the contract and be related to its subject matter. From a legal point of view, Contracting Authorities must choose the least intrusive and least burdensome option for potential suppliers when they must choose between several alternatives.

2.4 Demands for Contracting Authorities

Given the requirements of the general principles and their legislative reproduction in the Directives, Contracting Authorities in the EU operate in a highly rule-bound environment. Since regulations aim to standardize the awarding of public tenders, Contracting Authorities must adhere to them in every stage of a tender. This behavior contrasts with the private sector, where purchasers instead face market pressure when acquiring items from suppliers but do not have to comply with any regulation in addition to private law standards.

By enforcing predictability, the Directives heavily limit buyers' discretion and scope of actions in tenders. If they breach the regulations at any stage of the procurement process, procurement officials risk potential legal uproars and corresponding delays in the contract awards. Albeit the increased managerial efficiency pressure, they face significantly less severe consequences if they achieve unfavorable purchase prices. Therefore, they may choose to emphasize regulatory compliance more than economic performance. If procurement officials want to avoid problems in their supplier relationship, they must avoid regulatory misconduct (Flammer, 2018).

In sum, Contracting Authorities typically face much higher requirements than their private-sector counterparts. As displayed in Figure 5, the present work clusters these managerial requirements into five distinct sub-groups.

Figure 5: Contracting Authorities' Requirements in Tenders

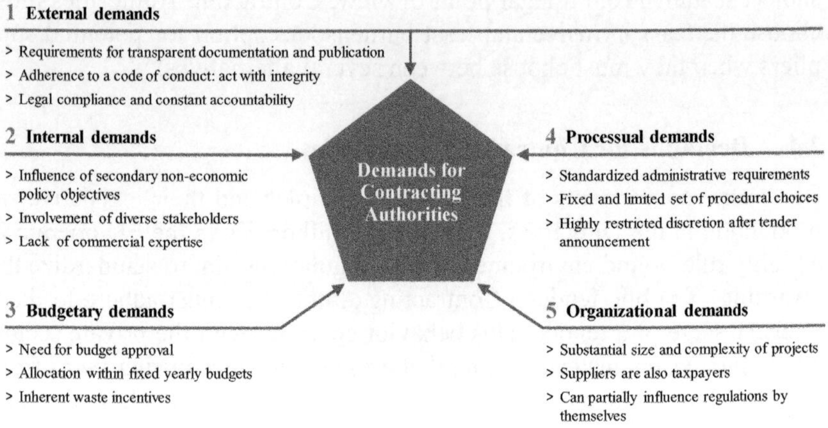

Source: Own illustration based on Telgen et al. (2007)

2.4.1 *External demands*

2.4.1.1 Transparency

The general procurement principles jointly place burdensome processual transparency requirements on Contracting Authorities. Transparency refers to the ability of potential suppliers to know and understand how a Contracting Authority awards a tender (Telgen et al., 2007). Since high transparency enables public oversight, Contracting Authorities will act cautiously and risk-aversely to circumvent any perception of misappropriation (McCue, 2000). Among other things, this requirement tends to induce a preference in procurement officials, in practice, to award contracts via highly transparent award procedures such as procurement auctions.

The publication requirements for tenders mirror the high demand for transparency in public procurement (Carayannis & Popescu, 2005). After the procurement officials prepare and compile the necessary information, they must inform the public about their plans for procurement by publishing a CN. In response to the publication, interested suppliers may request further documents and can ask questions that the procurement officials must answer publicly. The Directives set specific deadlines for the submission of offers or applications. Depending on the circumstances and the procedure that is chosen, these deadlines may vary. Thus, the CN needs to include an exact timetable for the respective deadlines.

2.4.1.2 Integrity

As non-private enterprises, Contracting Authorities must adhere to a specific code of conduct (Telgen et al., 2007). All stakeholders expect Contracting Authorities to act with integrity. Procurement officials must act as publicly announced and must avoid waste or misconduct. Regulators have acknowledged this demand for integrity by imposing significant burdens on procurement officials in the supplier selection phase. Not only the Directives but also most other public procurement legislation advocate for open procedures and usually restrict negotiations (Tadelis, 2012). Negotiated procedures may harm buyers' integrity in public procurement. Since negotiations allow for considerably more buyer discretion, they increase the risk of favoritism, kickbacks, and corruption.

Likewise, the general public, the media, suppliers, and other groups increasingly scrutinize and criticize public procurement (Wang & Bunn, 2004). These stakeholders demand that procurement officials conduct tenders in an equitable, transparent, and efficient way. Thereby, they discourage procurement officials from building close relationships with suppliers. Instead, Contracting Authorities may seek to include as many vendors as possible in order to ensure equal treatment and non-discrimination (Arlbjørn & Freytag, 2012). This motivation contrasts with the private sector, where purchasers seek to minimize this number to reduce their sourcing risks.

2.4.1.3 Accountability

The nature of compliance varies widely between public procurement and private purchasing (Johnson et al., 2003). While boards of directors and business plans manage the purchasing efforts in the private sector, regulations guide the actions of procurement officials (Larson, 2009). The high standards of transparency require procurement officials to justify their decisions at every stage of the tender process (Telgen et al., 2007). In the EU, potential suppliers can sue authorities if they do not comply with procurement law. Since authorities can be held legally responsible for not complying with regulatory requirements, these procedural rules guide their behavior. When carrying out tenders, authorities significantly care about compliance with regulations: Legal rules can be cumulative (e.g., European, national, and state law), contradictory, or even challenging to grasp.

2.4.1.4 *Internal demands*

In addition to external demands, Contracting Authorities have to meet secondary policy objectives that are not related to the contract award in the strict sense (Callender & Matthews, 2002; Schapper et al., 2006). As discussed in Section 2.2.3, these policy objectives may directly contradict primary efficiency objectives. Similarly, officials must serve many (and powerful) stakeholders in public procurement. Besides their responsibilities to the politicians who are often directly involved in tenders, procurement officials may also need to cater to the requests of diverse interest groups (e.g., citizens, taxpayers, voters, elected officials, public administrators, and procurement officials) that often have different or even contradictory objectives (Arlbjørn & Freytag, 2012).

Despite having increased external demands, the number of procurement officials who manage tenders is typically not comparable in private organizations – neither quantitatively nor qualitatively (Johnson et al., 2003). Often, officials are not explicitly focused on or trained in public procurement, and they tend to lack the necessary economic expertise. Specific cultural implications amplify this effect: Since Contracting Authorities traditionally care more about legal compliance, lawyers and administrative officials often make decisions about outcomes, while purchasing experts with a business background remain on the sidelines.

The lack of involvement of more strategically oriented and economically educated staff in procurement reflects the low strategic role that the procurement function still enjoys in many Contracting Authorities. In practice, many officials are still profoundly concerned about secondary interests, legal compliance, and risk avoidance. However, more professionalized procurement management might allow Contracting Authorities to fulfill their political and social objectives better (Ramsay, 2001).

2.4.1.5 *Budgetary demands*

The available budget drives public procurement decisions (Telgen et al., 2007). The available budget, at least in part, determines which solution the Contracting Authority can procure. Since procurement officials must not exceed their budgets, a cost-overrun of a tender will result in significant organizational disruption. Compared with private organizations, which generate revenue from the sales of goods and services, public bodies usually have fixed budgets and therefore predominantly draw their funds from joint tax revenues (Larson, 2009). Thus, no market-analogue incentive mechanisms ensure the frugal use of taxpayers' money.

Contracting Authorities might spend more money than necessary. Typically, hierarchically higher authorities allocate funds to other authorities on a budgetary basis. Money spent in the previous budgetary period largely determines the value of the upcoming budget. Under such a financing scheme, Contracting Authorities will experience future budget cuts if they do not exhaust their allocated budgetary resources within the same financial year. Authorities might face budget cuts if they had significantly lowered their expenditures. Public funding schemes also cause another symptom of waste. Contracting Authorities are likely to award many contracts to suppliers toward the end of the financial year to exploit the allocated budget and avoid future budget cuts.

2.4.2 *Processual demands*

2.4.2.1 Regulation requirements for procedures

Regulations place many administrative and processual requirements on Contracting Authorities. Limitations exist at different levels, from the EU to the local level. The lack of competitive pressure in public procurement primarily demands these restrictions. Without market pressure, regulation must ensure the efficiency of tenders.[19]

---

[19] Larger private-sector organizations must cope with principal-agent issues as well. Organizational, institutional, and personal objectives of private-sector purchasers can contrast shareholder interests regarding the best outcome of an acquisition. As a result, larger companies increasingly tend to formalize and institutionalize their purchasing functions.

In the EU, a robust regulatory emphasis on rules and predictability reduces the Contracting Authority's discretion throughout the whole tender (Schotanus & Telgen, 2007). Contracting Authorities might only possess substantial discretion in the early phases of a tender (Bajari et al., 2009). However, the Directives regulate the design of tenders as well: Therefore, Contracting Authorities might struggle to employ performance-oriented measures at all. They cannot freely choose and implement procedures according to their requirements (Wang & Bunn, 2004). Moreover, while designing the tenders, they must incorporate additional political and social goals.

The decision during tender design phase may still largely determine procurement performance because once procurement officials have informed the public about a tender (e.g., by releasing a Prior Notice (PN) or a CN on TED), the general principles and the Directives nearly vanish their discretion. Procurement legislation requires a standardized tender process that must fully comply with all its regulatory stipulations. Thus, Contracting Authorities must carefully craft the CN that fixated the award procedures, the analysis of submitted offers, and the selection of a supplier (Lundberg & Bergman, 2017).

2.4.2.2 Buyer-supplier relationships

Regulatory rules significantly impact the relationships between procurement officials and potential suppliers (Wang & Bunn, 2004). Regulations often require procurement officials to consider as many suppliers as possible during a tender. By contrast, private sector purchasers will instead try to reduce risk and build long-term relationships with only a few potential suppliers. Contracting Authorities will instead struggle to establish comparable long-term and stable partnerships with suppliers (Larson, 2009). They cannot promise to repeatedly award contracts to suppliers with whom they have worked in the past. To foster the principles of equal treatment and non-discrimination, the Directives are highly restrictive about including criteria such as previous projects and past suppliers in the award decision (Topp-Blatt, 2008). Although Contracting Authorities may profit from long-lasting supplier partnerships, particularly in complex tenders, regulatory rules significantly hamper their establishment and instead aim to ensure competitiveness in each tender.

Likewise, private-sector purchasers have a high degree of discretion when selecting the best supplier. For example, they can freely choose their most preferred contract award procedure. By contrast, regulation heavily restricts the same choice for Contracting Authorities (Tadelis, 2012). The Directives favor procurement auctions as the standard award procedures. Private-sector purchasers typically prefer negotiations to auctions, even if they purchase similar items as in the public sector (Bajari et al., 2009).

The public procurement regulators often allow the use of negotiations only in specific circumstances because negotiations have previously been found to be problematic: The more discretion there is in awarding contracts, the more room there is for favoritism, kickbacks, and corruption (Larson, 2009). Likewise, auctioned procedures may offer economic advantages in public procurement. First, regulators appreciate that auctioned procedures can promote competition between suppliers, leading to lower procurement expenditures (Tas, 2014). Thus, regulations often aim to involve as many potential suppliers as possible in a tender (Vaidya, Sajeev, & Callender, 2006). Second, Contracting Authorities can use auctioned procedures to determine previously unknown or non-existent market prices. Since acquisition needs in public procurement often require unique or exceptional solutions, a market price is often missing, or procurement officials do not know any potential suppliers.

2.4.2.3 Cooperation with other Contracting Authorities

Contracting Authorities may seek cooperation with other public organizations (a typical example includes purchasing groups in the hospital sector). From a competitive point of view, the Directives do not restrict such forms of cooperation (Telgen et al., 2007). However, other regulations may apply when establishing those cooperative vehicles. Most importantly, parties must comply with antitrust laws because the legal standards for transparency and accountability remain rigid. This form of purchasing cooperation often enables Contracting Authorities to achieve economies of scale and minimize process costs (Schotanus & Telgen, 2007).

2.4.3 Organizational demands

Distinct organizational roles and responsibilities characterize public procurement (Johnson et al., 2003). First, Contracting Authorities typically possess a substantial budget. The average value of public tenders significantly exceeds that of private procurement projects (Telgen et al., 2007). Public tenders often cover highly complex and long-term contracts (Bajari, Houghton, & Tadelis, 2014).

Second, Contracting Authorities as public organizations source from suppliers that act as their taxpayers at the same time (Telgen et al., 2007). From this perspective, suppliers' and clients' roles might reverse. Contracting Authorities face reciprocity requirements because they are buying from a supplier who is also receiving services from them. This complicated relationship places additional demands on buyer-supplier interactions at both the executive and operational levels – and provides another raison d'être for strict regulations in public procurement.

Third, although these regulations place a heavy burden on the behavior of Contracting Authorities, as part of the public sector, they can determine at least some of the regulations themselves. Besides, some public organizations do not only engage in procurement, but they also check for the regulatory compliance of other public authorities. Such Contracting Authorities act as players under the laws of the game but are also the referees.

3. Performance management in tenders

The analyses from the previous chapter showed that Contracting Authorities could not manage public tenders only according to their organizational needs (Wang & Bunn, 2004). Instead, procurement officials face several other demands in all phases of a tender. Most importantly, regulations considerably limit their scope of action in designing and managing a tender. Since procurement officials can only implement performance-oriented measures if the regulation provides them with the necessary freedom of choice, the present work needs to identify Contracting Authorities' scope of action before developing any measures.

However, public procurement differs from private purchasing not just in its strong regulatory focus on rules and predictability but also in its objectives. The particularities of public procurement impose heavy demands on Contracting Authorities. The degree to which they can adequately react to those demands determines the success of a tender. Thereby, the diverse demands determine the ultimate goals of Contracting Authorities in public procurement.

Any definition of procurement performance in tenders must consider these demands as well: Only if Contracting Authorities achieve a certain degree of goal achievement, they can reach high performance levels. Likewise, the degree of goal achievement represents the yardstick against which procurement officials can measure the impact of their managerial decisions because targeted and successful performance measures should be closely aligned with organizational goals (Beamon, 1999). The structure of this chapter follows this dependency:

> First, we will discuss the different and sometimes even contradictory goals of Contracting Authorities in public procurement.

> Based on these goals, we will derive a clear definition of performance that allows procurement officials to assess the effectiveness of any performance-oriented measures.

A. Rhode, *Public Procurement in the European Union*, Schriften zum europäischen Management, https://doi.org/10.1007/978-3-658-28073-4_3

3.1 Goals of Contracting Authorities

Before we discuss how Contracting Authorities can manage procurement performance in tenders, we must define the term procurement performance. Since performance is directly related to the degree of organizational goal achievement, we first need to identify the objectives of Contracting Authorities.

As shown in Section 2.4, the objectives of Contracting Authorities surpass those of their private-sector counterparts (Larson, 2009). In the private sector, managers will try to increase profits in order to maximize the overall market value of their companies (Jensen, 2002). To achieve this objective, they will focus on continuously adapting their purchasing operations to remain profitable in the long run. Due to market pressure, private companies threaten their existence if they fail to achieve this goal.

By contrast, Contracting Authorities do not aim to maximize profits because their organizational purpose is not profit-oriented. Instead, they aim to provide a wide range of public services (e.g., justice, health, social services, education, defense, and transportation). Thus, they pursue a diverse, sometimes even contradictory range of objectives. For example, a local authority could primarily want to secure or increase local employment. Thus, their procurement officials may prefer to award contracts to neighboring companies, although other suppliers may offer better value for money. Similarly, to promote sustainability, an authority will prefer sourcing from an environmentally friendly supplier and will be willing to accept higher procurement costs.

3.1.1 Development in stages

In recent decades, the role of procurement officials in the public sector has changed significantly (Telgen et al., 2007). Nowadays, most public organizations interpret procurement as an essential part of their operations. Different levels of maturity in public procurement as a management function require different actions from officials. Thus, if the procurement plays a more strategic role, its primary performance objectives will shift. The present work will employ a seven-stage framework developed by Telgen et al.

(2007). This framework shown in Figure 6 captures the development of public procurement as a managerial function that can deepen the understanding of performance management in tenders:

Figure 6: Development of the public procurement function

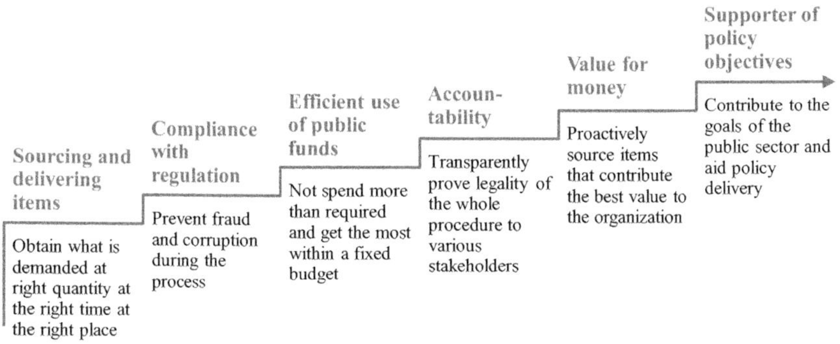

Source: Own illustration based on Telgen et al. (2007)

> In the first phase, officials primarily serve the procurement needs of other organizational members. They aim to fulfill organizational requirements and mostly provide an operational duty: Officials must ensure that they meet requirements in the right quantity, at the right time, and in the right place.

> In the second phase, officials must additionally comply with laws and regulations. They must ensure that not only are they meeting organizational needs but that they are also avoiding any managerial misconduct. In the EU, the Directives require them to comply with a comprehensive set of procedural rules to ensure evading such misconduct.

> In the third phase, a new economic perspective extends officials' managerial tasks. Officials' roles become more commercial by including increased efficiency as a goal. In this phase, officials face the fundamental dilemma of choosing between legal compliance and economic efficiency.

> In the fourth phase, officials maintain an economic perspective but gradually focus more on their political and social accountability. In addition to avoiding fraud and corruption, procurement officials must

justify their managerial decisions to external stakeholders who typically focus on reaching secondary procurement objectives.

> The fifth phase enhances the strategic role of officials. Not only must they minimize costs, but they must also optimize value for money. Officials must balance between lower cost and increased quality. Thus, officials must become proactive: By outsourcing certain parts of their service portfolio (via public procurement), they seek to improve the overall performance of the Contracting Authority. Still, they must meet organizational acquisition needs (the primary goal of the first phase) and comply with extensive regulations (the primary goal of the second phase).

> The sixth phase includes the needs and requirements of external stakeholders. Officials need to consider a wide range of political, social, and ecological goals. Governments try to utilize the monetary scope of public procurement to pursue strategies beyond economic considerations. In doing so, public procurement evolves from an operational function to a strategic policy instrument. For example, public tenders can aim to improve the creation of jobs, SME inclusion, diversity, innovation, sustainability, and foreign aid.

The EU Directives represent one of the most advanced and comprehensive regulatory systems for public procurement (Arrowsmith, 2008). Thus, the stipulations of the Directives unsurprisingly mirror the sixth development phase. Both latest reforms have further promoted the inclusion of policy-focused non-procurement goals. They have increased the managerial freedom to use public procurement as a policy tool. The Directives explicitly allow for the pursuit of an array of non-economic objectives. These goals can cover, for example (OECD, 2015):

> The promotion of environmental protection (e.g., using recycled goods, combating climate change, increasing the efficiency of the use of natural resources)

> Achievement of commercial objectives (e.g., preference for small and medium-sized enterprises, promotion of innovation)

> The pursuit of social objectives (e.g., supporting minority and women's enterprises, promoting social inclusion)

However, procurement officials do not decide on their own which non-economic goals to pursue. Instead, the higher-ranked political decision-makers determine them exogenously (Telgen et al., 2007).[20] Hence, the management of tenders has become progressively complicated. In today's EU, procurement officials must balance fundamental tensions between socio-economic objectives, national and international regulatory requirements, and economic interests. The growing complexity of regulations aggravates their ability to focus on their organizational goals while ensuring compliance. Often, officials must compromise because regulators often impose contradictory guidelines on them – as an attempt to translate different non-economic objectives into operational measures (Schapper et al., 2006).

3.2 Procurement performance in tenders

Contracting Authorities in the EU pursue different economic, legal, social, and political objectives. Given that any sound definition of procurement performance must be closely related to these goals, the present section aims to answer the following question: What does performance mean for procurement officials in Contracting Authorities given their managerial objectives?

3.2.1 Definition problems

The previous discussion shows that economic input-output relations do not fully reflect Contracting Authorities' objectives. More advanced and comprehensive regulatory systems introduce further non-economic goals into the management of tenders. However, procurement officials already care about legal compliance under rather simple regulatory regimes (see the second phase of public procurement development stages).

Thus, the range of requirements for public procurement officials nearly always surpasses those of their counterparts in the private sector. Unlike their private-sector counterparts (which typically rely on profitability as a single measure of success), procurement officials must weigh the different

[20] However, policy objectives are often broad and poorly defined – many different manifestations may even exist for the same political objective. Procurement officials may struggle to operationalize them as a basis for measuring their success.

performance objectives. They must assess their actions also in terms of (secondary) political and social objectives. However, this inclusion leads to a significant danger in public procurement performance management: Due to the lack of market efficiency pressures, officials may neglect the pursuit of economic goals (Murray, 1999).

3.2.2 New Public Management

How can politicians, regulators, and procurement officials alike react to this risk? After all, the Directives are not aimed at having procurement officials neglect economic aspects for the sake of achieving other social and political goals. Indeed, one may blame not only regulation but also the lack of training and education of officials for the significantly worse results in public procurement compared with private purchasing (Eßig, 2013).

Contracting Authorities may improve their outcomes by focusing more on economic efficiency in performance management. Even if economic input-output relations cannot fully operationalize procurement performance in tenders, Contracting Authorities may investigate private-sector strategy and analysis tools to adequately improve their performance management (Arlbjørn & Freytag, 2012). The popular concept of New Public Management (NPM) relies on the idea that public-sector officials can learn from managers in private companies. For tenders, NPM would imply that private-sector management methods can increase the procurement performance of Contracting Authorities (Minchuk & Mizrahi, 2016). For example, procurement officials could analyze how purchasers in private purchasing use procurement procedures (Hood, 1991). Contracting Authorities may benefit from learning from the private sector and mimicking their buying habits (Tadelis, 2012).

NPM follows a long tradition of public-sector management reforms. In recent decades, advocates of NPM have successfully influenced how governments run their operations: Inspired by the best practices in the private sector, many public authorities have privatized their services, adopted a more customer-focused approach, started measuring their performance levels, or aligned their incentive structures (Lane, 2002).

Developed in the late 20th century, NPM responded to the increasing financial problems of public administration and aimed to allocate taxpayers' money more efficiently (Christensen & Lægreid, 2002). NPM focuses on the implementation of two potential levers (Minchuk & Mizrahi, 2016). On the one hand, public administrations can transfer part of their operations to private companies through privatization. On the other hand, public administrations apply management approaches from the private sector to improve their operations, which remain their sole responsibility. Since privatization is the maximum form of public procurement where an authority outsources all parts of their operations to private sector companies, only the latter measure applies to the management of regular public tenders. NPM advocates claim that thereby, Contracting Authorities may solve the ultimate dilemma of achieving political or social goals without completely neglecting economic efficiency.

However, NPM recognizes that public officials may struggle when directly transferring managerial approaches from the private sector without adoptions. By proposing the 3-E concept, NPM acknowledges that performance management in the public sector is multifaceted. The 3-E concept is one of the most widely used frameworks for defining public sector performance (Boyne, 2002). Researchers have developed the performance criteria within the 3-E concept by following the production process used by public administrations. Public authorities should divide the production processes into different steps, objectives, inputs, results, and outcomes to measure their performance. They can then apply the following initial evaluation criteria to each of these identified elements:

> Economy: Officials should try to achieve a goal with the smallest amount of effort (minimum principle) or the best goal by all available means (maximum principle).

> Efficiency: Officials should endeavor to get the most out of their inputs for the actions leading to the outcomes.

> Effectiveness: Officials should aim to achieve all dimensions of their set objectives.

The 3-E concept states that all these dimensions have equal input in shaping performance management in the public sector. For public procurement, this implies that if a tender cannot meet all these criteria, Contracting Authorities should refrain from carrying it out.

3.2.3 *Implications for public procurement*

Because of its economic, social, and political dimension, regulators have referred to NPM as a yardstick for public procurement reforms, particularly in Anglo-American countries. In the EU, the latest reform efforts of the Directives rely on NPM (Bergman & Lundberg, 2013). Accordingly, the current Directives include all three performance dimensions of the 3-E concept.

First, the Directives provide Contracting Authorities with procedures that are designed to ensure that tenders can meet the criteria of economy. Until the 2014 reforms, procurement officials could choose between the most economically advantageous tender (MEAT) and the lowest price tender. These supplier selection rules directly mirror the economy dimension because they allow the procurement officials to choose between the minimum and maximum principle.

The 2014 reform defined MEAT as the standard award criterion. Thus, it stipulated that authorities should proceed according to the maximum principle, i.e., they should strive to achieve the best possible results with a fixed amount of resources. In other words, procurement officials must be sure to award the contract to the supplier offering the best value for money (Dimitri, 2013). The maximum principle allows Contracting Authorities to capitalize on all potential solutions within a specific budget (Bergman & Lundberg, 2013).[21]

Second, the Directives require Contracting Authorities to achieve efficient outcomes while fully complying with the applicable regulatory rules. Therefore, the Directives imply that one cannot measure performance purely in terms of economy. Instead, high performance requires compliance with the general principles and the Directives.

Third, regulatory compliance reflects the effectiveness dimension as well: On the one hand, regulations require purchasers to try to keep acquisition costs low – besides the absence of acting market forces. Regulators want

[21] However, even under the umbrella of the 2014 Directives, procurement officials can still pursue the minimum principle by heavily emphasizing the price component in a MEAT. Procurement officials might design such rules if they endeavor to procure a previously defined contract (output) at the lowest possible price (input).

to ensure an efficient allocation of taxpayers' money and provide officials with the necessary scope of actions. Likewise, officials should avoid any litigation costs to ensure transactional efficiency (e.g., by ensuring transparency to avoid favoritism). On the other hand, the regulations allow Contracting Authorities to include secondary, non-economic objectives for the sake of effectiveness – even at the expense of the primary economic objective. The Directives explicitly provide justifications for more expensive contract awards (e.g., environmentally friendly technologies) to achieve long-term policy objectives (e.g., reducing their CO2 footprint).

3.2.4 Defining procurement performance

Since the Directives rely on the ideas of NPM, the present work will define procurement performance in accordance with the 3E dimensions. The Directives use all three performance aspects to balance the fundamental regulatory tension between economy, efficiency, and effectiveness. Not only do the Directives provide a set of strict process-controlling rules (to ensure economy) and allow policymakers' objectives to be included in procurement (to achieve effectiveness), but they also recognize that procurement officials should source an ideal combination of high-quality and low prices (to achieve efficiency). To enable procurement officials to pursue efficiency, the Directives contain several procurement procedures that allow for the controlling of economy and effectiveness. Thereby, the Directives provide procurement officials with a clear managerial performance objective: They must choose, design, and conduct the procurement procedure that achieves the best value for money.

This interpretation of procurement performance largely correspondents with the often-cited framework by Schapper et al. (2006). Figure 7 shows the interdependencies between economy, efficiency, and effectiveness in performance management of public tenders.

Figure 7: The Compliance-Performance Cycle in public procurement

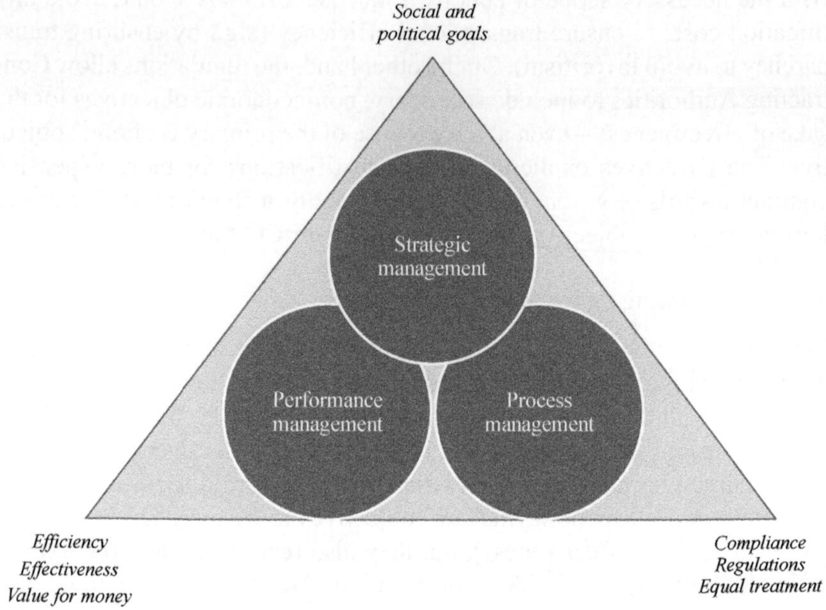

Source: Own illustration based on Schapper et al. (2006)

In harmony with the 3-E concept, Schapper et al. (2006) stated that performance management in public procurement is mostly related to the fulfillment of efficiency, effectiveness, and value for money . In public procurement, process management (focused on regulation and compliance) and strategic management (focused on secondary procurement goals) complement performance management. All three elements mutually depend on each other: Process management and strategic management influence performance management. However, different stakeholders are the primary managers of these dimensions. While higher ranked policymakers define strategic goals (i.e., outline effectiveness objectives) and lawmaking regulators control the procedures (to ensure economy), procurement officials should aim to increase aspects of performance (i.e., boost efficiency or value for money). Procurement officials cannot manage tenders independently of strategic and processual considerations. However, we argue that they should focus on their original efficiency task and not become too distracted by trying to comply with regulatory rules or the implementation of policy goals.

The Directives implement the same division of responsibilities. They differentiate between political, regulatory, and managerial categories of responsibility based on the dimensions of the 3E concept: Politicians define effectiveness for tenders, regulations enable economy, and Contracting Authorities implement efficiency. This division corresponds to the general procurement principles (also embodying political and social goals) that prescribe how regulators can implement economy while allowing procurement officials to efficiently source contracts from the best available supplier (Manso & Nikas, 2015). Following Schapper et al. (2006) and the Directives, we thus define procurement performance for Contracting Authorities as the managerial efficiency objective to ensure the best value for money in a tender.

Hence, procurement officials should manage tenders with the goal of obtaining the best price-performance ratio within the regulatory provisions of the Directives. Concentrating managerial responsibility into a single performance dimension possesses several upsides. Managerial tasks demand a clear definition of performance: Without such a yardstick, procurement officials cannot assess the positive or negative impact of their management decisions. Logically, managers cannot maximize performance in more than one dimension at a time unless the dimensions are monotonous transformations of each other (Jensen, 2002). If officials had to maximize performance in all three dimensions, they could not undertake any goal-oriented decisions.[22] By deliberately limiting the multi-layered definition of public-sector performance, the Directives provide officials with the clear managerial objective to increase efficiency. Moreover, the focus on efficiency (often in monetary terms) facilitates the performance measurement of single tenders. By contrast, one can hardly sensibly measure other

[22] Having a single managerial objective does not mean that procurement officials care only about efficiency. As stated, legal compliance profoundly affects the behavior of Contracting Authorities in public procurement. However, the Directives require procurement officials to focus their attention on improving efficiency when managing tenders. If they legally comply with one of the award procedures established by the Directives, they will be guaranteed to fulfill the other two performance criteria.

procurement principles, such as transparency and accountability (McCue et al., 2015).

This demand for efficiency has far-reaching managerial implications: The pressure on Contracting Authorities to use taxpayers' money efficiently has increased recently (Manso & Nikas, 2015). Despite the peculiarities of public finances, procurement officials often encounter limited resources in procurement – like private-sector purchasers. The concept of efficiency enables them to manage their scarce resources in terms of alternative uses.

The UK Treasury uses the term "good procurement" almost synonymously with efficiency (Van Weele & Eßig, 2017). It has defined "good procurement" as achieving the best value (output) for the money spent (input). Contracting Authorities should spend as little money as possible on high-quality items. Similarly, the UN Commission on International Trade Law (UNCITRAL) has defined "ensuring performance and efficiency" as the first of the main objectives for public procurement officials (Dimitri, 2013).

Therefore, we argue that the organizational reality of Contracting Authorities might not entirely reflect the development of the public procurement function that we sketched in section 3.1.1. In practice, procurement officials might still fail to generate their own policy objectives. In most (private and public) organizations, procurement still possesses an overwhelmingly tactical role as a supportive management function (Grandia, 2018; Kaufmann & Carter, 2004; Tassabehji & Moorhouse, 2008). Consequently, procurement goals remain operational: Procurement officials continue to focus on managing the efficient use of inputs to improve the achievement of organizational objectives.

While they are faced with secondary objectives, they do not define these objectives by themselves. Thus, political and social objectives still play only a minor role in managerial practice.[23] Although procurement goals become more comprehensive in advanced regulatory systems, the primary objectives defined in earlier stages remain fundamental. Logically,

[23] Even in the more advanced private sector, purchasing managers are often not involved in more strategic organizational issues (Cox, Chicksand, Ireland, & Davies, 2005).

procurement officials will more likely neglect to achieve policy objectives than renounce the acquisition of the necessary works, supplies, or services.

4. Contracting Authorities' scope of action in tenders

The previous chapter developed a definition of procurement performance that mirrors the regulatory stipulations of the Directives, the intentions of political decision makers, and the managerial reality of procurement officials. The present chapter employs this value-for-money definition as a yardstick for assessing performance-oriented measures in tenders.

The acquisition of both low value but high-volume contracts and high value but low volume contracts characterizes public tenders. Given this high heterogeneity, a single and standardized framework cannot achieve efficiency (Schapper et al., 2006). Instead, Contracting Authorities must manage their tenders within the scope of actions provided by the Directives to efficiently award contracts. The present chapter aims to identify this scope of actions throughout the whole tendering process.

Every tender in the EU goes through almost the same stages. In contrast to private procurement, regulatory requirements do not allow skipping, repeating, or executing in parallel with certain process phases (van Weele, 2014). Adjustments are often not possible or are painstaking (e.g., procurement officials must restart the entire tender process). Since procurement officials cannot compensate later for the errors or irregularities they committed earlier, they must design their tenders carefully.

Notwithstanding these restrictions, purchasers in public procurement and private purchasing go through the same phase of the acquisition of works, supplies, or services (Caldwell & Bakker, 2008). Therefore, the present work uses a model that was initially developed for private purchasing to analyze public tenders. Various academic models have described the purchasing process in the private sector. In general, such models include both the formal and informal activities that buyers conduct to meet their acquisition needs. As summarized in Figure 8, The present work employs a standard purchasing model described by van Weele (2014).

A. Rhode, *Public Procurement in the European Union*, Schriften zum europäischen Management, https://doi.org/10.1007/978-3-658-28073-4_4

Figure 8: Procurement and purchasing standard phases

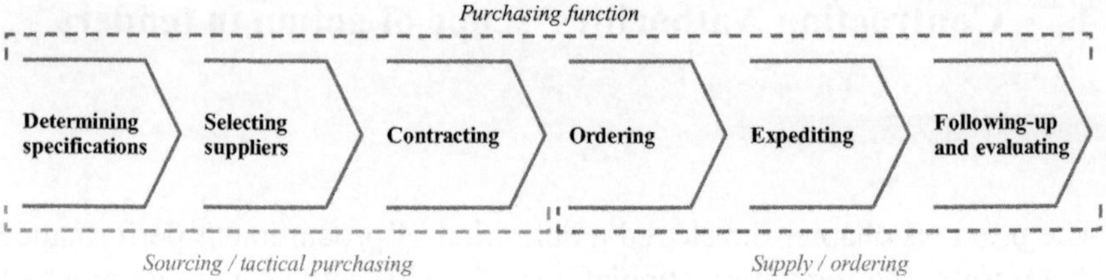

Source: Own illustration based on van Weele (2014)

This detailed model divides the entire purchasing process into six distinct steps. The model distinguishes between tactical purchasing (sourcing) and the order (supply) function. Thus, we can apply it to public procurement because the phases of a tender fully correspond with the steps of tactical purchasing (Caldwell & Bakker, 2008). Procurement officials initiate a tender by preparing a CN (which determines the specifications) for the publication on TED. With the publication, the Contracting Authority searches the market for potential suppliers and invites them to submit offers. This supplier selection phase ends when the Contracting Authority opens and compares the submitted offers. Once the procurement officials decide who gets the contract award, they inform the winning and losing suppliers of their decision and – after the expiration of statutory deadlines – publish the CAN (i.e., with the end of the contracting phase).[24]

While van Weele (2014) separated the specification phase from the supplier selection phase for private-sector purchasing, public tender phases are heavily intertwined in practice: When a Contracting Authority publishes

[24] Although the present work focuses on tactical purchasing phases during a tender, additional factor determining performance may exist within the later stages of public procurement. Once the buyer has awarded a contract, the expediting and evaluating begin. Since procurement officials must care about quality of the contract and cannot focus only on its price, the evaluation and monitoring phase may become complicated. Moreover, tensions between economic, strategic, or policy requirements affect procurement performance in practice. Different stakeholders may prefer different performance aspects and will interpret measurements differently (Caldwell & Bakker, 2008). The inclusion of political criteria adds further complexity. For example, when procuring coffee, the procurement officials might be satisfied with the final price, while other employees may hate the taste, and politicians may dislike the fact that the coffee is not fair trade.

the contract specifications, it has to estimate the practical feasibility of the potential solution and associated costs. Thereby, the specifications scope the market of suppliers and might even highlight a group of potential bidders. Therefore, the supplier selection phase depends on the previously defined specifications.[25] Figure 9 defines four distinct phases between the make-or-buy decision and the contract award. These provide Contracting Authorities with a standardized plan for action in each tender:

Figure 9: Stages in a public tender

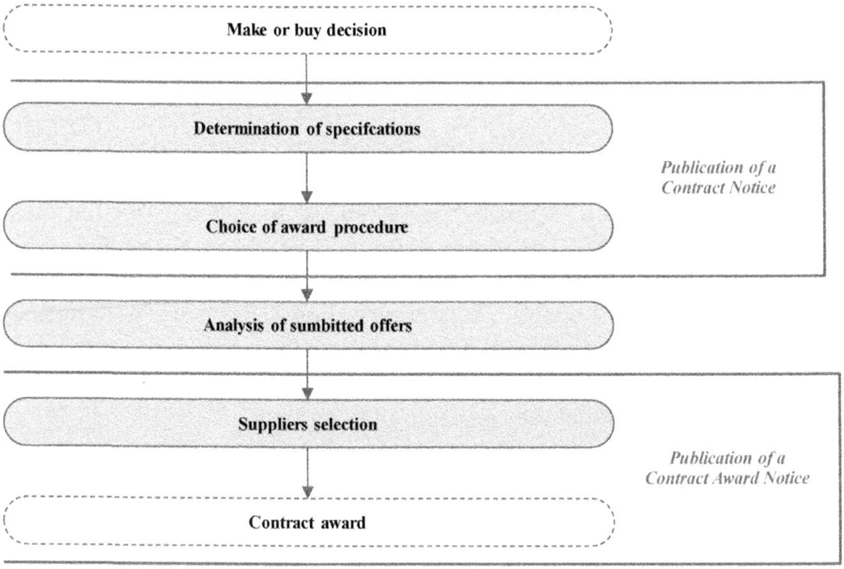

Source: Own illustration

[25] Contracting Authorities may formulate the specifications by already thinking of a certain supplier. Such behavior may predominantly arise in tenders offering innovative solutions or with monopolistic or oligopolistic supply structures (Arrowsmith, 2008). While such behavior contradicts the principle of equal treatment, it often occurs in practice when the buyer has already established a long-term relationship with a certain supplier (e.g., in repeat purchases).

4.1 Determination of specifications

4.1.1 General description

At the beginning of a tender, procurement officials must address the make-or-buy question (van Weele, 2014). To answer this question, a Contracting Authority must decide which works, supplies, or services it can produce alone and which it must purchase from external suppliers. In the following, we assume that the Contracting Authority has already assessed in advance whether it must purchase the required item or whether it can produce it on its own (i.e., it has already tackled the make-or-buy decision). Therefore, we will only discuss the case in which procurement officials decide to award the contract via a tender.

A Contracting Authority begins to assess a procurement need when it plans future activities, e.g., based on externally defined policy objectives. The Contracting Authority identifies the resources needed to carry out these activities successfully (Van Weele & Eßig, 2017). Since the authority has decided to procure these items externally, it initiates the procurement process by specifying the contract details according to its needs. Without such a specification, potential suppliers cannot react appropriately to the published tender. In the contract specifications, officials describe the works, supplies, or services that they are aiming to procure.

Procurement officials can more easily define the specifications of simple contracts or recurring tenders. However, they may struggle to formulate specifications when looking for more innovative or sophisticated solutions. Since they must define the specifications at the beginning of a tender, their content significantly influences its overall outcome: An incorrect need analysis (e.g., if the authority identifies and defines an inappropriate solution in the CN) means that a tender cannot be conducted successfully.

Public finance significantly affects the determination of specifications as well. Often, a Contracting Authority must not only prepare the specifications to enable suppliers to participate but must also apply for budget approval. Since such approvals can take a long time, the period between the first draft of the specifications and the actual tender can span, in the most severe cases, years. Applying for approval in parallel with the procurement process can solve this problem to some extent. However, such behavior involves the risks of funds that have not been approved or unnecessary transaction costs.

4.1.2 *Regulatory stipulations*

Although the Contracting Authority establishes the basis for the entire tender in this initial phase, the Directives remain relatively silent about concrete regulatory stipulations (van Weele, 2014). Instead, they grant Contracting Authorities a rather high scope of action. Procurement officials need to consider only a few limitations when conducting their need analysis. However, they must adhere to the general procurement principles. Accordingly, they must lay the foundation for a transparent and proportionate tender and award procedure.

For example, the principle of proportionality requires Contracting Authorities to consider economy and efficiency when defining specifications. Procurement officials should only specify a more expensive state-of-the-art solution if their organizational goals require an innovative approach. Likewise, the specifications should reflect only must-have characteristics and neglect nice-to-have features.

The strict regulatory provisions that are applicable after the publication of a CN implicitly require Contracting Authorities to define the specifications carefully (Arrowsmith, 2008). Once they publish the specifications, they can no longer amend them. If a Contracting Authority has defined the specifications incorrectly, it must typically cancel the entire tender and restart an entirely new tender. Because the same legal minimum deadlines and transparency demands apply to this new tender, poorly formulated specifications will significantly increase the transaction costs.

Likewise, a Contracting Authority may fail to award the contract to the most appropriate supplier if it does not formulate appropriate specifications. Therefore, in order to avoid contract award issues, Contracting Authorities should publish specifications that are as clear and complete as possible (Noch, 2016). Errors or omissions in the specifications can affect the overall success of the tender by opening the door to legal claims by losing bidders. Possible lawsuits by unsuccessful bidders may jeopardize the success of the entire tender.

4.1.2.1 Publication of a Contract Notice (CN)

The Directives do not heavily limit Contracting Authorities in defining specifications. However, they stipulate that procurement officials must initiate a tender by publishing a CN on TED that describes the scope of the contract. The publication on TED ensures that the CN complies with the formal norms and standards of the platform. The Directives require Europe-wide publication of the CN to encourage competition and allow the participation of all potential suppliers from across the EU.

The CN is an invitation to all interested suppliers to submit an offer in response, and it officially and publicly initiates the tender process. Since the CN constitutes an invitation to a tender, it should enable potential suppliers to decide whether to participate. Under certain circumstances (e.g., for innovative or sophisticated items), procurement officials might decide for the publication of a PN to inform potential suppliers about the planned tender.

The Directives require purchasers to publish CNs for each tender above the relevant monetary thresholds – not covering the previously mentioned exceptions. If the contract value exceeds a threshold, procurement officials must publish the CN on TED before informing potential suppliers elsewhere. Therefore, a Contracting Authority always needs to assess the total contract value to determine the publication requirements.

Since regulation demands non-discrimination and the equal treatment of all potential suppliers, the buyer's scope of actions significantly decreases after the publication of a CN. Thus, the CN considerably determines the success of a tender. First, it specifies the content of the final contract as well as the rights and obligations of the winning supplier during the implementation phase. Second, it establishes the basis for the application of the eligibility and award criteria. Third, it provides a common understanding of the technical, legal, and financial specifications to all potential suppliers: Only a shared understanding allows for the objective comparison of offers and legitimate evaluations of their value for money.

4.1.2.2 Prohibition of supplier involvement

The Directives require procurement officials to determine by themselves (i.e., without involving a supplier) precisely what works, supplies, or services they want to acquire. The general principles of equal treatment and non-discrimination prohibit procurement officials from contacting any suppliers privately before informing all potential suppliers by publishing a CN on TED. In the private sector, purchasing managers often work with potential suppliers as early as possible to clarify and define the specifications in detail (Erridge & Nondi, 1994). However, public procurement officials must publish specifications without checking their adequacy and suitability with potential suppliers.

4.2 Scope of Action of Contracting Authorities

Although the Directives provide for specific minimum standards for the specifications, procurement officials have some discretion in defining their content.

4.2.1 Publication of a Prior Notice (PN)

Contracting Authorities may inform potential suppliers of the planned procurement before the transaction by publishing a Prior Notice (PN) on TED. The Directives do not require the publication of a PN. However, a publication reduces the legal minimum time limits for the later tender initiated by the CN. To reduce these deadlines, the Contracting Authority must publish the PN at least 52 days but not earlier than one year before the publication date of the CN. However, the publication of a PN remains the exception for tenders in the EU (PwC et al., 2011). As a rule of thumb, purchasers directly initiate tenders with the publication of a CN.

4.2.2 Formulation of contract specifications

Procurement officials can choose between two generic kinds of specifications in a CN: A functional or a technical specification.[26] On the one hand, a technical specification describes the operational requirements of the procured good, work, or service that the winning supplier needs to fulfill. A

[26] As stated, buyers might decide for the prior publication of a PN. The specifications contained in a PN fully correspond with the specifications published in the CN. Thus, the fundamental choice between functional and technical specifications applies to tenders independent of a published PN.

technical specification describes the mechanical properties and characteristics of the items as well as the required activities of the winning supplier.

On the other hand, a functional specification defines the operational tasks, applications, and purposes of the supply, work, or service. Functional specifications are result-oriented: They describe the item's field of application from the view of the end-user. In 2004, the Directives approved the use of functional specifications.

4.2.3 Division of a contract into lots

Contracting Authorities must decide whether to acquire a fully functional item or its different parts. In the first case, a single supplier will implement the complete contract specifications (often including previous development and design phases). In the latter case, procurement officials break the contract down into smaller components (often referred to as lots) and award them separately. Procurement officials can but do not have to award these lots to different suppliers. When procurement officials award contracts in separate lots, they remain responsible for the coordination of the entire project.

The Directives regulate how to divide a contract award into lots. They aim to prohibit splitting an above-threshold tender into smaller parts to avoid compliance with the Directives. Procurement officials may engage in such inappropriate behavior to circumvent the strict rules of the Directives and to comply with only the less restrictive national regulations.

Hence, the Directives allow the division of a contract into smaller, coherent lots only for appropriate reasons (i.e., to better reflect procurement objectives). The awarding of complex work contracts might even require such a division if a single supplier cannot efficiently provide all the necessary components. For example, the Directives allow for the outsourcing of installation services to another supplier from the production process. The option of splitting a contract into several smaller installments may also serve the policy objective of increasing the involvement of small and medium-sized enterprises (SMEs) in public procurement.

4.2.4 *Publication and formulation of a price estimate*

To assess whether a tender falls under the regulatory umbrella of the Directives, Contracting Authorities must assess the monetary value of the entire contract (and, if necessary, of all the smaller lots). Otherwise, procurement officials would not be able to judge whether the contract exceeds the thresholds and whether it must apply to the Directives. Besides, Contracting Authorities usually require a monetary estimate of the contract value to apply for the respective funds before they launch a tender (European Commission, 2018). Procurement officials should estimate the value of the contract based on the total volume of services, supplies, or works for the entire term of the contract (including any options, phases, or possible renewals). The estimated value should comprise the full remuneration for the suppliers, including all types of expenses such as labor, materials, and transport (plus additional costs such as maintenance, custom licenses, operating costs, or travel expenses). Procurement officials should estimate the contract value based on experience, previous similar contracts, or preliminary market research.

Once the Contracting Authority has assessed the monetary value of the contract, it may share this information with potential suppliers in the CN. However, the Directives do not oblige to publish this information: A CN may conceal the Contracting Authorities' estimate from potential suppliers. Independent of this publication at the beginning, the Contracting Authorities should publish its estimate after the supplier is selected in the CAN to show the economic outcomes of the contract award publicly. This two-fold disclosure means that the present work needs to distinguish between two types of estimates. First, a CN might publish an estimate to inform potential bidders. Second, a CAN comprises an estimate to provide information about the tendered outcome. The present work defines the first as the ex-ante estimate and the latter as the ex-post price estimate to avoid confusion.[27] Not only do Contracting Authorities decide whether to publish an ex-ante price estimate, but they also enjoy the freedom to formulate it.

---

[27] In economic terms, the ex-ante estimate is a reference price supplied by first movers at the beginning of a tender. Past research has usually referred to such a reference price as either a first offer (in the case of a negotiation) or a starting price (in the case of an auction). Since tenders resemble procurements auctions in many characteristics, the present work will use the terms ex-ante estimate and starting price synonymously.

The Directives allow procurement officials to choose between an ex-ante estimate formulated as a price point or a price range.

4.3 Choice of the award procedure

4.3.1 General description

The choice of an award procedure significantly impacts the success of a tender (Bajari et al., 2009). In this step of the tendering process, the Directives are aimed toward enabling Contracting Authorities to choose the standardized award procedure that will most likely ensure the identification and selection of the best supplier. Therefore, the award procedure that is chosen must fulfill three criteria (Chong et al., 2016):

> Enable the best supplier to participate in the tender

> Ensure that the best supplier will be chosen from all participating bidders

> Limit favoritism or corruption

Related to the transactional outcome, procurement officials must define the reimbursement details of the award procedure in this phase. In public procurement, Contracting Authorities award suppliers on a fixed price basis. The CN does not specify the number of hours required to perform the required activities. Instead, the supplier needs to carry out the requested service or to deliver the requested works, supplies, or services at a fixed price and by a specified date.

4.3.2 Regulative stipulations

The Directives severely limit the range of possible award procedures. By establishing a fixed set of standardized procedures, the Directives aim to ensure that procurement officials treat interested suppliers equally and without discrimination (Chong et al., 2016). Under the regulatory regime of the Directives (i.e., above monetary thresholds), procurement officials can choose between the archetypes of the open procedure, the restricted procedure, the negotiated procedure, and the competitive dialogue.[28]

[28] Below the monetary thresholds, similar award procedures exist. Although only national laws govern these procedures, they usually correspond to the procedures above the

Moreover, the Directives do not permit a mixture of individual elements of different procurement procedures. Figure 10 compares the different phases of the four potential award procedures:

Figure 10: Different award procedure established by the Directives

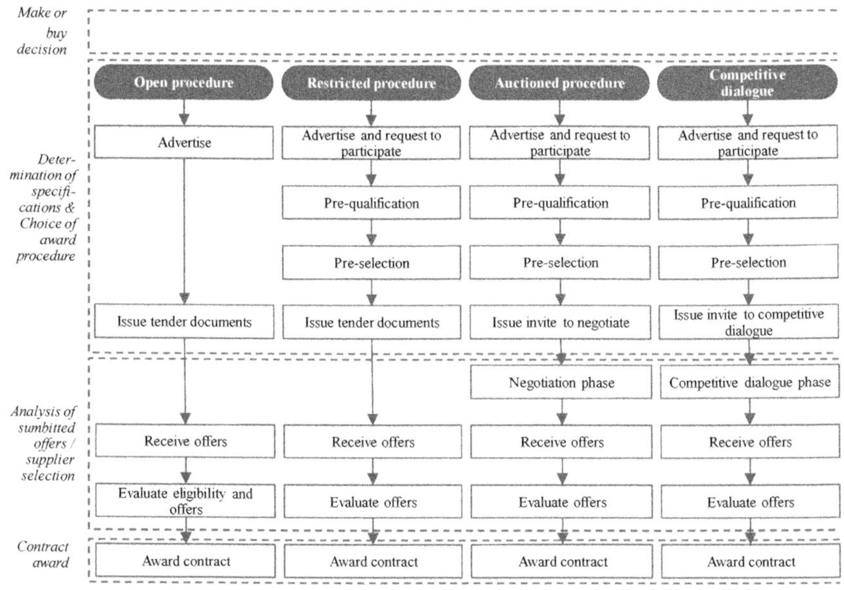

Source: Own illustration

4.3.3 *Scope of action for Contracting Authorities*

Contracting Authorities cannot freely choose between the available award procedures. Instead, EU Directives provide a clear hierarchy. However, the variety of public procurement procedures that procurement officials can use has increased over the years. The 2014 reform of the Directives reflects this development. The revision relaxed Contracting Authorities' choice between different procedures based on the specific circumstances of their

threshold. Since the present work focuses on tenders under the regime of the Directives, it will only discuss the latter ones. Besides the procurement procedures established by the Directives, no other procedures exist for above-threshold tenders.

needs, the characteristics of the procured items, or the market situation. Still, one can divide available procedures into standard procedures and exceptional procedures (Telles & Butler, 2014).[29]

On the one hand, Contracting Authorities may use standard procedures for any tender. On the other hand, purchasers can only use exceptional procedures as an alternative if the standard procedures have already failed or fail to apply to the given tender. This classification defines open and restricted procedures as standards. All other special procedures require more distinct reasons for their use. The Directives allow the use of the competitive dialogue and the negotiated procedures only under some circumstances.[30] Figure 11 shows that historically, open procedures have accounted for the most substantial proportion of all public tenders in the EU, but their importance has always depended on national market norms and standards.

[29] The recent reforms of Directives allowed Contracting Authorities to run electronic auctions as a device for awarding contracts. However, the Directives clearly state that electronic auctions are not a separate award procedure. Defining electronic auctions as a separate procedure would have contradicted the reform's simplification and flexibilization goals. Since an electronic auction is always a variant of an open, restricted, or negotiated procedure, the present work refrains from discussing it. Theoretically, its increased transparency might impact procurement performance by affecting the trust of bidders in the processes and lowering transaction costs (Pavel & Sičáková-Beblavá, 2013).

[30] Compared with other Contracting Authorities, public utilities can freely decide between the open procedure, the restricted procedure, and the negotiated procedure (with a prior call for competition) in all tenders.

Figure 11: Share of award procedures across EUR-Zone member states

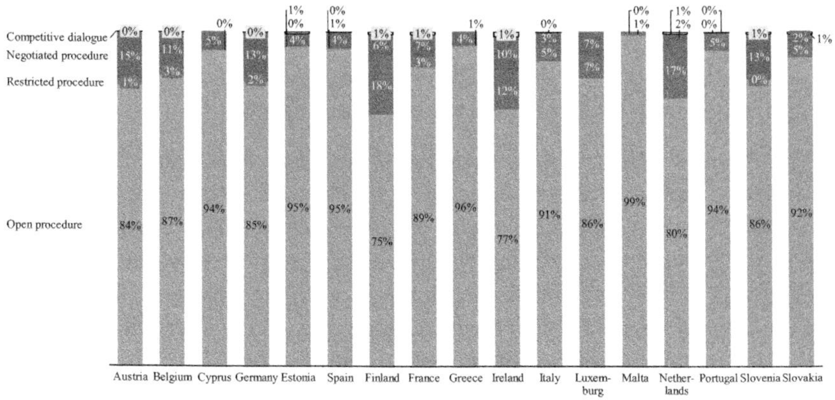

Source: Own calculations based on TED data 2012-2015 (European Commission)

4.3.3.1 Open procedure

Typically, regulatory systems in public procurement favor open procedures (Decarolis, 2014): For example, the World Bank encourages the introduction of open auctions into the public procurement systems of its receiver countries. In the open procedure, an unlimited number of interested suppliers may react to the published CN (Topp-Blatt, 2008). Thereby, any potential supplier can participate in a public tender.

Until the 2014 reform of the Directives, the open procedure used to enjoy absolute legal priority over any other procedure in the EU. The Directives favored open procedures because they allow maximum levels of competition and ensure equal treatment of all potential suppliers. Due to high competitiveness, potential suppliers should (in theory) make bids that are based on their minimum costs: They do not know the bids of other bidders and cannot enter further price negotiations.

The open procedure is the most strictly formalized and uniform award procedure (Leinemann, Ebert, & Kirch, 2016). After the publication of the CN, potential suppliers are given a maximum period of 52 days to prepare and submit their offers. If the procurement officials have previously published a PN, this period shrinks to 36 days. They can further shorten the timetable by allowing offers to be submitted electronically (minus 5 days) and by allowing responses to bidder inquiries to be made online (minus 12 days). Accordingly, in extreme cases, the deadline shrinks to a minimum of 15 days. Although procurement officials may profit from shortening the deadline, they must not shorten the response time too much because they might risk having too few or poorly prepared offers.

The submitted offers remain sealed until the end of the procurement auction. Once the procurement officials open the offers, they need to use the predefined criteria, established and published in the CN, to evaluate them. Thus, the procurement officials must evaluate each offer as it was received – without entering any further negotiations with the suppliers. The authority will award the contract to the best bidder, i.e., the bidder who offers the value for money as defined by the criteria of the CN. After this decision to award the contract, the open procedure does not allow for any kind of further negotiations.

4.3.3.2 Restricted procedure

Due to the 2014 reform, procurement officials can freely choose between an open and restricted procedure. The restricted procedure represents the only standard procedural alternative to the open procedure. The 2014 Directives impose no legal conditions to the use of a restricted procedure. In a restricted procedure, like the open procedure, all potential suppliers (without any restrictions) may apply to participate in a tender in a prior call for competition.

However, before the start of the procurement auction, the Contracting Authority decides whether potential suppliers can place offers based on their eligibility. Compared with the open procedure, a Contracting Authority checks the suitability of suppliers before they have submitted their offers and not after they have submitted all offers. The Contracting Authority can additionally limit the number of bidders by deliberately not inviting all eligible suppliers to the procurement auction. After the compulsory call for competition has ended, the procurement auction begins, and invited suppliers can submit their offers. Procurement officials must invite at least five potential suppliers to participate. The auction phase strongly resembles the procurement auction in an open procedure: Suppliers submit sealed bids and cannot renegotiate their submitted offers.

Before the 2014 reform, The EU Directives stated that procurement officials could opt for a restricted procedure only if an open procedure was not well-matched with the award conditions, e.g., when the admission of all possible suppliers seemed inappropriate. Besides, an open procedure was found to be impractical if:

> Only a limited number of suppliers can supply the required good, work, or service

> The conducting of an open procedure represents a disproportionate effort

> A prior open procedure did not produce an economically satisfactory result

> Security or urgency considerations make an open procedure impossible

If the Contracting Authority decided to use a restricted procedure, it had to record the reasons why it abolished the open procedure to obviate legal scrutiny. The 2014 reform has not altered the deadline for the use of the restricted procedure: The procurement officials must publish the call for competition at least 37 days before the publication of the CN. After the publication of the CN, procurement officials must allow the pre-selected suppliers 40 days to submit an offer. They might reduce this period to 36 days if they published a PN. As in the open procedure, electronically providing all necessary and related information reduces the time limit by five days: The total offer period lasts for at least 22 days. Thus, procurement officials can conduct a procurement auction in a restricted procedure in a shorter period than they can conduct an open procedure.

4.3.3.3 Negotiated procedures

The EU Directives contain negotiated procedures as an alternative to the auctioned procedures. Unlike the competitive dialogue (discussed in section 4.3.3.4), negotiated procedures are not an adapted variant of an open standard procedure, but they represent an entirely separate and independent set of procedures. Before the 2014 reform, the Directives only allowed the use of negotiated procedures if the standard procedures did not meet the requirements of the Contracting Authorities. They could opt for negotiated procedures only in exceptional cases (e.g., under extreme urgency or if an already conducted open or restricted procedure has failed). The 2014 reform of the Directives broadened this minimal field of application.

Auctioned procedures only remain mandatory for the procurement of standardized goods, works, or services. As a result, Contracting Authorities can use negotiated procedures more often. Thereby, traditional public procurement becomes more like procurement in the utility sector where the 2004 reform already allowed a more frequent use of negotiations. Compared with the auctioned procedures that rely on non-negotiable specifications (fixed in the CN), negotiated procedures depend on flexible contract specifications that procurement officials and suppliers jointly discuss (Topp-Blatt, 2008).

Although the Directives do not regulate the conducting of these negotiations, the general procurement principles continue to apply. Accordingly, Contracting Authorities cannot act freely during the negotiations. They must employ fair, reasonable, and uniform eligibility criteria and award criteria. Still, violations of the general principles of public procurement are more likely to arise in negotiations than in more transparent auctioned procedures. To ensure a minimum degree of transparency, the Contracting Authority must publish the results of the negotiations and must justify the use of negotiations (e.g., by stating that the time limits of other procedures were not sufficient).

A negotiated procedure usually consists of several stages with the final phase still involving several potential suppliers to ensure a minimal degree of competition. In general, the Directives define two different types of negotiated procedures: First, procurement officials can opt for the negotiated procedure with a prior call for competition.[31] In this case, the Contracting Authority initiates a tender by publishing a CN. This negotiated procedure includes a pre-qualification phase like the restricted procedure. In this first phase, the authority assesses the technical and economic eligibility of potential suppliers. Procurement officials must deem at least three candidates admissible for the second phase. Then, they begin to negotiate with all suppliers who passed the formal test of the first phase. Since Contracting Authorities must respect the principles of equal treatment and non-

[31] Some literature also uses the term "competitive procedure with negotiation" to describe this procedure.

discrimination, they must invite pre-selected suppliers to the negotiations simultaneously and in writing. This invitation must also specify the award criteria and the number of suppliers it invites to the negotiations.

Under the regime of the 2014 Directives, procurement officials can use a negotiated procedure with a prior call for competition when one of the following conditions applies:

> When contracts show any requirements that go beyond "off the shelf" purchasing. In other words, the works, supplies, or services must include design efforts, innovative solutions, or adaptations of available solutions.

> When no bidder has submitted a regular or an acceptable offer in an auctioned procedure (or in a competitive dialogue); this situation could indicate collusion among suppliers. However, the bids must have significantly exceeded the budget or failed to meet minimum quality requirements

> When procurement officials cannot specify the underlying contractual conditions alone with sufficient precision (by referring to defined standards, typical technical specifications, or technical references) but must develop them in cooperation with suppliers; due to unforeseen circumstances or lack of industry expertise, they might fail to specify the terms of the contract with sufficient accuracy or cannot estimate the costs associated with the contract

In the case of works contracts, procurement officials may use negotiations for nonstandard buildings or where the contract includes design efforts. Relevant situations for services or supplies include complex or sophisticated acquisition needs that require adaptation or design efforts – such as consulting services, architectural design, engineering services, or holistic ICT projects. However, procurement officials should not use a negotiated procedure when several potential suppliers can render the needed service or supply on similar quality levels.

Second, procurement officials can opt for the negotiated procedure without a call for competition. Compared with the previously discussed negotiated procedure with a prior call for competition, the Contracting Authority does not publish any notice before the tender. Instead, it enters directly into negotiations with potential suppliers whom it has found capable of supplying the necessary works, supplies, or services. In this highly flexible procedure, Contracting Authorities continuously need to comply with the general procurement principles, albeit the non-disclosure of a CN. They should talk to several suppliers – in particular, if the negotiations follow a discontinued auctioned procedure. Due to the massively decreased degree of transparency within this procedure, the EU Directives allow this procedure only for exceptional and rare occasions. Even after the reform in 2014, the negotiated procedure without a PN presents a procedure of final resort (Telles & Butler, 2014). Contracting Authorities may only opt for a negotiated procedure if

> Other procedures have yielded nonexistent or inappropriate outcomes
> Only one supplier can deliver the required item due to technical or legal exclusivity (procurement officials must explain why no other supplier is eligible)
> Unforeseen and exogenous circumstances cause a high level of urgency for the procurement (e.g., natural disasters)
> Unforeseen and exogenous circumstances have created a need for additional works, supplies, or services that previous contract award specifications did not cover

4.3.3.4 Competitive dialogue

The competitive dialogue is a multi-stage award procedure. The EU directives have established this procedure for the acquisition of particularly complex and high-value purchases (PwC et al., 2011). In the first phase, a CN invites all potential suppliers to apply for the contract (Topp-Blatt, 2008). This CN must state that the Contracting Authority wishes to enter a competitive dialogue and why it deviates from the standard procedures. In the next step, procurement officials select a group of the most suitable suppliers from the applicant pool. This pre-selection resembles the restricted procedure: They must select at least three potential suppliers. Next, the Contracting Authority enters into a dialogue with all the approved suppliers to develop and define the terms of the contract. The discussions aim to identify solutions that come as close as possible to the specifications. Based on this discussion, procurement officials select the most appropriate solution. They then summarize the results of the dialogue into detailed contract specifications. The pre-selected suppliers react by submitting their offers. During this dialogue, the Contracting Authority must adhere to the principles of transparency and equal treatment. They must ensure that all interested parties have access to the same information. Finally, the Contracting Authority selects the bidders based on economic value-for-money criteria. As in the open and restricted procedures, parties cannot renegotiate this final decision. The pre-selection of potential suppliers takes at least 37 days – procurement officials can shorten this period to 30 days if they publish the notices electronically. The Directives do not contain a deadline for the submission of offers during the dialogue phase.

Procurement officials may prefer to use the competitive dialogue for the procurement of complicated and difficult-to-specify items. However, the dialogue does not result in a contract award. Instead, they close the dialogue once it seems to have sufficient information about possible solutions, and then they initiate the actual award procedure. Thus, the next chapters will interpret the competitive dialogue as a variant of a negotiated procedure and will neglect to conduct a distinct further investigation of this award procedure. Compared with an auctioned procedure, the competitive dialogue allows for flexibility benefits because the procurement officials do not need to provide the specifications before the call for competition but negotiate them jointly with suitable suppliers. Accordingly, the arguments for why they should prefer a negotiated procedure also apply to a competitive dialogue.

4.4 Analysis of submitted offers

4.4.1 General description

In the private sector, purchasers typically draw up a bidder list to identify potential suppliers after they have implemented an award procedure. However, procurement officials must abandon this step. The Directives forbid them to draw up a list of suitable suppliers as this would contradict the fundamental principle of non-discrimination: Such a list might exclude a potential supplier and give preference to others. As mentioned above, the restricted procedure and the negotiated procedure with a prior call for competition also deliberately do not prevent any suppliers from participating in the pre-qualification phase.[32] Thereby, procurement officials do not inform a pre-selected group of suppliers about the tender, but they instead inform all potential suppliers.

The open procedure stands out because all interested bidders receive the tender documents. In all other procedures, only a group of pre-selected suppliers will get access to the tender documents. After sending out tender documents, the potential suppliers will prepare their offers for submission. During this tender phase, Contracting Authorities barely possess any options to influence the tender outcome. However, procurement officials must fulfill their informational duties by answering bidder requests – while, of course, adhering to the general procurement principles. After procurement officials have received offers from interested suppliers, they enter the phase of offer analysis.

In public procurement, the analysis of submitted offers differs from private purchasing as it much depends on the previous stages. When evaluating the suppliers and their offers, procurement must adhere to the criteria that they have published in the CN at the beginning of the tender. Since the CN defined the eligibility and award criteria, they already pre-determined the framework conditions for the supplier selection process that the procurement officials now must conduct.

4.4.2 Regulative stipulations

4.4.2.1 Reasons for exclusion

The Directives require the procurement officials to check whether they must exclude any submitted offers. This step includes a test of formal non-compliance with the chosen procurement procedure (e.g., late submission or lack of a legally binding signature).

In addition, the Directives prescribe a comprehensive list of criteria that procurement officials must examine before considering suppliers for the contract award. In the open procedure, officials conduct this task after the

[32] Only the negotiated procedure without a prior call for competition allows buyers to conduct a (non-public) pre-selection of a supplier. However, the Directives severely limit the use of this procedure. Even the 2014 reform (which otherwise promoted flexibility) did not reduce its restrictions on this procedure.

suppliers have submitted their offers. In all other procedures, they check these criteria as part of the pre-qualification process before inviting any supplier to submit offers. On the one hand, mandatory reasons lead directly to the exclusion of an interested supplier. The reasons include, for example, convictions for setting up criminal organizations, engaging in bribery, or committing fraud. On the other hand, Contracting Authorities can use optional criteria as further grounds for justifying the exclusion of a supplier. Authorities can but do not have to eliminate suppliers if they meet one of the following criteria:

- The supplier has filed for bankruptcy or cannot continue its business
- The supplier is about to cease its business activities
- The supplier has entered a payment procedure with its creditors
- The supplier has violated legal obligations
- The supplier committed a serious business offense
- The supplier has not fulfilled its social security or tax obligations

4.4.2.2 Eligibility criteria

Next, the Contracting Authority uses eligibility criteria to assess the suppliers that were not excluded in the previous step. Thereby, procurement officials analyze the extent to which suppliers can meet the contract specifications. Accordingly, these eligibility criteria serve to pre-select suppliers and usually serve as minimum quality requirements. The eligibility criteria are aimed at assessing the legal and economic suitability of the winning supplier. A supplier must qualify to carry out the task described in the CN by presenting evidence of a stable financial situation and the necessary technical and professional capabilities. In all award procedures, procurement officials will exclude suppliers that do not have the necessary expertise to perform the actions detailed in the contract.

The Contracting Authority must carry out this examination based solely on the background of the supplier and not based on the contents of the submitted offers. However, the chosen criteria must still be proportionate to the content of the contract award. In principle, one can divide the eligibility criteria into formal and material criteria.

> Formal criteria examine the suitability of suppliers based on submitted certificates (e.g., the entry in the commercial register).

> Material criteria check the suitability of a supplier based on economic, financial, or technical variables.

The criteria that are used must meet objective standards, and the procurement officials must have published them in the CN. Since the Directives do not explicitly define these criteria, the principles of public procurement form the primary yardstick for defining these criteria. However, the Directives define how suppliers can demonstrate their financial and technical capacity. Thereby, the Directives implicitly standardize the evaluation of eligibility criteria.

For both criteria, the Contracting Authority may require suppliers to provide evidence. However, the evidence required should match the contract specifications, should not undermine the protection of trade secrets, and should not discriminate against suppliers. For example, suppliers can submit one of the following documents to demonstrate their financial capacity:

> Bank statements

> Professional risk indemnity insurance

> Annual accounts

> Statement of the overall turnover or turnover in the area covered by the contract

Moreover, the Directives also list in detail the means for demonstrating technical capacity:

> Reference lists of previous similar contracts, possibly including proof of satisfactory performance

> Available tools, research, and production facilities as well as established quality control procedures

> Available supply chain management and tracking systems

> Number, qualifications, and experience of (managerial) staff

> Existing measures for environmental protection or respectively applicable certificates

Contracting Authorities must tell rejected suppliers why they were rejected. Eliminated suppliers can request more detailed information about their rejection. The Contracting Authorities have 15 days to respond with the requested information.

This discussion shows that the Directives provide several stipulations on how procurement officials must assess the offers submitted by potential suppliers. This comes as no surprise because both the Directives and the general principles aim to ensure the equal treatment of potential suppliers as one of their primary (economic and political) objectives. Compared to the other tender stages, procurement officials possess no leeway to improve the economic performance of tenders when analyzing the submitted offers. Instead, they should focus on legally complying with the rigid given regulations to avoid any legal uproar that might increase transaction cost.

4.5 Selection of suppliers

4.5.1 General description

After the suppliers (that the procurement officials did not previously exclude and found admissible) have submitted their offers, the officials must assess the technical and economic characteristics of their offers. After concentrating entirely on the bidders and their economic background in the previous analysis of the eligibility criteria, they now assess the contents and quality of the offers. Thus, the second evaluation differs significantly from the previous phase and must refer only to the contents of the submitted offers to ensure compliance with the general principles of public procurement.

Again, the scope of procurement officials' actions dramatically depends on their decisions during the previous tender stages. They must rely on evaluation criteria determined by the CN. For the detailed evaluation of the costs estimated by the supplier as well as the proposed execution of the contract, they must use the previously published award criteria. The Directives provide little discretion in this stage to reduce the risk of supplier discrimination (Arrowsmith, 2006).

Once the procurement officials have identified the winning supplier, they must inform all participating bidders of their decision (Jasper & Marx, 2018). The Contracting Authority must inform the unsuccessful bidders that they were not awarded the contract and provide reasons for their rejection. The losing suppliers can object this award decision within the next 15 days. Unsuccessful tenderers might appeal if they suspect a breach of public procurement principles. This period must pass before the contract award between the Contracting Authority and the winning supplier becomes legally effective After the contract award becomes legally binding, suppliers can only refer to secondary legal remedies (e.g., as indemnity claims). The Contracting Authority informs the successful bidders of its final decision unless a third party voices any formal objections or claims. By publishing the contract award notice (CAN), the Contracting Authority ends the tender.

4.5.2 Regulative stipulations

Compared with private-sector organizations, regulations minimize Contracting Authorities' discretion in the supplier selection phase. Public procurement legislation requires objective and transparent selection methods (Tadelis, 2012). For example, procurement officials must not discriminate in favor of strong brands or suppliers who have performed well in the past. Since infringements in the award phase may lead to costly court proceedings, the Directives contain strict administrative provisions that severely restrict the buyer's scope of action. Even if crucial unforeseen aspects emerge during the tender process, the Contracting Authority cannot alter the previously published award criteria. Instead, the procurement officials must abandon the tender and restart the entire process from scratch.

Depending on the nature of the procedure and the contract, the Directives contain detailed rules for the opening of offers (e.g., confidentiality, people present, and documentation requirements). During this stage, the procurement officials prepare the offers for the evaluation. They must treat all offers confidentially and cannot enter any further discussions with the interested suppliers. Negotiations with an individual supplier would contradict the general principle of equal treatment; by nature, negotiated procedures remain the notable exception. All other procedures forbid Contracting Authorities from establishing direct contact with potential suppliers. This prohibition of further negotiations protects potential suppliers; otherwise, the Contracting Authority could use its purchasing power to enforce lower prices. Suppliers cannot change the price or content of their offers under any circumstances. The Contracting Authority may only request additional information to remove misunderstandings or doubts. Procurement officials must exclude any renegotiated offers from the selection of suppliers.

Moreover, procurement officials must check whether to exclude offers that are too low to prevent ruinous price wars between suppliers and to ensure sufficient minimum quality levels. However, a Contracting Authority can only finally reject an offer if it has previously asked for detailed information about the nature of the offer's value.[33] Still, the Directives require procurement officials to award a contract based on the criteria determined in the CN. Although the EU Directives contain provisions that enable Contracting Authorities to exclude abnormally low offers, they do not clearly define abnormally low offers and provide no specific methods for identifying them. Even significantly undercutting other bids might not automatically justify the exclusion of an offer. Instead, Contracting Authorities cannot exclude an offer without previously asking the supplier for detailed information about the nature of the offer's value.

4.5.3 Scope of action for Contracting Authorities

Like the prior tender stage where procurement officials had to check the eligibility of potential suppliers, tight regulations provide procurement officials with no managerial discretion for assessing the submitted offers. The decisions during the supplier selection stage must rely on the specifications of the CN. However, within the design CN, Contracting Authorities have some discretion to design the supplier selection rule which they must apply in this late tender stage.

Until the 2014 reform of the Directives, procurement officials could choose between two economic principles when determining the award criteria. They could either award the contract solely based on the lowest price, which corresponds to a first-price sealed-bid procurement auction or based on the most economically advantageous tender (MEAT), which corresponds to a scoring procurement auction (Chong et al., 2016).[34] Most

[33] After the 2004 reform of the Directives, it is no longer permissible to exclude low-price offers that were enabled by legitimately obtained public subsidies for the supplier.
[34] Previous research has interpreted such tenders as lowest-price auctions (Asker & Cantillon, 2008). However, the lowest price mechanism can also be a kind of scoring rule. In

public international procurement laws (e.g., the United Nations and the World Bank) provide for those two main procedures (Ballesteros-Pérez, Skitmore, Pellicer, & González-Cruz, 2015). However, the 2014 reform of the EU Directives mandates the inclusion of quality criteria: Procurement officials must use a scoring rule to evaluate offers and cannot award a contract solely based on the lowest price. The present work still discusses both options because, even after 2014, they were still able to decide to almost entirely focus their award decision on the lowest price by increasing its relative importance compared with quality criteria.

4.5.3.1 Design of the supplier selection rule

The Directives define MEAT as a standard supplier selection rule: Procurement officials can include qualitative, technical, and sustainable aspects as well as the price in the award decision. A MEAT procedure takes monetary and non-monetary components into account. An underlying scoring rule that assigns dimensionless numbers to the various elements formalizes the MEAT procedure (Asker & Cantillon, 2008). The scoring rules must also weigh all qualitative and quantitative criteria. The Directives do not contain rules on the distribution of the different weightings between the criteria. Typically, not all award criteria possess the same weights. Instead, procurement officials use weightings to prioritize the criteria. Therefore, the weight distribution in practice varies considerably (Parikka-Alhola, 2008). In sum, the CN thereby communicates a binding evaluation matrix to all potential suppliers.[35] The procurement officials must not alter the matrix and must evaluate supplier's offers according to the published price and non-price attributes. The procurement officials must award the supplier that submitted the offer with the highest score according to the MEAT scoring rule.

However, a Contracting Authority cannot freely choose the quality criteria employed within a scoring rule. Instead, the regulation requires that they

---

such a case, the scoring rule is not responsive to both quality and price but only the price matters for the final score of the submitted offers.

[35] The Directives typically require that the weighting of the various criteria gets published. However, if the Contracting Authority cannot specify the award criteria or their weighting when publishing a CN, they must publish the criteria at the beginning of the second phase at the latest (e.g., with the call for tenders).

only apply proportionate criteria that are related to the subject matter of the contract. The chosen criteria must always include the price. Since regulation strictly separates award criteria from eligibility criteria, procurement officials cannot reuse an eligibility criterion as an award criterion: A supplier is either suitable or not suitable for the execution of a contract; more suitability does not present a sound contract award criterion. Thus, eligibility criteria must not relate to previous success rates of suppliers in similar contracts, and award criteria can only relate to the contents of the offers. The Directives contain a few examples of quality criteria: Delivery date, delivery time, completion time, operating costs, economic efficiency, craftsmanship, aesthetic and functional characteristics, after-sales service, technical support, profitability, and technical value.

The Directives imply two legal consequences (Parikka-Alhola, 2008): First, procurement officials do not have to rely on objective criteria. If the criteria depend on the subject matter of the contract, the regulation allows subjective criteria for scoring. In the procurement of works, for example, scoring rules can take aesthetic aspects into account. However, when deciding to include subjective criteria, procurement officials should explain the underlying indicators used for valuation. Second, awarding the offer that meets the MEAT criterion does not correspond with awarding the cheapest offer. Instead, factors other than price play an important role. However, the price can still act as the most critical criterion in MEAT scoring rules. Vice versa, MEAT scoring rules do not necessarily mean that quality plays a vital role in the award decision.

In theory, procurement officials can choose between three general types of MEAT scoring rules: Only quality, price to quality, and quality to price (Hyytinen, Lundberg, & Toivanen, 2018). For the first choice, the valuation rule combines different quality parameters. The Directives exclude this option because it does not consider value for money. For the other types, the scoring rule relies on either numerical or monetary values (Bergman & Lundberg, 2013). Accordingly, the scoring rule evaluates quality differences either in monetary terms or converts the price into a valuation corresponding to the quality valuation. Both rules define the MEAT as the one offer with the highest combined price and quality score.

Figure 12: Share of scoring rules versus lowest price rules across EUR-zone member states

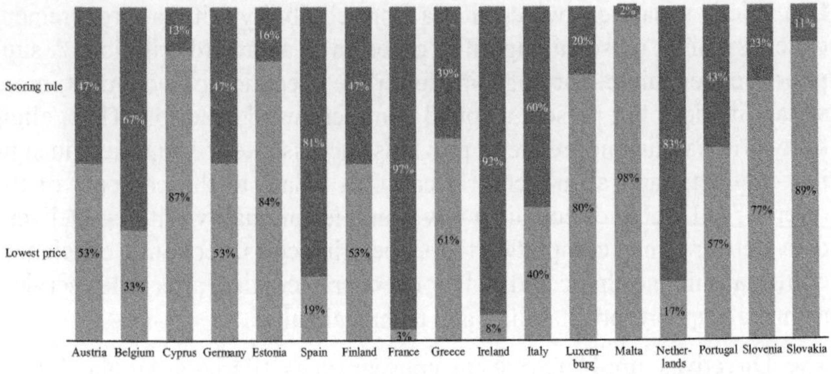

Source: Own calculations based on TED data 2012-2015 (European Commission)

Before the 2014 reform of the Directives, Contracting Authorities could opt for another award criterion: the lowest price. This criterion corresponds to a scoring rule that assigns 100% of the weights to a single economic variable: the price. The lowest price criterion followed a straightforward procedure. Procurement officials awarded contracts purely based on the price of the submitted (and evaluated as admissible) offers and excluded all other (relevant) aspects. The lowest bidder won and received the price of the cheapest bid – without the opportunity to negotiate price any further.

Already before the reform of the Directives, procurement officials preferred to award contracts on the basis of MEAT and used the price-only criterion mainly for lower-value contract awards: About 70% of the tenders that were awarded used the MEAT rules, corresponding to about 80% of contract values (PwC et al., 2011). Still, Figure 12 shows that the use of rules has massively varied across the EU member states.

5. Performance-oriented measures in tenders

As the previous chapter identified Contracting Authorities' scope of actions in designing tenders, the present chapter will discuss how procurement officials can use such design options to improve their procurement performance. Figure 13 summarizes the findings of the previous chapter and thereby outlines the structure for the current chapter. In sum, we discuss eight scopes of action that the Directives provide to Contracting Authorities. We investigate these scopes of action to determine whether Contracting Authorities can effectively use them to implement measures that will positively impact tendered outcomes.

We use a three-step approach to analyze the potential performance impact of each measure. First, we formulate a working hypothesis about how procurement officials can use their scope of action to implement the corresponding performance-oriented measure. We base each hypothesis on previous theoretical insights regarding the relation between performance and the use of such a measure. Previous research has allowed for the identification of performance-oriented measures at different tender stages. Second, we analyze prior empirical findings of studies that focused on procurement auctions regarding this measure. We thereby mainly focus on studies that took the informational and relational particularities of public procurement into account. Third, we use these empirical research findings to assess the validity of the working hypothesis. If we fail to come up with sufficient insights to support a hypothesis, we define a research gap that we will tackle in the 6th chapter, which presents the empirical investigation.

A. Rhode, *Public Procurement in the European Union*, Schriften zum europäischen Management, https://doi.org/10.1007/978-3-658-28073-4_5

Figure 13: Identified scopes of action of Contracting Authorities in public tenders

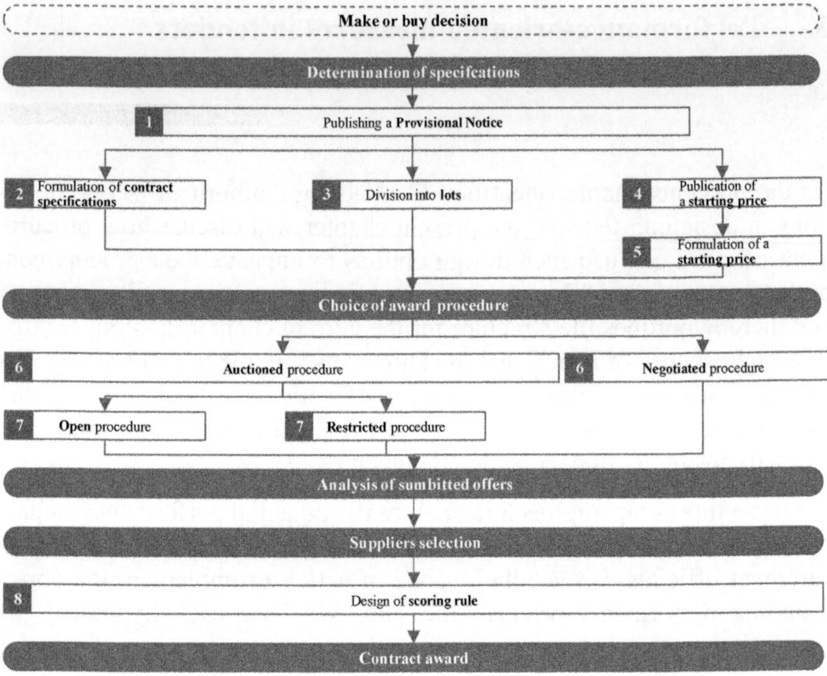

Source: Own illustration

5.1 Determination of specifications

To initiate the tender, Contracting Authorities must indicate their acquisition needs to potential suppliers. In this first phase, a high degree of discretion allows Contracting Authorities to implement several performance-oriented measures. Public procurement officials enjoy significant degrees of freedom only in this initial phase, i.e., before publicly informing potential suppliers about the tender.

5.1.1 Publication of a Prior Notice (PN)

5.1.1.1 Theoretical background and hypothesis development

As explained in Section 4.1, Contracting Authorities can inform suppliers of a tender by directly publishing a CN, or they can decide to publish a PN beforehand. The PN does not initiate the procurement procedure itself but informs potential suppliers about a future tender. A PN could increase bidders' interest because it may allow potential suppliers to prepare themselves to participate in the tender (Schmidt, 2015). If suppliers can prepare for the Contracting Authority's acquisition needs, they will be more likely to respond to a published CN. An extended preparation period may reduce the costs of participating in a tender. Likewise, the publication of a PN could enable potential suppliers to join their efforts. Particularly for complex or innovative solutions, suppliers can use the information entailed in a PN to prepare joint offers. These arguments led to the formulation of the first working hypothesis:

W1: The publication of a PN will increase bidders' interest, thus improving the procurement performance of Contracting Authorities in tenders.

The number of participants in tenders is not exogenously determined. Therefore, tenders resemble procurement auctions more than negotiations for which research usually regards the number of participants as fixed. Thus, we refer to prior auction theory studies as a theoretical foundation for investigating the effects of an increased number of interested suppliers in tenders. Other studies that have focused on public procurement have referred to auction theory as a scientific framework to investigate competition effects in tenders as well (Onur, Özcan, & Taş, 2012; Silva, Dunne, Kankanamge, & Kosmopoulou, 2008; Silva, Kosmopoulou, & Lamarche, 2009).

The relation between increased competition among suppliers and final prices is one of the standard questions of auction theory (Milgrom & Weber, 1982). Auction theory implies that auctioneers should design their procurement auctions to attract as many bidders as possible – regardless of the kind of auction. In English or second-price auctions, a higher number of bidders increases the likelihood that a bidder with a higher valuation will enter. In Dutch or first-price auctions, the number of bidders directly influences the behavior of bidders (i.e., the participants bid more aggressively). The performance effect of an additional bidder on the offers likely outshines the effects of other design choices (Bulow & Klemperer, 1996). This stipulation corresponds with the macroeconomic theory of supply: More bidders should encourage more competition so that the imperfectly competitive auction achieves an efficient result as the number of bidders becomes arbitrarily large (Hong & Shum, 2002).

The amplified competition resulting from increased bidder participation may prevent corruption and collusion (Che & Kim, 2006). In public procurement, the interface of public and private sectors typically produces the risk of corruption (Coppier & Piga, 2006). As more potential suppliers participate in a tender, it becomes more challenging to maintain a collusive arrangement – especially when new entrants become attracted to the tender. If bidders believe that, despite the agreement with other bidders, they might not win, their incentive to collude weakens. Correspondingly, the risk of corruption decreases because corruption usually requires successful collusion among bidders.[36]

However, the relation between the number of bidders and the auctioneer's performance might be non-linear (Milgrom & Weber, 1982). Its shape depends on the characteristics of the suppliers and the auctioned items. We consider the cost functions of suppliers for the analysis of competition effects. Previous authors have classified assumptions about suppliers' cost functions as a Private Value model, a Common Value model, or an Affiliated Value model.

First, in the Private Value model, bidders have different preferences and assess the value of the auctioned item differently. In such tenders, suppliers' cost estimates do not depend on how other potential suppliers assess the costs of a contract. Thus, even if suppliers learn about the evaluation

[36] Rose-Ackerman (1999) has argued that the number of bidders in procurement auctions is not essential due to competitive effects, but primarily because it affects the likelihood of collusion and corruption. Instead of attracting bidders to participate in the tender, procurement officials should focus on minimizing collusion. Increasing competition could be one but not the only way to achieve this goal. If other measures can effectively reduce collusion, increased competition might not further improve the buyer's performance. However, this alternate explanation, if it holds, would further support working hypothesis W1.

of others, they would not adapt their bidding behavior. Excellent examples of the Private Value model include demand auctions of arts and antiques (if the bidders do not act as speculators, investors, or resellers; in this case, their bids would depend on the valuation of other interested bidders).

Second, in the Common Value model, each supplier faces the same costs associated with the contract award (Milgrom & Weber, 1982). However, suppliers can observe the costs only afterward. Each supplier has different private information about the final costs. As a result, their assessments of the contract award may differ. Suppliers would adjust their bids if they learned about others' private information. The Common Value model captures the idea that the same input factor may influence suppliers' cost functions in tenders. A demand auction for oil extraction rights provides a typical example. Because all bidders might extract only the oil that is available in the auctioned area, they have a similar appreciation of the concession. However, nobody knows ex-ante exactly how much oil is in the ground. Thus, the bidders differ in their expectations of the potential amount of oil. Likewise, they might face different costs for the extraction and might have different expectations about the development of the oil price.

Third, auctions under the Affiliated Value model lie between the previous two extreme cases (Kagel, Harstad, & Levin, 1987). In auctions with Affiliated Values, the bidders' valuations share a Common Value component and a Private Value component. In practice, many auctioned items do not entirely meet the requirements of the Private Value model or the Common Value model. Instead, most real-life auctions share aspects of both models. Illustrative examples include art auctions with bidders acting as speculators, investors, or resellers: At such auctions, each bidder possesses an idiosyncratic appreciation of the artistic value of the item. However, the respective resale market price influences the valuation of all bidders. The theoretical implications (in different effect strengths) for Common Value auctions remain valid in an Affiliated Value model (if the auctioned items contain a Common Value component).

Applied to public tenders, the Private and Common Value models differ in their uncertainty concerning other bidders' preferences and the contract's specifications. In the Private Value model, the potential suppliers know only their valuation but not the valuations of others. In the case of the Common Value model, all potential suppliers share identical valuations of the auctioned contract. However, they do not entirely know the requirements and the objective value of the item. For working hypothesis W1, the distinction between Private, Common, and Affiliated Values matters because the models yield contradictory stipulations on the effects of increased competition on the auctioned outcome. Models describing a positive relationship between competition and performance levels rely on the Private Value model (Bulow & Klemperer, 1996). However, this assumed positive competition effect might reverse once values get affiliated (e.g., under the Common Value model).

With Affiliated Values, potential suppliers possess similar yet incomplete information about the value of the auctioned contract. In such an auction setting, the so-called winner's curse may arise (Kagel & Levin, 1986). This curse occurs as the winning bidder has the highest expected value for the contract and thus tends to overestimate its real value. Since bidding that is based purely on this information leads, on average, to a negative outcome (i.e., the winning bidder loses money), an adverse selection problem arises. Rational bidders incorporate this winner's curse into their strategy by bidding less aggressively. Once the number of bidders increases, rational suppliers will bid even more cautiously. Since more bidders enter an auction, more bidders will optimistically overstate their valuation of the contract. Accordingly, the likelihood that the winning bidder will suffer a loss grows, thus increasing the risk of the winner's curse.

For the Contracting Authority, a dominant winner's curse may increase the final price in tenders with high bidders' interest. Although increasing competition still leads to more offers, the winner's curse may become disproportionately more severe as more bidders participate. As a result, rational bidders will bid less aggressively. Contracting Authorities may want to limit the number of bidders in tenders in the case of a dominant Common Value component.

5.1.1.2 Existing empirical evidence

Since auction theory provides contradictory implications about whether the publication of a PN might improve buyers' performance, we will carefully investigate the empirical findings of the previous studies on public procurement. As implied by the previously discussed theoretical findings, empirical research did not provide a consistent and uniform picture of the performance effects of an increased number of bidders. Instead, diverse empirical findings matched the theoretical notion that differences in uncertainty about other bidders' preferences and the contract's value drive competition effects.

Brannman, Klein, and Weiss (1987) conducted a classical field study to test whether the dominance of a Private or a Common Value model affects auction outcomes with an increasing number of bidders. The authors used transaction data from auctions of oil production rights, municipal bonds, and timber sales. First, they investigated auctions of oil extraction concessions as an example of Common Value transactions. They showed that stronger competition improves the auctioneer's outcome and that participants do not adapt to the winner's curse.[37]

Second, the authors analyzed municipal bond auctions as an example of Affiliated Values. On the one hand, underwriters serve different clients and have different knowledge of the local bonds. On the other hand, future credit conditions have an impact on the present value of bonds for all underwriters. The authors reported that intense competition between bidders deteriorated the auctioneer's outcome.

Third, they analyzed wood auctions as an example of the Private Value model. The values of the auctioned items depend on the potentially higher transportation costs due to more remote processing locations. Their results showed that the outcome of the auctioneer improves with the number of bidders. The authors concluded that most bidders do not strive to avoid the winner's curse, although it occurs with affiliated values. Accordingly, auctioneers should try to attract more bidders to improve their performance. However, an average number of five to eight bidders already ensures a maximum level of competitiveness.

The findings by Brannman et al. (1987) correspond with a prior study by Kagel and Levin (1986), who empirically investigated competitive effects

[37] The authors negated the alternate explanation that Private Values are more pronounced as expected in oil extraction rights.

in Common Value demand auctions. They looked at auctions for contracts for a single inseparable commodity. In this apparent Common Value auction, participants bid more aggressively with a higher number of bidders. This increased aggressiveness led to negative economic results for suppliers. Although the winning bidder's curse occurred, bidders did not take this into account in their bidding strategy.

In another empirical study, Paarsch (1992) investigated the competitive effects in both Common and Private Value auctions. The author developed two models, which he used in an empirical analysis of 144 tenders for tree planting contracts. In contrast to Brannman et al. (1987), the reported results somewhat contradicted the implications of the Private Value model. Instead, Paarsch (1992) presented empirical evidence that complied with the Common Value model. He found that the competition effect tapered off when the number of bidders became large because of the anticipated winner's curse effect. Thus, the final price did not fall monotonously with more competition but only until the number of participants reached about five to ten.

Gómez-Lobo and Szymanski (2001) explored the relationship between costs and the number of offers in waste collection contracts in the UK. The authors found that more offers lowered the cost of the procured contracts. They reported another significant competition effect: The presence of two bidders reduced service costs by 12% to 13% compared with a single supplier.

Haile (2001) investigated Common Value auctions with a resale opportunity. The author reported that, at least to some extent, secondary market values determined the value of the winning bid in a procurement auction, thereby introducing an affiliated value component. Still, bidders behaved more aggressively when competing against more substantial numbers of participants. Thus, the outcomes for the auctioneer improved with increased competition, despite the existing Common Value components.

Gupta (2002) focused primarily on the number of participants required for a competitive tender environment. He analyzed highway construction contracts and found that the auctioneer's performance significantly increased as the number of bidders rose to the level of about six to eight suppliers.

He reported that, for example, an increase in the number of bidders from two to eight resulted in additional costs savings of 12% to 14%.

The study by Hong and Shum (2002) compared competition effects across three types of tenders: highway works, bridge constructions, and paving. In highway work contracts, they proposed that the Common Value component would significantly prevail. For this type of tender, they showed that the average procurement costs increased as competition intensified. For the other two types of tenders, the private-value components dominated their Common Value counterparts slightly: The authors likewise reported that more competition resulted in lower winning bids. Accordingly, bidders did not adjust for the increased winner's curse in those Affiliated Value tenders.

Millet, Parente, Fizel, and Venkataraman (2004) comprehensively analyzed competition effects in tenders. The authors distinguished between the number of invited bidders, the number of bidders who accepted the invitation, the number of bidders participating in the auction, and the number of bidders participating and actively bidding. For almost all forms of tenders that they studied, more invited and active bidders positively influenced the auctioneer's results. The number of active bidders and the number of offers submitted have a more considerable influence on the tendered result than on the numbers of invited and accepted bidders. The authors concluded that not only should auctioneers invite many suppliers, but they should also ensure that these suppliers participate actively.

Estache and Iimi (2008) focused on sectoral differences regarding the competition effect. They examined tenders from three infrastructure sectors: roads, electricity, and water. They found that increased competitiveness lowered final prices in all sectors. Nevertheless, the effect of an additional bidder diminished as competitiveness increased. In the road and water sectors, seven bidders ensured complete competition, whereas three bidders sufficed in the electricity sector. Their results suggested that improved competition reduces procurement costs by an average of 8% with the effect reaching its maximum between 4 and 14 offers.

Onur et al. (2012) analyzed competitiveness effects by investigating a data set comprised of public tenders in Turkey. They reported that every additional bidder lowered the final price by an average of 3.9%. However, they found that the number of bidders played a more significant role in tenders for works than for supplies and services. The authors argued that these empirical findings fit the predictions by auction theory because Private Value aspects are likely to dominate in tenders for works.

Grega and Nemec (2015) used a regression analysis to investigate field data published on public tenders in Slovakia. They reported that increased competitiveness significantly lowered final prices in public procurement.

Schmidt (2015) used a game theory approach to analyze competitiveness in public procurement empirically. He reported that the presence of another bidder decreased the contract price by an average of 4%. However, the influence of the expected number of submitted offers on the final price weakened with an increasing number of tenderers. The influence of additional bidders was rendered nonsignificant from certain high levels. Hence, more bidders may improve performance levels, particularly in tenders involving a smaller number of potential suppliers.

5.1.1.3 Assessment of the working hypothesis

The relation between increased competition and outcomes is probably the best-researched aspect of performance in tenders (Schmidt, 2015). The discussion of past empirical studies on competition effects in tenders has yielded two main insights: First, on the surface, the results of empirical studies may appear inconclusive. On the one hand, most studies have reported that increased competition leads to lower procurement costs. These studies have agreed that more substantial numbers of bidders decrease final prices and that a sufficiently competitive environment boosts performance. The number of submitted offers antecedes performance in tenders because an increased number of bidders increases competition. On the other hand, some authors have argued that the value of bids decreases with increases in bidders' participation in tenders with Common Value dominance: Due to asymmetric information, the economic impact of increased competition becomes inverted.

In real-world tenders, both common-value and private-value components play an essential role (Hong & Shum, 2002). Hence, in practice, procurement officials must consider two counteracting performance effects. First, more bidders have a positive effect on competition: With more bidders, the likelihood that a bidder with a higher valuation of the contract award will enter increases. Likewise, other bidders react by submitting more competitive offers to maintain their chances of winning. Second, more potential bidders might increase the winner's curse effect. Thus, rational bidders will bid less aggressively if they face increased competition.

However, both effects will not exert the same influence on procurement performance. The winner's curse effect requires a significant degree of Common Value uncertainty while the competition effects will occur in every auction – regardless of whether the Common Value or private model dominates. Therefore, we argue that Contracting Authorities, when designing their tenders, should generally strive to attract more potential suppliers. Only for some contracts will the winner's curse effect dominate over positive competition effects. Moreover, suppliers in public tender cannot observe how many other suppliers have submitted their offers. They can only anticipate (based on their market insights and prior experience) how many competitors might participate as well. The invisibility of others' bidding behavior might dampen the winner's curse effect. We argue that only in tenders with a high likelihood of aggressive bidding behavior (i.e., when general bidders' interest is high) will potential suppliers adjust for the winner's curse effect. This argumentation corresponds with previous empirical findings that already six to eight bidders will suffice to ensure a competitive environment. Only afterward might the competition effects taper off or even reverse (due to the winner's curse).

The stipulations of the Directives agree with the notion that sufficient competition among bidders should be ensured (Arlbjørn & Freytag, 2012). The Directives imply that increasing the number of bidders can prevent collusion, which otherwise would profoundly impede procurement performance. Even when the competition effect tapers off, an increase in the number of potential suppliers limits collusive behavior. The Directives incorporated this idea by demanding a minimum number of submitted bids in any procedure where procurement officials deliberately decide to limit competition, i.e., in restricted and negotiated procedures.

5.1.2 *Contract specifications*

5.1.2.1 *Theoretical background and hypothesis development*

As stated in Section 4.1, the 2004 reform of the Directives has allowed functional contract specifications. Nowadays, Contracting Authorities can choose between specifying a contract functionally or technically. Previous procurement research has briefly discussed the potential upsides and downsides of publishing functional and technical specifications (van Weele, 2014; Van Weele & Eßig, 2017). The main findings of these mostly theoretical considerations imply that the publication of functional specifications might yield several advantages for Contracting Authorities. Functional specifications should lower transaction costs and encourage more suppliers to submit offers. The next working hypothesis is as follows:

W2: The formulation of a functional specification in a CN will increase bidders' interest, thus improving the performance of Contracting Authorities in tenders.

Compared with functional specifications, technical specifications might possess several drawbacks. Typically, technical specifications rely on detailed technical drawings and activity schedules. Procurement officials will use such specifications to monitor the winning supplier's activities in detail. However, the high level of descriptive detail may result in over-specifications that become troublesome after the contract is awarded: The Contracting Authority may impose strict requirements on the winning supplier that result only in higher transaction costs but not in better functionality or improved quality.[38]

Potential suppliers may reflect this limited flexibility during the fulfillment stage by estimating increased costs and submitting correspondingly higher offers. Likewise, responding to highly detailed technical specifications increases the tender entry costs. Suppliers invest significant resources in participating in tenders, although they have a relatively low chance of winning the contract (Samuelson, 1985). Therefore, the entry costs that incur for

[38] The principle of proportionality implies that Contracting Authorities should formulate the specifications as effortlessly as possible from the perspective of potential suppliers. One may argue that, therefore, this principle requires the publishing of functional specifications.

preparing offers have an impact on the likelihood that suppliers submit bids. When deciding to participate in a tender, bidders must evaluate the resources required to assemble, prepare, and submit their offer (Hausch & Li, 1993). Therefore, excessive contract specifications may discourage some bidders from entering if they believe that the economic benefits of receiving a contract award do not justify the cost of submitting an offer.

Furthermore, overly precise contract specifications may shrink the supply market. Because strict technical specifications limit the scope of possible solutions, some potential suppliers may choose not to participate in the tender: either because they cannot provide a solution that meets the CN's technical requirements or because they face excessive production and development costs in meeting the requirements. In the latter case, their valuation (the difference between the cost estimate and the final price) of the contract award decreases, and they may refrain from participating in the tender.

Likewise, an over-specification increases the expected costs for suppliers in the event of an unforeseen adjustment need during the fulfillment stage. They must evaluate all potential technical changes in accordance with the contract specifications. As a result, further transaction costs can occur in two ways: On the one hand, the Contracting Authority will ensure that the selected contractor carries out his or her work by following the specifications of the CN. On the other hand, the selected supplier must obtain approval from the procurement officials before changing the technical specifications – preferably in writing.

In contrast, the increased flexibility of functional specifications can yield several advantages for suppliers and procurement officials. First, less rigid functional specifications can increase the potential suppliers' discretion during the offer preparation. Potential suppliers can apply their industry knowledge and expertise during the tendering process. Thereby, they can determine the technical details of their solution according to their cost functions. Likewise, functional specifications allow potential suppliers to propose new technologies not known to the procurement officials. Contracting Authorities can source solutions that they would not have thought of themselves. They can benefit from the knowledge and expertise of suppliers that the rigid requirements in alternative technical specifications would otherwise exclude. Thereby, functional specifications can lower tender entry costs and enable innovation in public procurement (Edler & Georghiou, 2007).[39]

Highly rigid specifications may harm performance levels in tender given the particularities of public procurement. The Directives forbid procurement officials from entering into discussions with potential suppliers before they publish the contract specifications. Otherwise, the Contracting Authority would disobey the general principles of non-discrimination and equal treatment. These two principles, along with the high transparency requirements, cause a rigid and limited exchange of information between procurement officials and potential suppliers. Thereby, potential suppliers cannot resolve ambiguities in the contract specifications before their fixation. In a given period after the CN publication, potential suppliers can submit written questions, which the Contracting Authorities must openly publish along with their answers.[40] After this question and answer period has ended, the Directives entirely prohibit suppliers from asking questions about the full content of the CN.

5.1.2.2 Existing empirical evidence

Like working hypothesis W1, the validity of working hypothesis W2 depends on the notion that increased competition causes lower procurement costs. Functional specifications may only improve procurement performance if more bidders' interest decreases the final price. Since the present work has already thoroughly discussed the existing empirical studies, we will refrain from repetition at this point and refer to Section 5.1.1 instead. However, we must note that – to the best of our knowledge – no previous empirical studies have investigated the relation between functional

[39] As discussed, public procurement differs from private purchasing due to its higher variety in (non-economic) objectives. If broader socioeconomic goals play a role in tenders (e.g., fostering small business activity), buyers must incorporate them into the CN as well. However, buyers might struggle to determine specifications as these somewhat intangible goals often refer to abstract policies. Including such goals may aggravate their ability to formulate specifications and select the most appropriate supplier.

[40] Contracting authorities must respond formally and in writing to all legitimate questions asked by potential suppliers. Buyers must publicly publish all their replies and make them available to all interested suppliers simultaneously.

specifications and the number of bidders as an antecedent of procurement performance.

5.1.2.3 *Assessment of the working hypothesis*

Since increased bidding activity will typically improve buyers' outcomes in tenders (see Section 5.1.1), we argue that functional specifications can improve outcomes by increasing the number of bidders. More flexible specifications will attract the interest of more suppliers. By contrast, rigid specifications will shrink the procurement market by excluding certain potential suppliers or even a whole group of suppliers.

Prior empirical research has so far neglected to investigate the relation between the formulation of contract specifications and performance in tenders. Still, previous empirical studies on competition effects have supported the idea that when more bidders are interested, procurement performance is likely to improve. Likewise, no theoretical or empirical research has suggested that the formulation of functional specifications might lower bidders' interest. Accordingly, we identified sufficient empirical evidence on competition effects in support of working hypothesis W2.

Thus, procurement officials should release functional specifications instead of technical ones. Functional specifications can only lower but not increase transaction costs for suppliers. These lower costs make it easier for potential suppliers to enter the tender. Functional specifications also directly ease the submission of offers by giving suppliers more discretion. Since suppliers will bear higher transaction costs when forming their offers based on technical specifications, they will be less likely to submit offers in reaction.

5.1.3 *Lots*

5.1.3.1 *Theoretical background and hypothesis development*

When defining the specifications, procurement officials must decide how many lots to award to potential suppliers. Since a Contracting Authority must coordinate the actions of different suppliers, splitting a single contract into several independent lots increases its administrative burden and transaction costs.

However, awarding a complex contract in smaller lots might expand the supply market. The Directives explicitly allow a contract to be split into several smaller tranches to meet the policy objective of greater participation by SMEs. Typically, the high monetary value of tenders would confront them with unacceptable financial risks. Accordingly, this secondary procurement objective points to an economic upside of awarding individual lots: Smaller contracts shrink the entry risks – particularly for smaller potential suppliers. As already argued in the previous two sections, the subsequent increase in competition between suppliers will likely have a positive effect on the performance of Contracting Authorities in public procurement. Thereby, we formed the next working hypothesis W3.

W3: The division of contracts into smaller lots will increase bidders' interest, thus improving the procurement performance of Contracting Authorities in tenders.

The division of procurement into smaller lots could lead to potential cost savings (Van Weele & Eßig, 2017). However, Contracting Authorities face a tradeoff when splitting a contract into smaller lots because their transaction costs could increase simultaneously. They will become fully responsible for coordinating the individually awarded suppliers and for ensuring a continuous flow of project-related activities during the fulfillment stage. Given this increased responsibility, additional transaction costs in the event of processual mistakes may easily outweigh or even exceed the potential cost-savings a priori. Procurement officials may only divide sufficiently valuable contracts into lots, so performance-enhancing competition effects become significant: The splitting of less valuable contracts will not widen the potential supply market as potential suppliers could neglect their financial risks.

Contracting Authorities need to balance another tradeoff between increased competition and lower economies of scale when they plan the number of lots and define their size. On the one hand, smaller lots lower the financial risks entailed in valuable contracts. On the other hand, winning a more massive contract allows economies of scale for the winning supplier.[41] If the chosen award mechanism ensures a competitive outcome,

[41] Economies of scale assume that when suppliers produce more, they can lower the average unit costs (Shepherd & Shepherd, 2004). Although past empirical studies have

procurement prices will thereby fall due to a lower cost estimate of the winning supplier. Thus, the procurement of items via a single holistic contract might create cost savings.

Lower economies of scale entail lower economic benefits for the winning supplier. Thereby, the reduced economies of scale could prevent suppliers from participating in a tender. Suppliers will only participate in a tender if they believe that the potential economic benefits of awarding the contract (albeit their relatively small chance of winning) outweigh the entry costs (Samuelson, 1985). Suppliers will be more likely to submit offers for more valuable tenders because higher contract values involve high economic benefits. Due to regulations, bidders typically incur high entry costs in public procurement – irrespective of the contract award value. While less complicated contracts typically entail lower entry costs, the economic benefits will decrease disproportionately as entry costs remain significant. Without a sufficient financial incentive, potential suppliers might not be willing to incur entry costs for the (small) chance of winning the tender.

5.1.3.2 Empirical evidence

In comparison with the vast array of studies on competition effects, we can only refer to limited previous empirical research that examined the effects of lots in public procurement.

Estache and Iimi (2008) examined the relation between lot sizes and the number of participating bidders in public tenders for large infrastructure projects. They stated that by splitting larger contracts into smaller lots, Contracting Authorities could profit from more competition for these lots. However, they reported that this performance-enhancing effect (i.e., from subdividing a contract into smaller lots) exists only for expensive contracts. With low contract values, the relative transaction costs for suppliers' participation in the tender may increase disproportionately. Therefore, a

concluded that economies of scale exist in a variety of industries, the scale concept implies that companies cannot realize declining average unit costs without any limitations. At some point, increasing output leads to rising average unit costs, a concept known as diseconomies of scale. A variety of factors can lead to those diseconomies, including fixed factors, administrative and bureaucratic costs, and transportation costs.

further reduction in the size of contracts that are already small will adversely shift the tradeoff between increased competition and economies of scale.

Onur et al. (2012) confirmed that the potential benefits of lot division remain limited. By analyzing an extensive data set of Turkish public tenders for services, works, and supply contracts, the authors found that higher-value tenders attracted the interest of more significant numbers of bidders. Since the relative share of entry costs compared with potential economic benefits for suppliers sink disproportionately, higher contract values facilitate their decision to enter. Accordingly, splitting a contract into smaller portions may indeed not increase bidders' interest at all.

5.1.3.3 Assessment of the working hypothesis

Albeit the limited empirical results on the relation between contract size and bidders' interest, we argue that with the necessary degree of caution, they support working hypothesis W3, which proposes that purchasers may profit from dividing contracts into smaller installments to attract more bidders. In doing so, they can expand the scope of potential suppliers and benefit from increased interest from bidders and thus improve their procurement performance. However, we argue that this performance-oriented measure might only be effective in high-value tenders.

Results from previous empirical studies have implied that contracts must reach a sufficiently high monetary value before Contracting Authorities should consider dividing them into several lots. Estache and Iimi (2008) reported positive effects of lot splitting on bidder participation. However, the authors derived this result from a tender data set for infrastructure projects. The final price (depending on the sector) of such projects averaged around EUR 10 to 40 million, and the standard deviation of the final prices in their data set ranged from around EUR 20 to 65 million. By contrast, Onur et al. (2012) analyzed a more diverse set of data across several types of contracts, items, and industries and reported that the splitting of contracts into lots did not increase bidders' interest. The contract award values in their data set averaged EUR 1 million (standard deviation = around EUR 3 million). For most potential suppliers in Turkey, such average values do not entail unacceptable financial risks.

Thus, the findings of Estache and Iimi (2008) on massive infrastructure projects and the results of Onur et al. (2012) on smaller tenders do not contradict but rather complement each other. Both studies provided sufficient empirical support for research hypothesis W3 – given a sufficiently large contract award. Their results also implied that an allocation of smaller lots would be likely to reduce the procurement performance for contracts with smaller award values: Disproportionately higher entry barriers due to lot splitting will lead to a lower number of submitted offers.

5.1.4 Release of a starting price

5.1.4.1 Theoretical background and hypothesis development

Contracting Authorities can publish an ex-ante price estimate in their CN. We argue that the release of such a starting price can impact bidders' behavior and thereby drive performance in tenders. Starting prices may drive the intrapsychic processes of the suppliers and interpersonal processes in economic transactions (Northcraft & Neale, 1987). For negotiations, researchers reported that starting prices could explain between 50% and up to 85% of the variance in final prices (Galinsky, Ku, & Mussweiler, 2009; Orr & Guthrie, 2005). Accordingly, negotiators may gain a first-mover advantage by publishing starting prices at the beginning of a negotiation.

Typically, Contracting Authorities do not use negotiations to acquire items or to transmit information to potential suppliers in public procurement (Bajari et al., 2009). Instead, the Directives favor the use of procurement auctions as a substitute for negotiations. However, Contracting Authorities act as first movers in tenders. Since they can thereby decide whether to release a starting price, Contracting Authorities might ask themselves if they can enjoy a similar first-mover advantage. Past research on negotiations and auctions has suggested that contracting authorities may enjoy a first-mover advantage by publishing starting prices in tenders. Therefore, we defined the next working hypothesis as:

W4: The release of a starting price will improve the procurement performance of Contracting Authorities in tenders.

Starting prices may influence the behavior and cognition of potential suppliers by exerting an anchoring effect on them. Anchoring is a heuristic (i.e., a mental shortcut for forming judgments and making decisions) on which individuals rely to estimate a number under uncertainty (Tversky & Kahneman, 1974). Anchoring occurs when people consider a given figure for an unknown number before estimating that number. The cognitive mechanisms of insufficient adjustment and selective accessibility can explain how starting prices positively anchor outcomes.

On the one hand, individuals tend not to move away from the anchor sufficiently (Epley & Gilovich, 2006). They start from the given number (i.e., the anchor) and adjust either up or down to reach a value that seems plausible while failing to move far enough away from the anchor. Thereby, an arbitrarily chosen anchor (e.g., a starting price) has an inappropriate influence on their (economic) assessments. Since tenders involve a significant degree of uncertainty for the suppliers, they might interpret starting prices as such an anchor and (insufficiently) adjust away when estimating the real value of the underlying contract. If suppliers face a low value, they might make corrections while preparing their bid but stop adjusting if they encounter the lowest amount they would accept in the case of a contract award: Thereby, a starting price will affect bidders' value estimations. Contracting Authorities might profit from this impact by deliberately publishing a starting price to influence the range of suppliers' counteroffers.

On the other hand, research has explained the anchoring effect by referring to individuals' selective accessibility: People tend to generate more arguments that are consistent with the anchor (Strack & Mussweiler, 1997). Anchor recipients ask themselves if the anchor represents a suitable outcome within the given uncertain circumstance. They look for alternative outcomes while accessing all the relevant attributes of the anchor itself. Afterward, when they try to evaluate the other outcomes, they look for similarities to the anchor. This process results in the anchor's potency: For example, a supplier exposed to a rather low-priced contract might attend more to production efficiency potentials than to the inherent risks of unforeseen cost increases.

In addition to the abovementioned behavioral explanations, which refer to the anchoring perspective, auction theory may provide an alternative explanation for the influence of starting prices on the final prices: The publication of a starting price could increase competition among bidders by making the values more predictable and reducing the winner's curse (Milgrom & Weber, 1982).[42] The release of private information entailed in the starting price might intensify competition among bidders by lowering the winner's curse. The release of information regarding the valuation of the contract may induce more aggressive bidding behavior, particularly in tenders with a Common Value dominance (Goeree & Offerman, 2003). By contrast, the release of information comprised in a starting price can worsen bidders' outcomes by reducing the relative value of their private information.[43] By lowering the uncertainty for other potential bidders, the release of a starting price could likewise motivate more bidders to enter. In tenders, potential bidders receive starting prices before they enter. Since starting prices precede the decision to enter, suppliers choose whether to enter a tender after considering the starting price. For example, they will be more likely to enter a tender when the starting price significantly exceeds their estimated costs in the case of a contract award.

Accordingly, Contracting Authorities may face a crucial question when deciding to publish the starting price in a CN: Does the starting price influence bidders' decisions to participate or is their interest fixed? The publication of starting prices may only matter if the number of bidders is not exogenously determined. Since increased competition among bidders is likely to improve procurement performance, they should entice as many suppliers as possible. By publishing a starting price, the Contracting Authority may provide potential suppliers with private information which lower their entry risks.

However, auction research also implies that the publication of a starting price does not come without any risks (Ku, Galinsky, & Murnighan, 2006). If procurement officials underestimate a starting price in a tender, they may discourage potential suppliers from participating. With a meager starting price, Contracting Authorities might fail to award a contract at all.

---

[42] For suppliers, tenders entail a high degree of uncertainty regarding the correct valuation of the contract. At least this conclusion holds if Private Values fail to capture all the contract characteristics. In practice, valuations of suppliers are typically affiliated as both Common Value and Private Value components play essential roles (Hong & Shum, 2002).
[43] However, a starting price release would not affect bids when only the Private Values model applies. In these auctions, the information conveyed by the price estimate would have no impact on the bidders' valuations.

Theoretically, deriving an optimal value of a starting price would require the nearly impossible task of obtaining an accurate picture of the distribution of the costs of all potential suppliers. By contrast, if procurement officials courteously formulate starting prices, they incentivize potential suppliers to demand a higher remuneration for the contract than necessary from an economic point of view.

Finally, auction theory implies that the effects of starting prices on performance should not be overestimated (H. Li & Riley, 2007) and that the impact of starting prices on the auction outcome is likely to remain low. Instead, the effects of an additional bidder should outshine the performance effects of other design options, such as the setting of starting prices (Bulow & Klemperer, 1996). Besides, suppliers might not attach too much importance to starting prices and may neglect them for the most part (Kamins, Drèze, & Folkes, 2004). For example, in open procurement auctions, compared with highly influential pricing signals provided by bids of other bidders, starting prices provided by the auctioneer lack credibility and thereby lack influence. Suppliers instead focus on other buyers' behavior or past similar tenders as pricing cues.

5.1.4.2 Existing Empirical Evidence

Since past research has investigated the effects of starting prices on outcomes in different economic transactions from various research perspectives, we divided up the discussion of existing empirical studies into four subsections to separately discuss the existing empirical evidence that is relevant to working hypothesis W4.

1. Negotiations

For negotiations, a plethora of studies has demonstrated that negotiators gain a first-mover advantage by releasing starting prices (Galinsky et al., 2009; Galinsky & Mussweiler, 2001; Schweinsberg, Ku, Wang, & Pillutla, 2012; Shalvi, Moran, & Ritov, 2010). Prior studies that have used laboratory and in-class experiments have claimed that by making the first offer, bargainers gain a first-mover advantage in negotiations: First offers provide positive anchors for outcomes. Independent of their monetary value, counterparties are likely to adopt starting prices as reference points and adjust their counteroffers to their numerical value (Kristensen & Gärling,

1997). Research has consistently reported the robustness of this anchoring effect – even when the anchors are unrealistic (Strack & Mussweiler, 1997) or recipients are forewarned (Wilson, Houston, Etling, & Brekke, 1996).

2. Demand Auctions

For demand auctions, past research has yielded mixed findings on the existence of a first-mover advantage. Some studies have reported that high starting prices yield lower final prices (Kamins et al., 2004; Ku et al., 2006). The framework of auctions leads to different performance effects of starting prices compared with negotiations. Since the number of bidders in auctions is typically not exogenously determined, the anchoring effect in auctions with high starting prices might reverse by inducing lower final prices (Ku et al., 2006). Since starting prices that are too high might prevent potential bidders from entering the auction, they might create barriers to entry. Thus, auctioneers might refrain from setting starting prices. Starting prices may cause a contrasting anchoring effect: In demand auctions, lower starting prices were found to result in more traffic (Kamins et al., 2004). Similarly, Reiley (2006) conducted a field experiment and reported that public starting prices harmed the performance of sellers in demand auctions. The publication of starting prices was found to reduce the number of bidders, the probability of a final deal, and the final prices.

Other studies have reported that starting prices are positively correlated with improved outcomes in demand auctions (Ariely & Simonson, 2003; Lucking-Reiley et al., 2007; Pinker, Seidmann, & Vakrat, 2003). Since bidders infer item values on the basis of starting prices, high starting prices anchor potential bidders and lead to higher final prices. Trautmann and Traxler (2010) confirmed these findings by analyzing field study data: They reported that starting prices increase auctioneers' performance. Brint (2003) argued that sellers could increase their results by having a high starting price, but only in a situation where counterparties possessed little price knowledge (e.g., without any reference or market price). Due to other available reference prices, first-mover's starting prices may struggle to influence bidders' behavior. However, other studies that have used field data have found no significant effects of starting prices on bidders' behavior, outcomes, and auctioneers' performance (Bajari & Hortaçsu, 2003; Hoppe & Sadrieh, 2007).

Galinsky, Ku, and Mussweiler (2009) tried to reconcile these conflicting insights by arguing that the number of actors in auctions is determined endogenously. The authors argued that the strength of the barriers to traffic meditates a U-shaped curvilinear relation between starting prices and outcomes. Without other significant entry barriers, the starting price could reduce the interest of potential bidders. Low starting prices may cause a contrasting anchor effect in auctions for three reasons: First, lower starting prices can lower the entry barriers for the bidder. Accordingly, the number of bidders participating in a demand auction will increase, thus leading to more competition. Second, low starting prices can lead to higher costs for early entrants. Therefore, these bidders will bid more aggressively at the end of a demand auction. Third, participants will receive a higher value from the increased activity and may be more likely to participate in the demand auction. Only if general barriers to entry (e.g., misspelled articles) prevent herding behavior, high starting prices may lead to assimilative anchoring effects. These barriers can limit general traffic in such a way that interpersonal effects due to herding behavior do not occur. Instead, the intrapsychological anchor effects remain more pronounced, leading to an assimilative effect of starting prices.

3. Housing transactions

Another line of research focusing on listing prices in housing transactions has led to more insights into the impact of starting prices on the auctioned results. A typical house sale begins with an auction-like process that structurally resembles public tenders. One party initiates the bidding process, and interested bidders submit offers. The auctioneer acts as the first mover and can publish a starting price. Sellers can decide to put the house up for sale, with or without a starting price. These prices initiate the economic transaction and may anchor recipients. A starting price in housing transactions typically indicates the monetary value that the auctioneer considers acceptable. In turn, the interested buyers interpret the starting price as negotiable and submit bids if they want to purchase the property. Thus, the starting price will usually lie close to the first mover's reservation price (to create some room for negotiation and competition). Either no bidder will accept the starting price, or several bidders may compete so that the auctioneer achieves a result better than the starting price. Alternatively, some housing transactions settle directly on the starting price (Case & Shiller, 2003).

Early research on housing transactions viewed starting prices as a mostly meaningless rite within the process initiation (Sheppard, 1999). Authors have traditionally treated house prices as an objective function of property and neighborhood characteristics. Starting prices would only serve the largely pointless purpose of initiating the tendering process. If at all, auctioneers would only use the starting price to promote visits. Accordingly, first movers would use attractive (i.e., low) starting prices to attract bidders' attention. By contrast, aggressive (i.e., high) starting prices could lower bidders' interest and reverse the anchoring effect.

However, empirical housing studies have exposed and refuted these beliefs. Experimental research has reported that starting prices have an assimilating anchoring effect on both real estate professionals and amateurs (Northcraft & Neale, 1987). The authors found that starting prices significantly influenced the valuations of amateurs and experts. Even though professional estate agents considered a starting price to be utterly uninformative, it strongly influenced their judgments.[44] Experts distinguished themselves from amateurs only by their denial of this influence.

Bucchianeri and Minson (2013) confirmed that high starting prices led to higher final prices by analyzing field data from more than 14,000 private housing transactions. They reported that higher starting prices were correlated with higher selling prices, which coincided with the effects of anchoring. Moreover, the heterogeneity of real estate prices in the same regional area significantly reduced the anchoring power of starting prices. The presence of houses with similar fundamental characteristics, listed or sold at different prices, provides bidders with anchor-disconfirming evidence.

By contrast, Gatzlaff and Liu (2013) reported a reversal of the first-mover advantage for the sale of income-generating commercial real estate. Complex commercial properties typically showed higher information asymmetries than simple residential buildings. Sellers often marketed these

[44] This finding corresponds with other classical studies on anchors. In such studies, individuals were exposed to a uninformative value that could still be a possible answer. Tversky and Kahneman (1974) reported that even such anchors exert significant suggestive effects on judgments.

properties without a starting price. The authors reported that vendors in their sample quoted starting prices for less than one-third of commercial property sales. For highly complex properties with more substantial information asymmetries, the probability decreased even more. Accordingly, the authors found that properties with public starting prices were correlated with lower end prices. They argued that sellers hid starting prices to maintain an information advantage and avoid trimming off particularly high bids. Hence, sellers did not use starting prices as a strategic anchor but instead concealed starting prices from interested buyers.

4. Tenders

Compared with studies on other kinds of economic transactions, the few studies that have analyzed starting prices in public tenders have all worked from the perspective of auction theory. The study by Silva et al. (2008) examined the publication of starting prices in US road construction tenders. Based on Milgrom's theorem No. 16, the authors proposed that the private information that was released from providing a starting price reduced the winner's curse and thereby increased competition among bidders. With typically affiliated values in tenders, the winner's curse occurs because the winning supplier is optimistic about the value of the item. A rational supplier incorporates this curse into its strategy by bidding less aggressively. Thus, the curse of a dominant winner would increase the final average prices in tenders. For some suppliers, however, this release reduces the value of their private information.

To examine their hypotheses, the authors analyzed a policy change regarding the publication of internal cost estimates (i.e., starting prices) using a difference-in-difference approach. They found that the release of the seller's information generally resulted in lower bids. In line with auction theory, they found that the level of overall cost uncertainty affected this relation because the effect of publishing information prevailed in public tenders for items that showed considerably less certainty. However, lower average supplier bids did not result in significantly lower winning bids. Instead, the authors reported a nonsignificant correlation between the publication of starting prices and final prices. Only the average bid fell after the policy change. Thus, the published price estimates did not lead to significantly lower procurement costs and correspondingly higher performance levels for the Contracting Authorities. The released information concerned only the upper end of the bid distribution. The publication of a starting price did not induce other suppliers to adjust their already less optimistic and more realistic valuations.

A subsequent and directly related study by Silva et al. (2009) used a similar approach but specifically focused on the behavior of new entrants. Coming from an auction theory perspective, the authors argued that the winner's curse should particularly affect new entrants, who typically possess less information about the auctioned contracts. Given this cost uncertainty, they should bid more aggressively than incumbent firms. The authors found that the information asymmetry between entrant and incumbent firms became less pronounced after the publication of starting prices. Accordingly, the released starting price likely increased the profit margins of new entrants and increased their economic prospects after the tender entry. However, the authors did not report any significant relation between the release of price estimates and buyers' procurement performance.

5.1.4.3 Assessment of the working hypothesis

Many empirical studies have focused on the relation between the publication of a starting price and economic outcomes: Authors have analyzed various types of economic transactions based on different theoretical frameworks and have reported contradictory empirical results. Previous empirical evidence has provided several insights into the performance effects of starting prices in tenders but has not provided sufficient evidence to conclude that Contracting Authorities can improve their procurement performance by publishing a starting price. Each research stream has provided several reasons for why the publication of a starting price in public tenders could boost or harm procurement performance. Accordingly, empirical studies to date have not provided enough support for working hypothesis W4.

Instead, the present work reports a research gap that we will examine empirically in Chapter 6. We will go through each previously discussed stream of research separately to assess why the current state of research has not sufficiently supported working hypothesis W4. Furthermore, we will discuss these studies to identify implications for the empirical investigation conducted in the present work.

1. Negotiations

Previous anchoring studies have implied that starting prices may affect outcomes in all economic transactions that represent a choice environment involving risk and uncertainty. However, the advantages of going first might not arise in public procurement because negotiations and tenders differ in their informational and relational mechanisms. Insights of past research have at least scrutinized whether a first-mover advantage exists in public tenders.

For example, tenders and negotiations differ in the richness of communication that exists between the buyer and supplier (Drolet & Morris, 2000). Such differences may cause effects of anchors to differ between the two transactional settings. Anchor effects that might affect outcomes by driving suppliers' behavior based on communicative and psychological means might work in distinctively different ways in public tenders compared with private-sector price negotiations. In negotiations, the buyer usually discusses the acquisition in detail with the supplier before signing the contract. Unlike tenders, negotiations take place in a face-to-face manner, and all senses are involved: Not only do both buyers and suppliers exchange verbal messages, but they also use body language and facial expressions as a means for communicating their meaning. The transactional outcomes can depend heavily on the human factor.

By contrast, purely written messages in tenders offer relatively little indication of such underlying meanings. In public tenders, the impersonal and fact-based price determinations leave little room for personal interactions (Kaufmann & Carter, 2004). Regulatory burdens heavily restrict the exchange of information and the opportunities for social interaction between the parties. Procurement officials receive information primarily in the form of suppliers' bids. The more impersonal price determination typically forbids personal meetings and exchanges.

Moreover, starting prices in tenders may lack the extremity required to anchor bidders effectively. Prior negotiation research has argued that the first-offer extremity determines the first-mover's success (Thompson, 2015). Therefore, factors that elevate or reduce the first-offer extremity determine the first-mover's success (Maaravi, Ganzach, & Pazy, 2011). Hence, negotiation researchers have recommended to first movers, in practice, to begin as extremely as reasonably possible. However, Contracting Authorities cannot adhere to this advice due to regulative restrictions demanding a realistic calculation basis (see Section 4.1.3). Compared with extreme first offers in negotiations, starting prices in public procurement thus are often interpreted as acceptable by recipients.

Similarly, several negotiation studies have demonstrated that making the first offer may result in relational disadvantages (Loschelder et al., 2016; Loschelder, Swaab, Trötschel, & Galinsky, 2014). When the first movers possess little information about the item or market, they risk making an unacceptable offer. Moreover, starting prices might create impasses by motivating people to walk away from a negotiation (Ames & Mason, 2015). Schweinsberg et al. (2012) argued that counterparties' reactions depend on their assumptions about power levels. An extreme starting price may mainly increase the risk that a low-power negotiator will leave the transaction without a deal.

This risk might particularly arise in tenders because regulations tend to lower suppliers' bargaining power by mainly placing the risk on their side (Tadelis, 2012). However, applying findings of negotiation research to tenders still requires great caution. Since most negotiation research so far has focused on the impact of first offers after the involved parties have agreed to negotiate, the reported adverse effects of starting prices have referred to impasses that arise during the negotiation. The decision to enter a transaction differs psychologically from the decision to end one (Yip & Schweinsberg, 2017). Without a prior entry decision, no transaction takes place at all, and caring about potential impasses becomes obsolete. Thus, starting prices in negotiations may cause different reactions in recipients than in public tenders, where suppliers process starting prices before they decide whether to enter.

In general, negotiation studies may have underestimated the risk of impasses created by starting prices (Galinsky et al., 2009). Most of the studies have demonstrated the first-mover advantage in laboratory negotiations. While authors have provided consistent experimental evidence that starting prices cause a first-mover advantage due to anchoring effects, they neglected to provide an experimental replication. The lack of access to current and reliable transaction data remains one of the largest in negotiation research. Researchers can easily manipulate and control for the influence of a single starting price in laboratory studies. However, researchers have struggled to identify a starting price in field studies because markets usually offer several candidates (Lin, Huang, & Zeelenberg, 2006). Thus, we cannot directly transfer the insights provided by laboratory studies to real-world markets.

Likewise, real-life attitudes with financial consequences encourage elaborate thinking, which reduces the potency of anchors compared with experimental approaches (Epley & Gilovich, 2006). Also, an experimental framework conceals the risk of bottlenecks by creating artificial incentives to enter into agreements and not terminate transactions. Both reservations may particularly apply to starting prices in tenders. On the one hand, public procurement usually involves rather valuable contracts with considerable financial consequences for winning suppliers. Suppliers may engage in more elaborate information processing, which may then influence starting prices. On the other hand, the number of submitted offers likely antecedes performance in public procurement. Therefore, the release of a starting price may decrease performance levels if it reduces bidders' interest in the contract award.

2. Demand auctions

Previous auction studies have provided another basis for deriving hypotheses on the impact of starting prices in tenders. Still, these studies have only yielded inconclusive results on the relation between starting prices and final prices. Instead of providing uniform implications, existing empirical studies suggest that the first-mover advantage strongly depends on transactional specifics. Not only might starting prices in tenders affect intrapsychic processes, but they might also catalyze interpersonal processes, which might reverse anchoring effects by lowering the number of submitted bid.

For negotiations, prior research has demonstrated the first-mover advantage under the premise that the involved parties have already entered the transactions (Schweinsberg et al., 2012). In tenders and auctions, potential suppliers receive starting prices before they enter the transaction. Since starting prices precede the decision to enter, bidders choose whether to participate after considering the starting price. Thus, they will likely refrain from entering a procurement auction when the starting price undercuts their estimated costs. Since auctions without a starting price do not deter the entry decisions of potential suppliers, auctioneers might deliberately conceal starting prices to avoid lowering suppliers' interest.

Previous research has implied that this impact of starting prices on bidders' interest strongly depends on transactional structures. Ku et al. (2006) showed that depending on the occurrence of herding behavior, contrasting or assimilative anchoring effects will prevail. While their results imply that assimilative anchoring effects might only occur in procurement auctions with high barriers to entry, their findings might not apply to public tenders. In such first-price sealed-bid auction settings, contrasting anchoring effects due to herding behavior might not appear. Refraining from disclosing a starting price may lower the entry barriers for suppliers but cannot create sunk costs for early entrants because bidders submit only one offer. Likewise, bidders cannot derive value from the increase in bidding activity because the numbers of offers get published after the contract award.

Still, other empirical evidence has suggested that starting prices may create barriers to entry in tenders. Studies on demand auctions have likewise reported that starting prices increase the chances of not selling an item while decreasing the numbers of bids and bidders (Lucking-Reiley et al., 2007; Pinker et al., 2003). Since starting prices precede the entry decision in tenders as well, suppliers will refrain from entering when the starting price undercuts their estimated costs.

Finally, a study by Brint (2003) suggested that an assimilative anchoring effect only exists for items without a clear starting price. This characteristic might apply to some tenders but not to all of them. Similarly, the strength of the assimilative anchoring effect appears to decrease if bidders have access to anchor-disconfirming evidence (Bucchianeri & Minson, 2013). High level of heterogeneity of tenders may give rise to this effects in public procurement: Contracting Authorities acquire both unusual items without any comparable values as pricing clues and standardized items with transparent market prices as further reference points.

3. Housing transactions

The discussed similarities between list prices in housing sales and ex-ante price estimates in public procurement valorize the empirical findings of housing studies: Both kinds of starting prices might similarly influence bidders' cognitive processes and behavior. However, the existing field studies have not produced consistent empirical findings. On the one hand, Bucchianeri and Minson (2013) reported that high starting prices led to higher final prices by analyzing private housing transaction data. On the other hand, the findings by Gatzlaff and Liu (2013) implied that the assimilative anchor effect might reverse in transactions involving more complex items with more significant information asymmetries: Transactions that provide a starting price may be correlated with lower sales prices. Particularly in tenders for expensive contracts, procurement officials might not reveal starting price information to profit from stronger information asymmetries. Compared with private purchasing, increased complexity, higher information asymmetries, and reduced informational exchange characterize public procurement (Tadelis, 2012). Thus, Contracting Authorities might have good reasons to deliberately conceal starting prices to maintain an information advantage and to avoid cutting off lower than expected offers.

4. Tenders

Compared with research focused on negotiations, demand auctions, and housing transactions, existing empirical studies on the relation between starting prices and outcomes in public procurement have remained limited. No studies have investigated whether starting prices exert an anchoring effect on potential suppliers.

Only the study by Silva et al. (2008) investigated how the release of starting prices affects final prices in tenders. However, they did not focus on Contracting Authorities' release behavior. Instead, the authors tried to empirically validate Milgrom's Theorem No. 16 (Milgrom, 1979) by investigating the impact of a policy change on bidders' behavior. Moreover, they reported a nonsignificant relation between the publication of starting prices and final prices. The authors were able to replicate the finding that the release of buyers' information entailed in a starting price increased competition among bidders. They argued that the release of information only leads to an upward revision in the costs of bidders who had an optimistic assessment of the costs associated with the implementation of the project. Since starting prices influence bidders' behavior only when they are optimistic, starting prices did not impact final prices, on average.

However, these insights are not sufficient to conclude that Contracting Authorities cannot improve their procurement performance by disclosing starting prices. Likewise, their results do not imply that Contracting Authorities should not care about the publication of starting prices. Some methodological difficulties do not allow for the generalizing of their findings on the performance impact of starting prices in tenders. First, in their study, they failed to investigate anchoring effects as a possible alternative explanation for the impact of starting prices on outcomes. Second, the study possessed a limited scope by only looking at road construction projects in two US states. The previous discussion of other empirical and theoretical studies on public procurement showed that the performance impact of starting prices depends heavily on contract characteristics. Accordingly, a sample that consists only of contracts for road construction projects is not sufficient for assessing the relation between price estimates and final prices in tenders in general (and for investigating anchoring effects in particular). Third, the study followed a difference-in-differences method, which might limit the validity of its results due to the potential endogeneity of the policy change (Besley & Case, 2000). Thus, their results may oversimplify any causal inference regarding the relation between price estimates and procurement performance (Bertrand, Duflo, & Mullainathan, 2002). Instead, a structural regression model may allow for a better understanding of the (anchoring) effect of starting prices on bidders' behavior and transaction outcomes.

5.1.5 Formulation of a starting price

5.1.5.1 Theoretical background and hypothesis development

Since the present work aims at identifying the scope of action that the Directives leave to procurement officials for managing tenders, we must recognize that a Contracting Authority possesses the first-mover freedom not only to publish a starting price but also to define its form and precision. Moreover, procurement officials can choose whether to formulate this starting price as a price point or as a price range.

Previous research has implied that different kinds of starting prices might impact bidders' cognitions, thereby affecting outcomes, even though the starting prices on their own comprise nearly the same informational value from a purely rational point of view (Loschelder, Stuppi et al., 2014; Mason, Lee, Wiley, & Ames, 2013). Most negotiation studies have shown that accurate starting prices exert particularly strong anchor potency (Loschelder, Stuppi, et al., 2014; Mason et al., 2013). Increased precision may enhance the impact of the starting price on the final prices in public tenders as well: Recipients might interpret a precise starting price point as more credible than the other kinds of starting prices (i.e., a round starting price point or a starting price range). Despite the difference in many relational and informational aspects between negotiations and tenders (Bajari et al., 2009), intrapsychic mechanisms responsible for the increased anchoring potency of precise starting prices might work in public procurement as well. Therefore, we built the next working hypothesis:

W5: The formulation of a precise starting price procurement will improve the procurement performance of Contracting Authorities in tenders.

Researchers tend to refer to two intrapsychic mechanisms to explain why increased precision promotes the anchoring potency of starting prices (Loschelder, Stuppi, et al., 2014). On the one hand, researchers have used the social-relational attribution of competence explanation. Recipients may attribute more competence to precise starting prices. Suppliers may assume that Contracting Authorities need all the numbers to estimate the value of the tendered contract. Therefore, precise starting prices may seem more plausible and may thereby enjoy increased anchor potency.

On the other hand, the scale granularity explanation refers to a serial adjustment in the counterparties' cognitive processes. Precise offers may induce a finer-grained mental scale, which may lead the recipients to adjust the starting price bit by bit in smaller steps. Precision reduces the overall adjustment in price and induces more conciliatory counteroffers.

These intrapsychic mechanisms can only explain how the precision of starting prices disclosed as price points might affect the procurement performance of Contracting Authorities. However, first movers may choose to formulate starting prices as ranges. These price ranges might also affect buyers' performance by influencing the behaviors and cognitions of interested suppliers. The respective findings of Ames and Mason (2015) for negotiations imply that Contracting Authorities can achieve better deals by formulating (imprecise) starting price ranges.

In general, Ku et al. (2006) argued that starting prices in auctions may affect outcomes by influencing the counterparties' intrapsychic processes and by influencing the interaction between parties. Since starting price ranges have affected outcomes in negotiations on exactly these two levels, they might also affect outcomes in tenders alike.

First, starting price ranges may improve relationships by inducing politeness and lowering the extremity of suppliers' counteroffers. Counterparties might interpret starting price ranges as politer than equally aggressive price points. In turn, they might respond by submitting less extreme bids. Second, price ranges possess an informative effect by shaping counterparties' assumptions about the first mover's reservation price and the item's underlying value. Suppliers may use these assumptions to establish a framework for probable tender outcomes. According to the selective attention explanation, they will focus on the more attractive value at the end of the price range. Using bolstering starting price ranges (a CN advertising a contract at a starting price range that goes from €900,000 to €1,100,000 versus a starting price point of €1,000,000) may be particularly beneficial. The ambitious figure within a bolstering starting price range might exert an informational influence on recipients by boosting its anchor potency compared with similar starting price points.

5.1.5.2 Existing empirical evidence

Since the past empirical findings of the different degree of precision of starting price points and starting price ranges yield different insights for performance management in tenders, we will discuss them separately.

1. Starting price points

Despite the many studies on anchoring in negotiations, researchers have only rather recently begun to study anchoring precision effects (Loschelder, Friese, & Trötschel, 2017). Most studies have reported that precise anchors outperform round anchors. For first movers in negotiations, increased starting price precision leads to better outcomes (Loschelder, Stuppi, et al., 2014; Mason et al., 2013; Thomas & Park, 2013; Thomas,

Simon, & Kadiyali, 2010). Increased starting price precision promotes the first-mover advantage in auction settings.

Studies on housing transactions conducted in laboratory settings (Cardella & Seiler, 2016; Thomas et al., 2010) and those based on transaction data (Beracha & Seiler, 2014; Janiszewski & Uy, 2008) have both claimed that increased precision in anchors leads to higher selling prices. Accordingly, recipients will interpret precise starting prices as indicative of a more reasoned and better-informed seller. More precise starting prices tend to lead to lower adjustment compared with corresponding rounded equivalents. Thereby, the increase in precision should lead to a lower negotiated discount and an improved performance for the first-mover.

However, other recent studies have identified potential disadvantages of increased anchor precision in economic transactions (Loschelder et al., 2016). A high level of precision can backfire because recipients might interpret an overly precise starting price as a lack of first-mover competence. In line with the attribution-of-competence account, precision loses some of its anchor potency once it exceeds a certain level. Anchors that are too precise may undermine the first-mover advantage as counterparties may interpret them as a sign of decreased competence; the competence attributed to the first mover may cause an inverted U-shaped relation between precision and final prices. Experienced negotiators believe that other experienced negotiators will not make an exact first offer. Consequently, recipients will attribute lower competence to a precise offer without a plausible justification. Accordingly, the scale-granularity explanation fails to capture the relations between precision and final prices.

Social attribution processes might drive another disadvantage of increases in anchor precision. Overly precise starting prices can create barriers to entry, which might reduce a supplier's likelihood of entering the transaction (Lee et al., 2018). The authors showed that starting prices that are too precise might create barriers to entry because they prevent potential counterparties from entering into a transaction. Based on starting price precision, first-offer recipients form assumptions about the first mover. Recipients believe that starting prices indicate the first mover's reservation price. Because precision implies less room for concessions, counterparties will see precise first movers as less flexible. A constricted bargaining space lowers the attractiveness of entering the transaction. Similarly, Backus, Blake, and Tadelis (2016) argued that first movers may use round starting prices to signal flexibility and that they will accept poorer outcomes to shorten transaction times.

Yan and Pena-Marin (2017) referred to another intrapsychic mechanism to discuss another potential disadvantage of increased precision. Compared with precise numbers, round values suggest completion and more likely correspond to counterparties' goals. Round starting prices imply that the deal will soon close and are likely to induce less aggression. In their study, the counterparties accepted round starting prices rather than equally extreme precise ones. When the counterparties faced precise starting prices, they responded with lower counteroffers. The authors concluded that a so-called roundness advantage depends on the counterparties' cognitive focus. The benefits of round starting prices increase when counterparties focus on the task of accepting an offer rather than on formulating a counteroffer. In the latter, the increased anchor potency of precise starting prices will prevail.

2. Starting price ranges

Ames and Mason (2015) studied how starting price ranges influenced negotiation outcomes. The authors argued that first movers could achieve better deals by using starting price ranges compared with equally extreme starting price points. The authors examined three distinct kinds of range offers in detail.

First, the authors found that a bolstering range offer (e.g., a seller asking for \$5,000 to \$5,200 vs. a point offer of \$5,000; and vice versa, a buyer offering \$4,800 to \$5,000 vs. a point offer of \$5,000) yielded improved outcomes without damaging the relationship between parties. The bolstering range offers outperformed the point offers of equal value: The former enjoyed lower rates of impasses, received less aggressive counteroffers, and led to improved outcomes. Accordingly, first movers may use bolstering range offers in negotiations when they need to claim value and nurture the relationship with the counterparty.

Second, the authors studied bracketing range offers, which span point offers (e.g., a seller asking for \$4,900 to \$5,100 vs. a point offer of \$5,000; and vice versa, a buyer offering \$4,900 to \$5,100 vs. a point offer of

$5,000). Compared with point offers, less aggressive bracketing range offers yielded better outcomes and positively affected negotiators' relationships. Consequently, first movers may use bracketing range offers in negotiations when they wish to maintain a fruitful relationship with the counterparty.

Third, the study analyzed back down range offers, which contain a point value and a more modest figure (e.g., a seller asking for $4,800 to $5,000 vs. a point offer of $5,000; and vice versa, a buyer offering $5,000 to $5,200 vs. a point offer of $5,000). The authors found that first movers should avoid using back down range offers. On the one hand, these offers led to worse negotiation results than point offers. On the other hand, they did not offer any relational benefits compared with bracketing range offers.

5.1.5.3 Assessment of the working hypothesis

Previous studies on anchor precision have provided heterogeneous insights into the relation between anchor precision and performance. Prima facie, the results of increased numerical precision and imprecise range anchors even conflict with each other because price ranges are arguably less precise than any other round point price. Consequently, the results of Ames and Mason (2015) might contradict other implications on the potential performance benefits of increased anchor precision in public tenders. Ames and Mason (2015) already acknowledged the seemingly contradictory implications of research on range anchors and increased anchor precision. The authors proposed that future research should jointly examine their effects. However, no other study so far has jointly analyzed both types of anchoring effects in any form of economic transaction.

When transferring existing research findings to public tenders, existent research gap widens even further. For tenders, researchers have so far neglected to investigate precision effects. No studies have examined how procurement officials should formulate starting prices to increase their performance. The structural differences prevent a direct transfer of anchoring insights from negotiations to tenders – both for starting price points and starting price ranges. Even though the intrapsychic mechanisms responsible for assimilative anchoring effects of increased precision may remain valid, interpersonal processes shaped by starting price precision that affect outcomes might work differently.

We currently do not know how interpersonal precision effects work in tenders. The number of participants in public procurement is not exogenously determined. In most tenders, bidders' participation precedes the buyer's performance because an increased number of interested suppliers surges competition for the contract award (see section 5.1.1). Potential entry barriers created by increased starting price precision might outweigh the positive effects of increased anchor potency.

Consequently, the present empirical findings are not sufficient for providing a definite recommendation to procurement officials on how to formulate starting prices. Current research implies that each available type of starting price might improve the Contracting Authorities' outcomes. Depending on the study, precise starting price points (e.g., €499,999), round starting price points (e.g., €500,000), or starting price ranges (e.g., €490,000 to €510,000) may have the most positive impact on performance.

Accordingly, studies have not provided enough support for both working hypotheses W5. Instead, the present work acknowledges another research gap that we will examine empirically in the following chapters. To deepen the understanding of the nature of this research gap, we will go through each previously discussed research stream separately.

1. Starting price points

Anchors may affect outcomes by influencing suppliers' cognitions in different ways in tenders than in negotiations. Thus, the implications of negotiation research on the increased potency of precise anchors might not apply to public tenders. In contrast, some findings imply that the potential disadvantages of starting price precision might mainly prevail in public procurement.

Most previous studies have reported that precise starting prices enjoy an improved anchor potency compared with round starting prices. Studies have reported a positive impact of increased anchor precision on outcomes with regularity in negotiations (Loschelder, Stuppi, et al., 2014; Mason et al., 2013) as well as in auctions (Janiszewski & Uy, 2008). Consequently, procurement officials might strive for increased precision when they formulate public starting prices as well. However, the relation between precision and anchor potency might not be linear (Loschelder et al., 2016). When precision exceeds an appropriate level, it loses its anchor potency, thus leading to an (inverse) U-shaped relation between anchor precision and final prices. In public tenders, starting prices that are too precise might undermine precision benefits as well. An inverse U-shaped relation between precision and transaction prices might be particularly likely as it primarily occurs with the participation of professional and expert suppliers (Loschelder et al., 2016). Potential participants in tenders are likely to possess a high level of expertise because they are likely to operate in an industry where the public sector is their most crucial customer.

Additionally, precise starting prices might create barriers to entry because potential suppliers might associate the precise first-mover with inflexibility (Lee et al., 2018). If this inflexibility discourages potential suppliers from participating, it will create higher entry barriers that might reverse the potential benefits of precision. Suppliers weigh transaction costs against potential gains when entering a tender (Levin & Smith, 1994). If increased precision conveys a smaller difference between the starting price and the buyer's reservation price, interested suppliers will assume that the potential economic gains of participating are low. They might refrain from preparing and submitting an offer in response to a tender with a precise starting price.

2. Starting price ranges

The form of the starting price may drive buyers' performance in tenders as well. Ames and Mason (2015) studied the performance effects of starting price ranges. The authors found that starting price ranges exerted an informational effect and a politeness effect.[45]

In public tenders, starting price ranges may yield an informational effect by shaping the potential bidders' assumptions about acceptable settlement values. Moreover, potential suppliers might interpret starting price ranges as politer than equally aggressive starting price points. Therefore, starting price ranges may induce politeness by lowering the extremity of suppliers'

[45] However, recommendations by researchers to practitioners not to employ range offers (Thompson, 2015) and to formulate starting prices that are as precise as possible (Neale & Lys, 2015) cast some doubt on the effectiveness of range offers outside of laboratory settings.

offers. If recipients interpret a range anchor as politer compared with an equally extreme point anchor, they also might be more likely to participate in a tender. Procurement officials could profit from increased bidding activity by awarding a contract at a lower cost base. Using bolstering starting price ranges may be particularly beneficial in tenders: In addition to the range's politeness effect, the ambitious figure within a bolstering starting price range might exert an informational influence on recipients by boosting anchor potency compared with starting prices with similar values.

5.2 Choice of the award procedure

As discussed in Section 4.3, the Directives contain a menu of procurement procedures from which Contracting Authorities can choose:[46]

> Open procedures: All interested suppliers may submit an offer

> Restricted procedures: Only those suppliers invited by the Contracting Authority after the pre-selection phase may submit offers

> Negotiated procedures: Contracting Authorities negotiate a contract directly with suppliers that have qualified in a pre-selection phase

Since the open and restricted procedures are both auctioned procedures, Contracting Authorities must first decide whether to award a contract through a procurement auction or by negotiating with potential suppliers. If procurement officials opt for an auctioned procedure, they must choose secondly between an open and a restricted procedure. Since these two types of decisions may distinctively drive procurement performance, this section will discuss these measures separately.

Although the Directives set the open procedure as the standard format, purchasers can switch to a restricted or negotiated procedure. After the 2014

[46] Procurement officials can also use the competitive dialogue – particularly for the procurement of complicated and hard-to-specify contracts. However, the dialogue itself does not result in a contract award. Instead, procurement officials close the dialogue once they feel sufficiently informed about possible solutions and then invite suppliers to submit offers. Thus, the competitive dialogue is a sub form of a negotiated procedure. Compared with an auctioned procedure, the competitive dialogue allows flexibility because procurement officials do not need to determine specifications before publishing a CN but after negotiating them jointly with suitable suppliers. Accordingly, a competitive dialogue might provide the same flexibility advantages as the negotiated procedure.

reform, they can always opt for a restricted procedure instead of an open procedure. Compared with the restricted procedure, the regulation still limits the discretion of the Contracting Authority to use a negotiated procedure. However, the present work aims to analyze the decision to choose an award procedure from a performance-oriented perspective. Thus, we assume that, if necessary, procurement officials can reasonably substantiate why they deviated from the open procedure. Accordingly, the present section ignores that the Directives may restrict a buyer's choice of which procurement procedure to apply.

5.2.1 Choosing between an auctioned procedure and a negotiated procedure

5.2.1.1 Theoretical background and hypothesis development

As a device for transmitting information between buyers and suppliers, procurement auctions and negotiations may be substituted for each other (Bajari et al., 2009). In principle, procurement auctions represent a specific form of negotiations in which bidders submit their offers simultaneously and in a transparent manner, instead of engaging in the usual separate and successive negotiations. However, negotiations and auctions differ in many processual aspects.

From the research perspective of the present work, the use of a negotiated procedure may represent an archetypical example of how Contracting Authorities can improve their performance by implementing the best practices from the private sector. In the private sector, purchasers can freely choose the award procedure and typically prefer to use negotiations to satisfy their acquisition needs. Given the increased impact of auctions on competition, the avoidance of auctioned procedures in the private sector is puzzling. Should Contracting Authorities in public procurement try to avoid auctions whenever possible and instead employ negotiated procedures?[47]

[47] After the reform of the Directives in 2014, a Contracting Authority can opt for a negotiated procedure to satisfy non-standard acquisition needs. This reform reflects past criticism of practitioners and academics alike that the auctions might not always outperform other procedures in public procurement. However, the Directives continue to heavily restrict the use of negotiations without a prior call for competition.

Compared with auctioned procedures, the buyer's discretion in negotiations increases: Thereby, negotiations can have a positive impact on purchasing performance in several respects (Ax & Schneider, 2005). First, procurement officials can refine contract specifications because they can quickly adapt their needs and find innovative solutions in joint discussions with suppliers – particularly for complex contracts. Second, negotiations reduce the likelihood of adaptations of the specifications after the contract award that would increase procurement and transaction costs. Third, officials can ask potential suppliers to justify the different elements of their offers during a negotiation. Thereby, they can better control for illegal behavior such as collusion and low-balling offers (i.e., intentionally low but economically unfeasible offers, which suppliers will renegotiate after they win the tender).

Due to high degrees of transparency and formalization, auctioned procedures in public procurement may create significant transaction costs. In practice, procurement officials may try to avoid an auctioned procedure to reduce transaction costs (Kosilek & Uhr, 2002). However, intense and time-consuming interpersonal exchanges in a negotiation are not likely to reduce but are more likely to increase transaction costs. Theoretically, the creation of more complete specifications in negotiations creates higher pre-award transaction costs that are compensated for by a lower risk of post-award adaptions (Tirole, 2009).[48] Particular for complex and high-value contracts, potential post-award adaptions present one of the biggest performance obstacles in public procurement (Bajari et al., 2009). In line with these arguments, we built the next working hypothesis:

W6: Compared with an auctioned procedure, the choice to go with a negotiated procedure will improve the procurement performance of Contracting Authorities in tenders.

Procurement officials may refrain from auctions when procuring complex and customized contracts (Bajari et al., 2009). During a public tender, the

[48] The validity of this argument does not depend on the 2014 reform of Directives that, in certain circumstances, allowed renegotiations. Before the reform, potential contract adjustments led to even higher transaction costs. Since procurement officials could not renegotiate contract specifications with the winning supplier, they had to completely reissue a tender to acquire a newly specified contract.

Contracting Authority alone defines the specifications and determines only price-related issues along with suppliers. Accordingly, procurement auctions are usually fixed-pie transactions that are primarily focused on determining final prices. In negotiations, on the other hand, both sides can develop creative solutions to expand the size of the pie: Parties can discuss other issues alongside costs (e.g., quality levels, delivery conditions) to improve the suitability of contract specifications.

However, increased discretion may result in performance disadvantages as well: Increased freedom in the selection of contractors gives rise to favoritism and corruption in tenders (Chong et al., 2016). By contrast, auctioned procedures lower the risk of corruption as they allow the free entry of all qualified bidders and demand objective criteria for the selection of bidders (Hyytinen et al., 2018).[49]

5.2.1.2 Empirical findings

Empirical studies on private purchasing and public procurement alike have argued that auctions may allow for the realization of more favorable purchasing prices compared with negotiations (Gattiker, Huang, & Schwarz, 2007; Jap, 2002; Mithas & Jones, 2007). These empirical studies correspond with the notion of auction theory that open procedures will foster levels of competition. Increased competition among bidders will lower costs until bids decrease to economically minimum costs (Milgrom & Weber, 1982). By stimulating competition between suppliers, fair market prices may be discovered: Competition keeps the final price as low as possible because bidders must submit truthful bids. Likewise, competition aggravates collusion and corruption, thereby ensuring the equal treatment of potential suppliers and further improving procurement performance. Auctions will particularly enjoy performance advantages if they can attract many potential suppliers to submit offers. With a sufficiently high level of

---

[49] Theoretically, Contracting Authorities may prefer to allow collusion if the winner's curse is severe (Hong & Shum, 2002). With a significant Common Value dominance, the information pooling resulting from bidders' discussions can mitigate the winner's curse effects. While the U.S. government allowed joint bidding in the past, the Directives explicitly forbid such behavior. Moreover, such a policy change would massively contradict the general principles. Accordingly, in the present work, we refrain from discussing pooling as a performance-oriented measure.

competition, the auction mechanism will motivate suppliers to place bids at an economic minimum (Bulow & Klemperer, 1996). Procurement officials may fail to achieve the same cost-optimal outcome in other procedures that restrict competition and thereby allow potential suppliers to add a premium to their submitted offers.

However, previous empirical studies have shown that increased competition does not always improve buyers' outcomes (see Section 5.1.1). When the winner's curse occurs, Contracting Authorities may wish to restrict entry by favoring negotiations over auctions. Likewise, the empirical evidence of the downsides of low flexibility in a procurement auction substantiates the potential upsides of negotiations as they present the procedure with the highest degree of buyer discretion.

Bajari et al. (2009) compared the performance effects of auctions and negotiations in tenders. The authors hypothesized that negotiations would outperform open procedures because they allow for a pre-agreement exchange of information between the Contracting Authority and potential suppliers. By contrast, auctions may stifle communication: A contracting Authority can no longer profit from suppliers' expertise. To test their hypotheses, the authors examined a set of US work contracts from 1995 to 2000. Their results showed that, due to incomplete specifications, auctions for high value and complex contracts performed poorly. Likewise, auctions lost their competitive advantage for transactions with only a few available potential suppliers.

Awarding fixed-price contracts through open procedures may backfire. The authors argued that the restricted flow of information in an open procedure would lead to some economic downsides. Parties limit their informational exchange to the price, even though other qualitative considerations particularly matter for complex contracts. The lack of communication and the need to proceed quickly without creating detailed specifications increased the risk of contractual changes in later stages, ex-post haggling, and increased transaction costs. In negotiations, however, buyers can refine their specifications, express their underlying needs, and identify unexpected and innovative solutions.

Lalive and Schmutzler (2011) studied the procurement of railway services in Germany, comparing negotiations and auctions. They reported evidence that negotiations are correlated with higher final prices. Their results indicated a significant efficiency-enhancing effect of auctions. However, their data set mainly consisted of simple contracts. Accordingly, the procurement officials in their data set could precisely and thoroughly define their contract specifications.

Decarolis (2014) implied a caveat for the employment of open procedures in public procurement. He investigated tenders in Italy where regulators introduced first-price auctions. His result showed that such competitive auctions induced more aggressive bidding behavior, leading to lower final prices. However, they also yielded adverse performance effects: Since lower prices increased the risk that the winning suppliers could not deliver what they initially promised, post-award adaptions of the contract specifications became significantly more likely. The necessary adaptions equalized at least 50% of the cost savings of lower winning bids. Accordingly, the author argued that procurement officials should cautiously use open auctions in an environment where suppliers might fail to deliver on their promises.

5.2.1.3 Assessment of the working hypothesis

When making the decision to go with an auctioned procedure or a negotiated procedure, Contracting Authorities face the general dilemma that the chosen procedure should maximize procurement performance while preventing manipulation, corruption, or favoritism.

Given the plethora of empirical findings on the effect of increased competition on outcomes, past versions of the Directives have unsurprisingly favored open auctions: Regulators aim to define mechanisms that minimize the overall transaction costs and the potential for corruption. Auctioned procedures combine performance advantages (by attracting many suppliers and providing strong incentives to bidders to bid at their actual costs) and compliance benefits (by ensuring a high degree of transparency and non-discrimination).

However, the empirical findings show that these desirable effects depend on two critical assumptions: On the one hand, a sufficiently large number of potential suppliers must exist. On the other hand, auctioneers must be able to formulate complete contract specifications that define parties' rights and obligations across all future contingencies (Heinrich, 1999). If these assumptions hold, we argue that Contracting Authorities should opt for auctioned procedures to award contracts.

However, we agree with Bajari et al. (2009) that Contracting Authorities may prefer negotiated procedures to auctioned procedures once ex-post adaptions of contract specifications become likely. Since negotiations between procurement officials and suppliers can avoid ex-post transaction costs, their potential cost savings may outweigh the auctions' potential performance benefits. Therefore, procurement officials must identify projects that stand out in their level of complexity. Common aspects of complex contracts incapacitate fixed-price auction procedures for their acquisition: Potential post-award adaptions increase transaction costs and might in severe cases even require the restarting of the entire tender process.

Moreover, empirical studies also imply that Contracting Authorities in auctioned procedures might miss out on the closer exchange with qualified and knowledgeable suppliers. Procurement officials might prefer negotiations that allow for a more vivid exchange of information and reduce the risk of post-award adaptations – without necessarily increasing final prices (Tirole, 2009). The particularities of public finance may pressure procurement officials to proceed quickly (without the ability to produce complete specifications). Thereby, they might increase the risk of contractual incompleteness and potential post-award adaptations in tenders.

Accordingly, empirical research findings support working hypothesis W6 that Contracting Authorities should prefer negotiated procedures versus auctioned procedures. We acknowledge contracting research findings that have shown that, from a regulatory perspective, negotiations increase the risk of corruption and other kinds of misbehavior. In public procurement, suppliers may bribe officials to obtain a contract through direct negotiations and to avoid an open procedure (Søreide, 2004).

In the present work, we were able to avoid addressing such counterarguments because our aim was to identify measures that Contracting Authorities can use in public tenders to improve their performance. In Chapter 4, we argued that reaching higher performance levels of Contracting Authorities largely corresponds to getting the best value for money in public procurement. Engaging in collusive behavior with suppliers in negotiations would obviously go against this efficiency objective. Thus, we could rule out the possibility that performance-oriented procurement officials would exploit their increased discretion in negotiations to engage in unlawful relationships with suppliers. The increased risk of collusion and corruption in negotiations would not falsify working hypothesis W6.[50]

5.2.2 *Open vs. restricted auctioned procedures*

5.2.2.1 *Theoretical background and hypothesis development*

As previously discussed, open procedures might induce higher procurement performance through increased competition, less corruption, and more transparency. In practice, Contracting Authorities may deny the feasibility of an open procedure because only a limited number of suppliers can deliver the item or because its implementation involves a disproportionate effort.

In comparison with the open procedure, the restricted procedure deliberately limits the number of offers. The corresponding reduction in the competition may cause higher final bids as well as an increased risk for corruption and collusion. To prevent these potential downsides, the Directives require procurement officials to ensure a sufficient level of bidders' interest in a restricted procedure: They must invite at least five bidders to submit an offer. Moreover, they must ensure that they do not always select the same group of suppliers in the pre-qualification in the event of renewed contracts.

The current section interprets restricted procedures as a hybrid form of tendering that falls between the opposites of an open procedure and a negotiation: A restricted procedure enables part of the competitive pressure of an open procedure while increasing buyers' discretion. Moreover, a restricted procedure lowers transaction costs as procurement officials have to assess

[50] To proactively lower concerns about low transparency in negotiations, procurement officials may combine the negotiated procedure with a clear set of rules to qualify appropriate suppliers (Kelman, 2002). In a previous call for competition, procurement officials can transparently evaluate the eligibility of potential suppliers. Otherwise, Contracting Authorities may struggle to plausibly and transparently award contracts in a negotiated procedure. For the same reasons, the Directives treat negotiations without a previous call for competition as a last-resort procedure (Spagnolo, 2012).

a smaller number of offers compared with the open procedure. Both higher levels of flexibility and discretion lower the transactions costs of running a restricted procedure. In line with these arguments, we built the next working hypothesis:

W7: Compared with an open procedure, the choice to go with a restricted procedure will improve the procurement performance of Contracting Authorities in tenders.

The first main argument in favor of restricted procedures reflects one of the advantages of negotiations versus open procedures. If procurement officials cannot enforce critical quality dimensions via the contract specifications, open auctions suffer from high asymmetric information and potential ex-post transaction costs. While negotiations allow both to be reduced by engaging in an active exchange of information with suppliers before the contract award, restricted procedures might lower them by incentivizing appropriate supplier behavior after the contract award.

If buyers cannot fully define and enforce appropriate behavior in suppliers, they face a principal-agent problem and a moral hazard in (public) procurement (Baker, Gibbons, & Murphy, 2002). By restricting competition and thus increasing the discretionary power of procurement officials, restricted procedures might act as a reputation-based mechanism to alleviate non-contractibility of high-quality contract rendering and delivery (Spagnolo, 2012). In tenders, contracting Authorities can use the economic opportunities that arise from future (renewed) contract awards as a motivational tool for suppliers. If a Contracting Authority repeatedly engages with the same group of suppliers, bidders have an incentive to behave in the buyer's interest to build a reputation for winning future tenders. With high levels of competition in open procedures, this incentive typically remains low as suppliers have only small chances of winning subsequent contract awards continuously.

By restricting competition, the Contracting Authority can increase a supplier's chance of winning a contract (Hallwood, 1996). By increasing the bidder's economic interest to win the transaction at hand as well as potential renewals in restricted procedures, they will emphasize the importance of reputation: They may attract more reputable suppliers or incentivize reputational behavior from suppliers.

By restricting competition, procurement officials can compensate for a common disadvantage of public procurement in the EU:The regulation prohibits them from basing the contract award decision on previous relationships and the supplier's reputation to ensure the equal treatment of suppliers (Banerjee & Duflo, 2000). Since procurement officials cannot use suppliers' past performance as an award criterion, they might fail to select a reputable contractor in an open procedure. A restricted procedure will allow them to filter out less reputable suppliers by lowering their incentives and chances to participate in a tender (Kim, 1998). By allowing the consideration of reputation and the establishment of longer-lasting relationships with suppliers, the restricted procedure may improve buyers' performance. Since restricted procedures indirectly strengthen the significance of suppliers' reputation, they install an informal governance mechanism as a remedy for incomplete contract design. Compared to less reliable suppliers, reputable and more long-term-oriented suppliers will not read incomplete specifications strategically to determine where they will fail and behave accordingly, although auctions that award contracts based on a fixed (unit) price entail such incentives.

Likewise, restricting competition will attract more reputable suppliers due to lower entry barriers. In complex tenders conducted in an open procedure, suppliers might avoid entering an auction due to the amount of effort required to prepare adequate tender documents. Restricted procedures require the same level of effort from suppliers – but only in the second stage of the tender with a limited number of competitors. Thus, particularly qualified suppliers enjoy a higher relative chance to win the contract award and will bear the high tender entry costs.

Furthermore, Contracting Authorities may want to limit the number of bids submitted to lower their transaction costs for analyzing submitted offers and selecting a winning supplier. With high interest from bidders, procurement officials may have to evaluate many offers. These evaluations can be costly and time-consuming. Thus, they may want to limit offers because the fundamental analysis of the eligibility of the suppliers and the content of their offers can become costly – particularly for complex tenders that attract many bidders. By allowing only suitable suppliers to submit offers, a restricted procedure allows procurement officials to save their resources while evaluating offers. Restricting the number of offers avoids unnecessary costs related to filtering out unsuitable suppliers. Likewise, more bidders in open auctions increase transaction costs as the Contracting Authority must issue full tender documents to all interested suppliers. However, the electronic transmission of electronic documents can significantly reduce these kinds of transaction costs.[51]

5.2.2.2 Existing empirical evidence

Until recently, empirical studies have failed to investigate how different types of auctioned procedures affect procurement outcomes (Hyytinen et al., 2018). Fortunately for the taxpayers, recent research has begun to assess how restricted procedures affect buyers' procurement performance.[52]

Chong et al. (2016) focused on the potential abuse of restricted procedures. The authors reported that compared with open auctions, Contracting Authorities used restricted procedures for more complex tenders. Buyers might want to take advantage of increased discretion when tendering more complex contracts. However, the authors reported that lower institutional quality was correlated with the use of restricted auctions as well. Since buyers more frequently used restricted award procedures in adverse institutional environments, their results suggested that increased discretion within restricted procedures gives rise to potential abuses. Although the authors could not directly prove that such illegal behavior exists, they provided additional indirect support for their argument: The introduction of the Directives (which, before the 2014 reform, strongly favored open procedures) affected the tendering behavior of Contracting Authorities only when the institutional environment was weak. These authorities used significantly fewer restricted procedures after the introduction of the Directives, whereas higher quality buyers did not change their choice of open or restricted procedures after the Directives became effective.

---

[51] Restricted procedures do not uniformly lower transaction costs. For example, the statutory time limits are shorter under the open procedure than under the restricted procedure.
[52] Usually, past research has focused on the positive competition effects of (open) auctioned procedures. For example, Domberger, Hall, and Li (1995) collected data on public tenders in Australia. They reported that increased competition after the regulatory introduction of auctions led to significantly reduced prices. Moreover, buyers profited from maintained or even enhanced quality in the service rendering.

Chever, Saussier, and Yvrande-Billon (2017) analyzed data from social housing tenders in France. The authors aimed to investigate the potential advantages of using restricted auctions when tendering small, simple contracts. Theoretically, buyers might prefer the restricted procedure for complex contracts. Increased transaction costs due to contract incompleteness should occur only rarely in simple tenders. Thus, the use of restricted auctions for low-value contracts seemed puzzling. However, their empirical investigation showed that restricted procedures did not result in higher final prices. Instead, buyers might use restricted procedures to reduce transaction costs while still ensuring a high degree of competition. Accordingly, the authors reported no evidence of corruption or favoritism. In line with the previously discussed theoretical considerations, the authors argued that, even when corruption occurs, buyers may profit from restricted auctions by attracting more reputable suppliers and lowering transaction costs.

Coviello et al. (2018) analyzed the effect of buyers' discretion on procurement outcomes for public work contracts in Italy. They compared tenders above the monetary thresholds (awarded through an open procedure) and below those (awarded through a restricted procedure). The authors reported that increased discretion within the restricted procedures did not significantly affect the tender outcomes (e.g., the winning bid, the likelihood of a cost overrun, or the probability that the contract award would go to a local supplier). However, higher discretion increased the probability that the same supplier would win repeatedly. While this award behavior may signal an increased risk of corruption, it did not deteriorate average procurement outcomes. Thus, the increase in the probability that the buyers would award the same supplier indicated not only corruption but also relational benefits. Increased discretion allows buyers to award the same (reputable) suppliers because of value-for-money considerations. Likewise, awarding the same supplier may reduce transaction costs: The authors reported that discretion reduced the total duration of the works and led to the selection of larger firms with typically better governance. Thus, the positive effects of increased discretion may, in sum, dominate negative ones. The authors concluded that even if discretion does not directly improve outcomes, it reduces transaction costs for the screening of offers.

5.2.2.3 *Assessment of the working hypothesis*

When procurement officials decide whether to use an open or restricted auction format, they should not overlook the plethora of theoretical and empirical studies that highlight the performance benefits of open auctions (Decarolis, 2014). Empirical research has implied that the past version of the Directives reasonably defined the open procedure as the standard. Many arguments underpin why reduced competition between bidders in tenders may lead to higher procurement costs in restricted procedures. To limit the harmful effects of decreased competition, the Directives require Contracting Authorities to request offers from at least three suppliers in restricted procedures. However, this minimum legal requirement most likely does not ensure full competitiveness: The past empirical studies on competition in public procurement have shown that a fully competitive procurement environment requires six to eight participants (Estache & Iimi, 2008; Gupta, 2002; Paarsch, 1992).

Theoretical considerations have implied that a restricted procedure may reduce transaction costs when the contracts are difficult to specify. Particularly for complex transactions, a restricted procedure could act as a remedy for incomplete contract specifications by attracting more reputable suppliers. However, the increased discretion creates more room for corruption and favoritism. Empirical studies have replicated the finding that restricted procedures in public procurement entail this dilemma. Chong et al. (2016) reported that procurement officials might exploit the increased discretion. However, the countervailing effects due to improved supplier reputation resulted in a nonsignificant relation between the use of a restricted procedure and average tender outcomes. Coviello et al. (2018) confirmed this reasoning by reporting that restricted procedures did not significantly affect final prices, although they increased the probability that the same firms win repeatedly. It was only the results of Chever et al. (2017) that implied that the primary reason procurement officials employ restricted procedures is to exploit the increased discretion to engage in illegal behavior.

Accordingly, restricted procedures yield a tradeoff between the benefits of discretion and the downsides of increased competition like the negotiated procedure. To check working hypothesis W6 for this tradeoff, we employed the same argumentation as in the previous section: Performance-oriented procurement officials will not engage in corruption or collusion despite the opportunity because such behavior would interfere with their primary performance objective. A Contracting Authority striving for lower costs will use the increased discretion only to improve contract-award efficiency, i.e., to exploit the relational benefits of restricted procedures.

From this performance perspective, officials may use the increased discretion to establish more stable relationships with reputable suppliers.[53] Empirical findings have shown that increased discretion, on average, does not impede performance levels, even though some procurement officials engage in improper behavior. This result implies that sincere procurement officials can effectively use their increased discretion to improve their outcomes and lower transaction costs. In sum, the previous empirical research findings support working hypothesis W7: Compared with an open procedure, Contracting Authorities can use a restricted procedure to improve their performance in tenders.

5.3 Selection of suppliers

5.3.1 Design of the supplier selection rule

5.3.1.1 Theoretical background and hypothesis development

After the submission phase, Contracting Authorities need to identify the offer with the best value for money; otherwise, their performance levels will suffer a great deal (Rezende, 2009). The regulation's emphasis on rules and predictability forces procurement officials to always award the bidder with the highest score on the award criteria (i.e., on the scoring rule) published in a CN – another example of how the different tender stages are intertwined in public procurement.

The regulatory change to require a scoring rule (MEAT criterion) for supplier selection corresponds to a shift in the Directive's definition of

[53] They might still worry that the decreased degree of competition between bidders will cause collusion that will drive up the award values. However, past empirical research has not given rise to the suspicion that restricted procedures suffer from increased collusion among suppliers.

performance: Away from a low price orientation to a multi-criteria approach that takes into account quality and price (Dimitri, 2013, p. 149). Since procurement officials might struggle to measure and thus evaluate quality characteristics, a scoring rule requires them to bear additional transaction costs for the planning and execution of a contract award. However, a scoring rule provides officials with flexibility in weighing lower prices against higher quality levels. Therefore, its efficiency depends on the chosen award criteria and their weighting. The designed scoring rule should at best correspond to the utility function of the Contracting Authority to solve the tension between higher quality and lower costs (Bergman & Lundberg, 2013). Therefore, the Directives provide procurement officials with a relatively high degree of freedom in choosing and designing the award criteria (Jasper & Marx, 2018). Standardized and prefabricated award criteria will fail to capture the often heterogeneous characteristics of contracts adequately.

By contrast, procurement officials must select and design suitable award criteria without any legislative guidance. If they fail to define the right award criteria, they might end up not choosing the best available supplier. Consequently, procurement performance depends on using a well-designed scoring rule with appropriate award criteria for selecting the winning supplier. Especially in tenders for complex and multi-faceted contracts, procurement officials might struggle to identify and weigh award criteria that completely fit their acquisition needs.

Until the 2014 reform of the Directives, procurement officials could decide whether to stick to the lowest price or to include additional qualitative criteria in the scoring rule. Even before the 2014 reform, the Directives strongly preferred the use of scoring rules, but afterward, they required their use – even for the procurement of standardized contracts (e.g., for raw materials). However, by setting the price weights close to 100%, Contracting Authorities may still choose to run a quasi-lowest price tender.

Still, we believe that the current version of Directives does not prescribe the use of scoring rules without any reasons. A strong focus on the price in the scoring rule would contradict the thrust of the 2014 reform. Notably, this change in the regulatory regime gave rise to the next working hypothesis:

W8: The assignment of significant weights in the scoring rule to quality criteria will improve the procurement performance of Contracting Authorities in tenders.

Contracting Authorities must balance an inherent tradeoff in the supplier selection phase (Decarolis, 2014). They always face uncertainties regarding both the actual quality and the final costs. Regarding the quality, buyers' performance might suffer from asymmetric information and moral hazards: Suppliers have an incentive to cheat on the promised quality levels after winning the contract award. Regarding the costs, procurement officials face an optimization problem: They do not know how much it will cost the suppliers to achieve alternate, better quality levels. Procurement officials may require quality standards that unfavorably affect the marginal relation between required quality and associated costs, thus increasing the costs more than economically needed.

Demand auctions' natural assumption of exogenously fixed item quality does not apply to tenders. Thus, a Contracting Authority cannot design the scoring rule only according to their perceived importance of quality, but they must consider uncertainties of cost and quality (after the contract award) as well. By pronouncing the quality criteria in scoring rules, procurement officials may increase competition between suppliers with high marginal quality costs and suppliers with low marginal quality costs (Che, 1993). Such quality discrimination can improve procurement performance by preferring better value for money suppliers. Since procurement officials cannot adequately assess the final costs or the quality that is delivered, they must set the right incentives for high value for money suppliers by assigning significant weight to the quality award criteria.

By contrast, the increased weight applied to the lowest price criterion may affect bidders' aggressiveness (Ballesteros-Pérez, González-Cruz, Pastor-Ferrando, & Fernández-Diego, 2012). With complex contracts, moral hazards leading to increased overall transaction costs may increasingly arise (e.g., winning a contract by deliberately underestimating the final costs). Similar to the theoretical effect of restricted auctions (see Section 4.2.2.2), scoring rules may help to prevent such behavior by pronouncing reputation in the supplier selection phase (Saussier & Tirole, 2015). Since scoring rules that focus on the price may reduce entry incentives for reputable suppliers (as they incentivize low-balling bids from their less reputable counterparts), procurement officials should only assign significant weight to the price in a scoring rule if they can ensure that only reputable supplier can surpass the previously set quality thresholds (Decarolis, 2014). Contract complexity makes it more difficult to define the quality and increases cost uncertainties; thus, complexity raises the danger of additional future transaction costs. The more complex the contract gets, the more a scoring rule mainly focused on the price may backfire – even when procurement officials can pre-select suppliers at a previous tender stage (Asker & Cantillon, 2008).

However, some authors have provided arguments for a high focus on the price component in scoring rules (Bergman & Lundberg, 2013). Quality criteria might be more challenging to design and less intuitive than the lowest price criterion. Thus, procurement officials may focus on the lowest price if they can verify the quality of, for example, standardized products (Dini et al., 2006).[54]

The increased importance of the lowest price also might decrease the risk of corruption in public procurement (Tran, 2010). A higher weight assigned to the lowest price limits Contracting Authorities' discretion in evaluating offers. The lowest price rule is transparent and hard to manipulate. By contrast, particularly in price-to-quality scoring auctions, external stakeholders will have trouble scrutinizing the officials' evaluation of quality criteria (Bergman & Lundberg, 2013). In such tenders, officials transform the price into a score and add it to the quality score. Thereby, they use a price-adjusted highest-quality method. By using a price-to-quality scoring rule, procurement officials can disguise the preferences behind their award decision. The opaqueness of the rules allows them to avoid treating all suppliers equally. By using non-linear functions of price scores, procurement officials can easily discriminate against certain suppliers

[54] However, we are questioning whether this objection can withstand the test of reality. First, compared with the US governmental institutions, European Contracting Authorities have historically used the lowest price rules less frequently. Thus, suppliers and procurement officials alike should know how to engage in scoring auctions. Second, while the principle of lowest-price tenders might be straightforward in theory, in practice, procurement officials may struggle to define appropriate minimum quality requirements in a preselection phase.

because they must reduce their prices by different amounts to achieve a given increase in the overall score.

5.3.1.2 Empirical findings

Although in practice, the scoring rule heavily influences the award decision, it has attracted relatively little attention from the academic community (Lundberg & Bergman, 2017). Accordingly, we only find some empirical studies that discussed the relation between scoring rules and tender outcomes.

Wong, Holt, and Harris (2001) initiated this line of limited research by conducting an empirical survey among procurement officials. They reported that the lowest price criterion does not necessarily lower final prices compared with the scoring rule. Instead, the authors argued that procurement officials favor scoring models not only because they allow quality to be considered in the award decision, but also because they might realize an increase in the value for money.

Molenaar and Johnson (2003) confirmed the potential value for money advantages of scoring models in practice by using another survey approach. They found that a scoring rule lowers the procurement official's perceived tradeoff between higher value and lower costs. Particularly for the procurement of more complex contracts, scoring rules allow procurement officials to identify and source from the best available option.

Lewis and Bajari (2011) empirically investigated the effects of the lowest price criterion and scoring rules in the procurement of highway construction contracts in California between 2003 and 2008. In the past, procurement officials had to rely on the lowest price and just defined minimum quality thresholds for such tenders. The authors argued that this selection mechanism offered the advantage that the procurement officials could pick the cheapest yet most reliable contractor. However, without the newly introduced scoring rules, suppliers had no incentive to outperform the specifications and deliver a better than required item. In a structural analysis, they found that direct procurement costs in tenders with scoring rules rose by about 8% compared with the lowest price tenders.

From a broader point of view, however, the benefits resulting from a reduction of around 30% in the completion time in the case of a scoring rule compensated for this rise in costs. A scoring rule allowed for the faster completion of construction projects without quality compromises. By valuing time, scoring options provide suppliers with specific incentives for accelerated delivery. Thus, suppliers who can accelerate construction beyond standard targets will do so to maximize their profits from the contract award.

They concluded that scoring rules allow for welfare gains because they lower the information asymmetry between suppliers and Contracting Authorities regarding the marginal costs of providing higher quality. They noted that already small incentives induced by (sub-optimal) scoring rules could positively impact outcomes. Thus, the potential increase in the problem of designing the right scoring rules should not prevent procurement officials from employing them in practice.

Decarolis (2014) provided empirical evidence for the undesirable performance effects of lowest price rules in the procurement of service contracts. Buyers can quite easily design selection rules that assign more weight to the price. However, they thereby increased the risk of awarding bidders who cannot fulfill their quality promises. Cost-overruns, renegotiations, and retendering become more likely and might push up ex-post transaction costs, which level out the ex-ante cost savings. Thereby, the author provided empirical support for the existence of moral hazard in lowest price tenders.

Lundberg and Bergman (2017) examined the effect of lowest price and scoring rules in the selection of suppliers in tenders of local and central authorities in Sweden. The authors proposed that buyers should not employ the lowest price as the supplier selection method when facing cost and quality uncertainties. Accordingly, the authors reported that buyers should employ the lowest price method only when facing low uncertainties (e.g., when they procure standardized contracts or when they can control the quality). However, the authors found that Contracting Authorities should prefer the use of scoring rules with higher degrees of uncertainty. In practice, procurement officials use scoring rules more often when they feel uncertain about costs and about the quality that is being delivered. However, they also found that the design of award criteria also depended on local habits and organizational inertia and not only on economic considerations.

5.3.1.3 *Assessment of the working hypothesis*

We argue that the 2014 reform of the Directives reasonably forbade lowest price tenders: Both theoretical implications and empirical studies have substantiated this regulatory decision. Since Contracting Authorities considered awarding a contract to the lowest bidder to be effortless and straightforward, they had a long tradition of preferring the lowest price criterion (Waara & Bröchner, 2006). However, they used the lowest price method not out of economic consideration but mainly due to local habits and institutional inertia. When the procurement officials feel uncertain about costs and about the quality that is being delivered, they should prefer designing more complex scoring rules.

Empirical studies have found that the lowest price rule may backfire, especially in oversupplied markets. Instead, research has demonstrated the benefits of scoring rules to attain better value for money. Empirical studies have shown that the lowest price criterion becomes increasingly disadvantageous with increased contract complexity. Instead, scoring rules that consider both price and quality outperform first-price mechanisms, although they add complexity to the supplier selection phase.[55]

However, Contracting Authorities should not only apply significant weights to quality criteria in complex transactions.[56] Instead, we argue that procurement officials should always include quality criteria with significant weights in their scoring rules because cost uncertainty affects simple tenders as well. Even with the most straightforward tenders, procurement officials should dispense with the lowest price rule because suppliers' solutions always differ in more dimensions than price. A combination of

---

[55] A scoring rule should preferably convert quality levels into monetary values and not vice versa in order to foster the transparency of award decisions (Bergman & Lundberg, 2013).

[56] Only Grega and Nemec (2015) reported that in comparison with the MEAT criterion, the lowest price criterion created a cost savings of about 1% in public tenders conducted in Slovakia. However, we argue that their econometric set-up was flawed because they did not include any control variables that could capture variations across tenders. Since the empirical investigations of the present work (see Section 6.2) imply that any econometric models will fail to capture the impact of single variables on procurement performance without the inclusion of such control variables, we did not include their findings in this section.

factors based on price, quality, delivery, and technology will effectively incentivize more reputable suppliers. Accordingly, previous empirical studies have supported working hypothesis W8, which proposes that assigning significant weights to quality characteristics in supplier selection will improve the procurement performance of Contracting Authorities in tenders.

6. Research hypotheses and empirical approach

In the present chapter, we will develop the research hypotheses and discuss the set-up of the empirical investigations. First, we summarize the status quo of the present work to derive concrete research hypotheses for empirical investigations.

Figure 14 shows that previous research has yielded sufficient support for six of our eight working hypotheses based on past empirical studies on tenders and procurement auctions. For these six working hypotheses, recent research has yielded sufficient empirical evidence to provide Contracting Authorities with clear implications for how specific measures will influence their procurement performance.

However, so far, the available empirical studies cannot provide any well-grounded recommendations to Contracting Authorities regarding how the release of a starting price in a CN may affect their procurement performance. Thus, the present work will empirically investigate if Contracting Authorities in tenders enjoy a first-mover advantage like negotiators in private-sector purchasing.

A. Rhode, *Public Procurement in the European Union*, Schriften zum europäischen Management, https://doi.org/10.1007/978-3-658-28073-4_6

Figure 14: Working hypotheses on performance-oriented measures in tenders

	Working hypotheses	Previous empirical evidence
W1	The publication of a PN will increase bidders' interest, thus improving the procurement performance of Contracting Authorities	Sufficient evidence to support hypothesis
W2	The formulation of a functional specification in a CN will increase the number of submitted bids, thus improving the procurement performance of Contracting Authorities	Sufficient evidence to support hypothesis
W3	The division of contracts into smaller lots will increase the number of submitted bids, thus improving the procurement performance of Contracting Authorities	Sufficient evidence to support hypothesis
W4	The release of a starting price in a CN will improve the procurement performance of Contracting Authorities	No sufficient evidence to support hypothesis
W5	The formulation of a precise starting price in a CN will improve the procurement performance of Contracting Authorities	No sufficient evidence to support hypothesis
W6	The choice for a negotiated procedure instead of an auctioned procedure will improve the procurement performance of Contracting Authorities	Sufficient evidence to support hypothesis
W7	The choice for a restricted procedure instead of an open procedure will improve the procurement performance of Contracting Authorities	Sufficient evidence to support hypothesis
W8	The focus on quality criteria versus price criteria in the supplier selection rule will improve the procurement performance of Contracting Authorities	Sufficient evidence to support hypothesis

Source: Own illustration

Moreover, procurement officials must decide on the level of numerical precision for starting price publications in the CN: For example, they can estimate the monetary value of a contract at "1,000,000 EUR" (an imprecise price point), "999,999 EUR" (a precise price point), or "900,000 EUR to 1,100,000 EUR" (a price range). Since the different kinds of starting prices might yield differing anchoring effects, albeit providing nearly the same information from a purely rational point of view, we will further investigate these starting prices distinctively.

6.1 Conceptual model and hypotheses

6.1.1 Publication of a starting price

First, we focused on working hypothesis W4, which proposed that the release of a starting price in a CN will improve the procurement performance of Contracting Authorities. We wanted to investigate whether the release of a starting price would anchor potential suppliers in tenders and thus yield a first-mover advantage. We aimed to demonstrate that the relation between starting prices and performance levels in public procurement arises independently of other tender conditions. Hence, this section will first examine the determinants of the likelihood that procurement officials will disclose a starting price in a tender.

6.1.1.1 How tender characteristics affect the release of a starting price

Procurement officials may prefer to disclose starting prices for certain kinds of tenders. The likelihood of starting price disclosure may depend on buyer, market, and contract conditions. Previous empirical research has shown that tender design decision might depend on such organizational variables (Bergman & Lundberg, 2013). First, lower procurement expertise and a low degree of professionalism might lower officials' likelihood of releasing a starting price. The calculation of starting prices requires effort. The Directives entail that procurement officials base their starting prices on realistically calculated internal cost estimates. If procurement officials in a Contracting Authority lack the necessary competence or resources, they will refrain from publishing starting prices. They might assess their own cost calculation as somewhat unreliable and therefore want to conceal it from external stakeholders.

The significance of the procurement function and corresponding professionalism and the degree of available resources are likely to vary across the different kinds of Contracting Authorities. For example, a public utility company operates closer to the market and may face private competitors. The resulting pressure for efficiency guides their procurement efforts, and they invest more resources and training into the management of their procurement efforts.

By contrast, for example, local authorities operate nearly independently of any market forces. Moreover, they might lack the personnel resources to provide sufficient and dedicated procurement expertise. In sum, local authorities might be less likely than public utilities to publish a starting price in a CN. Furthermore, expectations of suppliers may instigate the disclosure of starting prices for certain Contracting Authorities (e.g., suppliers in the defense sector might expect starting prices to be released). In public procurement, such expectations exist, particularly given the high level of asymmetric information between Contracting Authorities and potential suppliers governing the whole tender process. Although regulatory rules and standards do not affect the private sector, such expectations affect the behavior of private auctioneers as well: For example, demand auctions of arts and antiques continuously begin by publishing an appreciation of the auctioned item (i.e., a starting price).

Second, differences in national market norms may affect the likelihood of starting price disclosure. The regulatory requirements for Contracting Authorities differ between EU countries. Because member states individually transpose the Directives into national procurement law, different national regulations might exist for the publication of starting prices in CNs. Likewise, procurement law in the EU is dichotomous because the Directives only apply to tenders whose contract values exceed uniform monetary thresholds.

For tenders below thresholds, national regulations differ between member states. The two regulatory systems influence each other: If national law requires starting prices for smaller tenders, procurement officials might be more likely to publish starting prices for contracts above threshold projects even though they are not legally required. Besides, different national market norms might drive the decision to publish starting prices. Market norms may still mirror past legal differences between member states before the Directives took effect. Differences that continue to exist for the procurement of below-threshold contracts may accentuate varying market norms between EU states.

Finally, the monetary value of an auctioned contract could influence the likelihood of starting price disclosure. In compound (and thus more valuable) tenders, the distribution of bids by potential suppliers may be broader, especially given the significant information asymmetries in public procurement. Hence, Contracting Authorities might not provide starting prices to avoid cutting off potentially low bids. Alternatively, procurement officials might deliberately disclose starting prices in high-value tenders to reduce information asymmetries and to effectively anchor suppliers given the increased cash-flow uncertainty. Accordingly, the present work hypothesizes:

H1: The buyer (the type of Contracting Authority or the main field of activity), market (the country of origin), and contract conditions (the value of the ex-post price estimate) will affect the likelihood of starting price disclosure in a tender.

6.1.1.2 How the release of a starting price impacts procurement performance

Most past anchoring studies have implied that the disclosure of a starting price in a tender causes an assimilative anchoring effect, which yields a first-mover advantage. The present work argues that contrasting anchoring effects due to herding behavior fail to appear in public procurement because most tenders are conducted as sealed-bid procurement auctions: Like in demand auctions, refraining from disclosing a starting price may lower entry barriers for suppliers. However, early entrants will not suffer from sunk costs because potential suppliers may submit only one offer during a tender. Likewise, other potential suppliers cannot derive higher value from the increased bidding activity because procurement officials do not publish the numbers of offers until the release of the CAN.

Given the potentially positive impact of starting prices on performance (demonstrated in private-sector negotiations and demand auctions alike), it is puzzling why many Contracting Authorities seem to conceal starting prices from potential suppliers in public tenders. Previous empirical studies (see Section 5.4) have implied that the anchoring effect of starting prices depends on transactional structures affecting recipients' behavior.

Therefore, we focus on investigating the various structural particularities of public tenders. First, in contrast to private-sector negotiations, the number of participants in public tenders is not exogenously determined. Section 5.1 demonstrated that the number of submitted offers profoundly affects procurement performance in tenders. The degree of competition between potential suppliers influences their bidding behavior and the risk of collusive behavior and corruption (Che & Kim, 2006). Thus, if the publication of starting prices lowers the number of offers by creating entry barriers, the final prices may increase.

For negotiations, prior research has demonstrated the first-mover advantage solely under the premise that the involved parties have already entered into a transaction (Schweinsberg et al., 2012). Since most previous anchoring studies have used experimental research designs, they may have underestimated the risk of impasses potentially created by starting prices (Galinsky et al., 2009). Negotiations conducted in simulated experiments conceal the risk of impasses by creating artificial incentives for reaching agreements and not quitting the negotiation.

In actual tenders, potential suppliers receive starting prices before entering. Because starting prices precede the entry decision, suppliers choose whether to enter a tender after considering the starting price. They will refrain from entering when the published starting price heavily undercuts their estimated costs in case of a contract award. Because tenders without a starting price do not exert a similar kind of deterring effect on a supplier's entry decision, procurement officials might deliberately conceal starting prices to avoid lowering suppliers' interest.

First, previous empirical studies on demand auctions have likewise reported that starting prices increase a seller's chances of not selling an item while decreasing the numbers of bids and bidders (Lucking-Reiley et al., 2007; Pinker et al., 2003). This risk of entry barriers might particularly arise in public procurement because regulations lower suppliers' bargaining power by allocating risk primarily on their side (Tadelis, 2012). As such low-power players, they might be particularly likely to walk away from a tender when confronted with a starting price (Schweinsberg et al., 2012).

Second, buyers' interests in both maintaining an informational advantage and not preventing lower than expected bids may limit the disclosure of starting prices in tenders. Particularly in high-value tenders for complicated contracts, Contracting Authorities might not reveal starting price information in order to profit from higher information asymmetries (Gatzlaff & Liu, 2013).

Third, starting prices in public tenders may lack the extremity required to anchor bidders effectively. Prior negotiation research has argued that the extremity of first offers determines the first mover's success (Loschelder et al., 2016). Compared with competitive first offers in negotiations, starting prices in tenders may be interpreted by potential suppliers as acceptable. The Directives stipulate that procurement officials should estimate starting prices based on realistic calculations. However, other studies have confirmed the assimilative anchoring potency of less extreme starting prices in other economic transactions besides negotiations: reserve prices and minimum bids in demand auctions (Kamins et al., 2004) and list prices in housing sales (Bucchianeri & Minson, 2013). Starting prices in housing and public procurement may have many similarities because bidders perceive both as a negotiable yardstick and not as a binding ceiling.

Likewise, the alternative explanation from auction theory predicts that the release of a buyer's information entailed in a starting price increases competition among bidders by lowering the likelihood of significant information asymmetries (Silva et al., 2008). Accordingly, based on findings from prior empirical research, we hypothesized:

H2: The release of a starting price in a CN will improve Contracting Authorities' procurement performance.

However, the strength of the relationship between a starting price and the final prices might depend on salient anchor-disconfirming evidence provided by other available tenders. Brint (2003) found that starting prices significantly anchored counterparties only for items that did not have an apparent reference price. Accordingly, Bucchianeri and Minson (2013) reported that the presence of similar auctions listed at different prices significantly decreased the anchoring potency of starting prices. Similarly, the presence of tenders for similar contracts at different final prices may provide bidders with salient anchor-disconfirming evidence in public procurement. We hypothesized:

H3: The salience of tenders for similar contracts procured at different prices will decrease the anchoring potency of starting prices.

6.1.1.3 How the release of a starting price impacts the number of bidders

Furthermore, we aim to analyze the relation between starting price disclosure and the number of bidders in a tender. First, the number of bidders as a proxy for procurement performance is closely related to research hypothesis H2. Past anchoring studies have implied that starting prices might create barriers to entry in tenders (Galinsky et al., 2009; Lee et al., 2018). If starting prices lower the number of bidders, lower procurement performance will result (Brannman et al., 1987). The effect of an additional bidder may even outshine the effects of other design options such as the release of a starting price (Bulow & Klemperer, 1996).

Second, the impact of starting price disclosure on the number of bidders provides a test of both the anchoring and the alternative winner's curse hypotheses. The two alternative explanations imply different directions for the coefficient for the number of bidders. Due to barriers to entry that have the potential to arise, the anchoring hypothesis would propose a negative relation between starting prices and the number of offers in the case of a release. According to the conflicting winner's curse hypothesis, the publication of a starting price will lower information asymmetries (Silva et al., 2008).[57] Given the rigid exchange of information in public procurement, the release of a starting price may reduce the risks associated with entering the tender. Thus, tenders with a published starting price should, on average, attract more bidders. However, given that most of the previous empirical research has supported the existence of anchoring effects in all kinds of economic transactions, we hypothesized:

H4: The publication of a starting price in a CN will lower the number of bids that are submitted.

6.1.2 Formulation of a published starting price

After creating concrete research hypotheses to follow the previous working hypothesis W4, which proposed that the release of a starting price in a CN will improve the procurement performance of Contracting Authorities, we now turn to working hypothesis W5. We aim to empirically examine whether and how the formulation of a precise or imprecise starting price in a CN affects tender outcomes.

Previous studies on starting price precision have provided heterogeneous insights into the potential relation between precision and performance

[57] As discussed in Section 5.1.5, this hypothesis proposes that the tendered contracts show Common Value uncertainty. On the basis of past empirical studies (Hong & Shum, 2002), we assume that affiliated contract values prevail on TED as both Common Value and Private Value components matter in practice.

levels. The results of empirical studies focused on the increased numerical precision of price points and the implications of studies concerning price ranges have conflicted with each other already. The existing research ambiguities increase when we consider the particularities of public procurement. The manifold transactional differences prevent a direct transfer of anchoring insights from research on negotiations to tenders. Even though the intrapsychic mechanisms responsible for assimilative anchoring effects of increased precision may remain valid in public procurement, interpersonal processes shaped by starting price precision might work differently than in negotiations. Regulation as the main differentiator between public procurement and private purchasing heavily affects the buyer-supplier relationship in tenders. Since interpersonal anchoring effects caused by different degrees of starting price precision will work by influencing this relationship, regulation will heavily shape precision effects as well.

Consequently, we cannot provide procurement officials with a clear answer for how to formulate starting prices in tenders. By choosing the "best" kind of starting price, they may improve procurement performance in tenders while complying with the legal requirements of the Directives. However, current research implies that each available type of starting price might improve the Contracting Authorities' outcomes. Depending on the study, precise starting price points (e.g., €499,999), round starting price points (e.g., €500,000), or starting price ranges (e.g., €490,000 to €510,000) may have the most positive impact on performance. Accordingly, the present work derived several sometimes-opposing hypotheses on the relations between starting price precision and outcomes based on the insights discussed in Section 5.1.5.

6.1.2.1 How starting price precision affects procurement performance

Most previous studies on starting price precision have implied that increased precision will enhance the starting price's impact on the final prices in tenders. Potential suppliers might interpret precise starting price points as particularly credible. Public tenders differ from negotiations in many relational and informational aspects. However, these dissimilarities most likely do not affect the intrapsychic mechanisms responsible for the increased anchoring potency of precise starting prices in economic transactions (Loschelder et al., 2017). Therefore, we hypothesized:

H5: The increased numerical precision of starting price points will improve the procurement performance of Contracting Authorities.

Still, the attribution of competence might offer the best explanation for why precise starting prices may enjoy increased anchor potency in tenders (Loschelder et al., 2016). Professional and experienced bidders participate in public procurement. Therefore, we must acknowledge the danger that bidders might interpret very precise starting prices in tenders as less plausible. The release of an exact starting price may signal that the responsible procurement officials have a low level of competence and professionalism. As a result, the relation between starting price precision and performance might be an inverse U-shape. We hypothesized in accordance:

H6: Very high precision in starting price points will reduce Contracting Authorities' procurement performance.

6.1.2.2 How starting price precision affects the number of bidders

Other findings from previous empirical research have implied additional potential disadvantages of increased starting price precision in public tenders. Precise starting prices might create barriers to entry because counterparties might associate the precise first movers with inflexibility (Lee et al., 2018). We looked at the number of bidders because decreased competition among potential suppliers may increase final costs for the Contracting Authority (see Section 5.1.1).

In public tenders, precise starting price points might discourage potential suppliers from participating. Suppliers weigh transaction costs with potential gains in the case of a contract award when entering a tender. If increased precision conveys a small difference between the starting price and the Contracting Authority's reservation price, interested suppliers will assume that the potential economic gains in case of a contract award are small.[58] Thus, increased starting price precision might create barriers to entry by increasing the suppliers' perception of procurement official's

[58] In public tenders, procurement officials may have a reservation price in mind. According to the Directives, the results of tenders are not always legally binding for the awarding of a contract. Procurement officials might decide to rerun an auction or even change to another award procedure if the first tender did not yield satisfactory outcomes.

inflexibility and by lowering the attractiveness for suppliers to enter the tender.

H7: Increasing the numerical precision of starting price points will reduce the number of offers that are submitted.

The disadvantages of increased anchor precision might be particularly severe as the number of offers submitted approximates procurement performance in most tenders. When more bidders participate in a tender, the procurement officials can award a supplier that offers a better value-for-money deal. Moreover, an increased amount of competition between bidders reduces collusive behavior and corruption. If increased precision reduces bidders' interest, the buyers' performance levels will deteriorate.

6.1.2.3 How starting price ranges affect procurement performance

Besides, the present work will explore the performance effects of starting price ranges. Ames and Mason (2015) found that starting price ranges exert an informative or politeness effect in negotiations. Starting price ranges tend to improve negotiated outcomes by affecting the counterparty's intrapsychic processes and by influencing the interaction between parties. In public procurement, starting prices may affect outcomes alike by exerting an influence on the same two levels. Starting price ranges may yield an informational effect by shaping the potential suppliers' assumptions about acceptable settlement values in tenders. Counterparties might interpret starting price ranges as politer than equally aggressive starting price points. Therefore, starting price ranges may induce politeness by lowering the extremity of suppliers' offers. Disclosing bolstering starting price ranges in a CN may particularly benefit Contracting Authorities. In addition to the politeness effect yielded by all kinds of starting price ranges, the ambitious figure within a bolstering starting price range might exert an informational influence on suppliers by boosting its anchor potency compared with starting prices of similar value. Following Ames and Mason (2015), we hypothesized:

H8: Compared with other kinds of starting prices, starting price ranges will improve Contracting Authorities' procurement performance.

H8a: Compared with other kinds of starting price ranges, bolstering starting price ranges will improve Contracting Authorities' procurement performance.

H8b: Compared with other kinds of starting price ranges, bracketing starting price ranges will not improve Contracting Authorities' procurement performance.

H8c: Compared with other kinds of starting price ranges, back down starting price ranges will not decrease Contracting Authorities' procurement performance.

6.2 Steps in the empirical investigation

6.2.1 Data collection

The empirical part of the present study used data on public tenders published by the European Commission. The data set consisted of standard forms filled out by Contracting Authorities in the EU. Contracting Authorities publish these forms on TED. Typically, procurement officials use the publication of a CN on TED to initiate the tendering process. Amongst other elements (e.g., the contract specifications), the CN may contain a starting price that may anchor potential suppliers. The published starting price reflects the value that the Contracting Authority estimates for the contract award. In every tender, Contracting Authorities must come up with such an award estimate to determine the applicable regulative umbrella of the contract at hand.

The present work has identified three levels of data within tenders published on TED: First, contract award notices (CANs) contain the results of the tender. Second, contract awards (CAs) inform potential suppliers about the specific award details. Because Contracting Authorities can award more than one contract in different lots at a single tender (see Section 5.1.3), a CAN may include several CAs. Third, contract notices (CNs) contain information about the announcement of a tender (e.g., a CN can contain a starting price).

6.2.2 Data cleaning

We collected tender data from a published set of open procedures that were conducted without any cancelations or corrections from January 2012 to December 2015. We focused on open procedures as they represented the by far largest share of tenders within the analyzed data set (see Figure 11) and were defined as the standard procurement procedure by the Directives before their 2014 reform. The data published on TED consist of unverified standard forms that have been filled out by procurement officials responsible for managing the respective tender. We found that many standard forms filling were incomplete, inconsistent, or erroneous. Accordingly, the empirical investigation relied on previous data-cleaning steps that we defined following Onur et al. (2012). In their paper, the authors analyzed tenders published in the Official Gazette of the Republic of Turkey. Because their initial set of tenders also consisted of manual entries, they faced similar inconsistencies in the data recording process. Because we acknowledge that many inconsistencies in the data set of the present study are due to manual data entry as well, we relied on an approach that was similar to Onur et al. (2012) before engaging in any econometric investigations:

> Phase I: We excluded all incomplete observations (i.e., those tenders that were missing data on the variables necessary for the econometric specifications)

> Phase II: We excluded data inputs that seemed likely to be incorrect (i.e., by using inherent data logic checks and excluding outliers)

Figure 15: Data cleaning steps applied in the empirical investigations

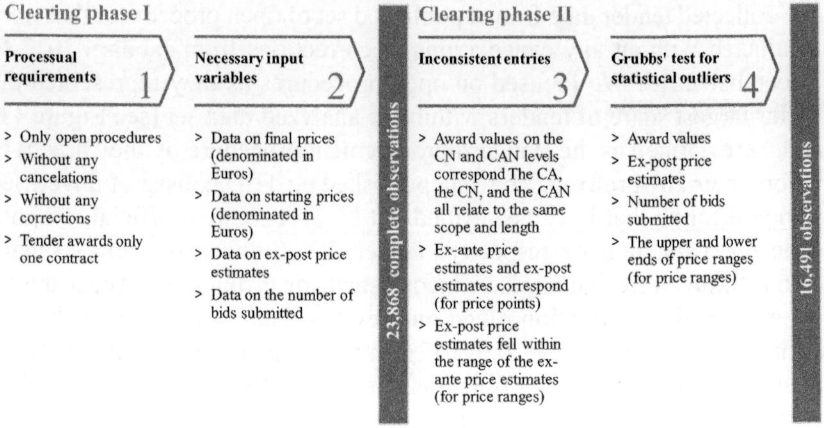

Source: Own Illustration

Figure 15 shows how the data cleaning proceeded in more detail. In Phase I, we ensured that procurement officials correctly conducted and recorded the tenders in the data set. The included observations had to fulfill several requirements of the empirical investigations.

Because procurement officials can award more than one contract in a tender, a CAN may include several contract awards (from different lots). We linked manually added starting price data from the CN with information about tender outcomes published in the CAN to address the outcome-related research questions addressed in the present work. We could not run sensible econometric analyses without unequivocally linking information on final prices (contained in CANs) with starting price data (contained in CAs). Only a direct link ensured that the starting price and the final price referred to the same contract. Thus, we limited the data set to CANs that contained only a single contract award to ensure that this link occurred on a single contract level. In other words, we excluded all tenders that consisted of more than one lot.

Moreover, the observations had to include data on final prices, data on starting prices (denominated in Euros), data on ex-post price estimates, and data on the number of bids submitted. If observations did not cover all this information, we could not sensibly include them in the econometric models. To run the econometric analyses, we thereby depended on these first two data-cleaning steps, which resulted in a data set with 23,868 observations.

The next step in data cleaning was aimed at ensuring correct and sensible econometric results. We could have run the econometric analyses without conducting the additionally defined manual sanity checks. However, we would have obtained distorted results if we had not implemented these further data-cleaning steps. Because some of the manual data inputted in TED were probably incorrect, we applied several manual sanity checks within the observations. We excluded inconsistent and contradictory observations by utilizing the information contained in the multiple standard form fillings regarding the same input variables. In the following steps, we excluded different erroneous data inputs:

- We controlled for whether the award values on the CN and CAN levels corresponded to each other.
- We checked for whether values in the CA, the CN, and the CAN were related to the same scope and length of the contract.
- For tenders with starting price points, we verified that the starting prices (published in the CNs) corresponded with ex-post price estimates (published in the CANs).
- For tenders with starting price ranges, we checked whether the point values of the ex-post price estimates (published in the CANs) fell within the range of the starting prices (published in the CNs).
- We applied Grubbs' test for statistical outliers to the nondichotomous variables (awarded values, ex-post price estimates, the upper and lower ends of price ranges, and the bids that were submitted). We excluded all outliers – Onur et al. (2012) performed a similar step to handle data outliers manually.

6.3 Data analysis

These filtering steps resulted in a data set containing 16,491 observations. To test the hypotheses on the release and formulation of starting prices that we defined in section 6.1, we had to divide the data set into tenders above and below the monetary thresholds. The empirical investigation of an anchoring effect yielded by a starting prices release required this division.

For the empirical investigation of anchoring effects of starting prices, we needed to exclude all tenders with ex-post price estimates below the applicable monetary thresholds. Although the Directives require the publication of CNs on TED only for tenders whose contract award values exceed the respective monetary thresholds, some procurement officials also publish CNs for below-threshold tenders on TED – maybe as a sign of good managerial practice or to profit from increased competition for tenders published on TED (PwC et al., 2011).

If we would include such below-threshold tenders in the empirical investigation, the econometric models could not clearly identify the potential anchoring effect of a starting price. Because Contracting Authorities must legally publish tenders on TED only for contracts above threshold values, the publication on TED itself could signal the contract value estimate. The publication of a CN on TED will send out this value signal independent of whether the CN contains a starting price. This signaling will distort the reported relation between starting prices and outcomes because we could not single out two cofounding value signals – one by the mere publication of a CN on TED and the other by the potential release of a starting price in the CN.

By contrast, the investigation of precision effects did not require such a division because we focused only on tenders with an advertised starting price. Therefore, we did not exclude any tenders on TED that fell below the monetary threshold from the data set. This inclusion increased the data set by an additional 909 observations.

6.3.1 Variable definitions

The present section contains the definitions we applied to the final data set to answer the research questions from the present work. First, to encapsulate the procurement performance levels of tenders, we used the difference in the natural logarithms of the award value and the ex-post price estimate. This index aids the interpretation of the regression results. A log difference's high value implies that the contract's price exceeded the costs estimated by procurement officials, thereby indicating poor performance. In other words, a high value means that the procurement officials achieved a worse-than-expected outcome. However, a low value means that the procurement officials achieved an outcome that was better than expected. When a log difference takes on a low value, this implies that the contract's price was below the estimated costs, thereby indicating a high procurement performance.

Because the data set covered a wide range of different tenders that were conducted, its award values and ex-post price estimates showed high heterogeneity. The log difference enabled us to encapsulate this heterogeneity and compare the performance levels of all tenders in the data set. Past field studies on public procurement have used similar dependent variables as performance indicators (Silva et al., 2008; Silva et al., 2009).

Second, we recorded information contained in CANs on buyer, market, and contract characteristics to capture as many variations as possible between the observations. As stated, CANs contain additional information about the contract details. We used this information to define variables that control for the impact of other potentially influencing factors on performance. We captured variations in the tenders by including information about the various types of awarded contracts (i.e., services, supplies, or works). Besides, we classified the tenders according to Common Procurement Vocabulary (e.g., chemical products or industrial machinery). The Common Procurement Vocabulary (CPV) is a single classification system developed to describe the contract's subject matter. Moreover, we captured variations within market conditions by incorporating data on the Contracting Authority's country of origin (e.g., Germany or France) and the year of publication (i.e., 2012 to 2015). Likewise, we captured variations within the different types of Contracting Authorities (e.g., central government or local authorities) and the relevant Contracting Authority's operating sector (e.g., defense or education).

Third, we used the information contained in the CNs to construct the dummy variables that indicated the disclosure of a starting price. Next, we used several variables to distinguish between the different kinds of published starting prices: We distinguished between observations with starting price points and observations with starting price ranges. For starting price points, we measured their numerical precision by including an interval-scaled, continuous index variable. For this variable, we divided the number of digits by the number of significant figures to derive a relative index of precision. Lee et al. (2018) used a similar approach to define the precision of starting prices (in housing transactions). The authors excluded trailing zeros from the overall number of digits and afterward counted the remaining numbers as precise ones. However, we could not follow their approach exactly because the starting prices we analyzed contained decimals (e.g., a starting price of €940,000.33 is more precise than a starting price of €940,000). The significant figures are the digits of a number used to express the degree of accuracy, starting from the first nonzero digit. We divided this absolute measure of precision by the number of all digits to calculate a relative precision index (e.g., €123,900.00 contains four significant figures and eight digits overall; the index value is 0.5). By comparing the individual precision index with the median value of the index, we constructed further dummy variables to establish whether a starting price point was round or precise.

To determine the kind of starting price range, we compared the value of the ex-post price estimate with the upper and lower ends of the starting price range. For example, we categorized a starting price range as a bolstering range type if the starting price range was €100,000 to €200,000 and the ex-post price estimate was €200,000.

Fourth, we measured the value heterogeneity of tenders for similar contracts. For each class within the Common Procurement Vocabulary (CPV) code, we calculated the standard deviation in award values to reflect the variation for similar tenders. Bucchianeri and Minson (2013) used a similar variable to capture the price heterogeneity within similar housing sales. The CPV categorizes the possible types of awarded contracts and assigns standardized codes to them. Its hierarchical nine-digit tree structure allows for the consolidation of its codes. The first two digits of the code determine the CPV division, and the first four digits refer to the CPV class. We used the CPV division to classify the observations in the econometric specifications. If a contract referred to more than one CPV, we used the first CPV mentioned for the classification.

6.3.2 *Descriptive statistics for tenders above threshold values*

For all the observations in the final data set above threshold values, Table 2 presents the descriptive statistics for all the variables we used. Panel A reports summary statistics for each of the nondichotomous variables, and Panel B reports frequencies for the dichotomous variables. To allow for comparisons, Table 2 reports the statistics for the pooled set of tenders well as for the set of tenders that disclosed a starting price and the set of tenders that did not release one.

Table 2 shows high heterogeneity within the tenders included in the data set. Award values ranged widely from a low of €39,972 to a high of €22.4 million, with a mean price of €1.46 million. The average tender received 4.33 offers with a high of 25 offers and a low of 1 offer. The average performance level was at -0.25; indicating general procurement performance within the data set. The ex-post price estimate averaged €1.97 million or 134.9% of the award value. Of interest, 71.3% (10,441) of the tender disclosed a starting price.

Panel A shows that the award value of tenders that released a starting price ranged from €40,443 to €22.2 million with a mean award value of approximately €1.44 million. The average tender that published a starting price received 4.41 offers, and the average procurement performance was at -0.28. In comparison, tenders without a starting price published in the CN ranged from €40,443 to €22.4 million with a mean price of €1.49 million. These tenders received, on average, 4.14 offers and showed an average performance index value of -0.18. Compared with tenders without a starting price, tenders that published a starting price, on average, had a similar monetary scope, received more bidders' interest, and enjoyed a better procurement performance.

Panel B shows how observations varied according to the buyers' characteristics. For example, central government buyers accounted for 46% of the tenders with a starting price but accounted for over 55% of the tenders without a starting price. By contrast, sectoral contracting authorities increasingly relied on tenders with a starting price (4.1%) compared with those without a starting price (3.1%). Moreover, the likelihood of starting price disclosure differed between national markets. As a striking example, Slovenian contracting authorities issued 18.2% of the tenders without a starting price but only published 1.3% of the tenders with a starting price. Conversely, tenders by buyers from Slovakia were nearly always issued with a starting price (overall share of 12.9%); they accounted for only 0.8% of the tenders without a starting price.

Table 2: Descriptive statistics for observations above the threshold values

Variables	**Statistic**	**All tenders** 14,643 observations	**Tenders without a starting price** 4,202 observations	**Tenders with a starting price** 10,441 observations
Panel A: nondichotomous variables				
Number of submitted offers	M	4.33	4.14	4.41
	SD	4.08	3.8	4.18
	Min	1	1	1
	Max	25	25	25
Award value [€]	M	1,455,179	1,489,839	1,441,230
	SD	2,672,849	2,790,663	2,623,950
	Min	39,972	40,443	39,972
	Max	22,400,000	22,400,000	22,235,754
Ex-post price estimate [€]	M	1,827,332	1,754,938	1,856,467
	SD	3,309,361	3,326,664	3,302,084
	Min	130,081	131,000	130,081
	Max	28,500,000	27,396,642	28,500,000
Procurement performance (log (award value – ex-post price estimate))	M	-0.25	-0.18	-0.28
	SD	0.33	0.27	0.34
	Min	-1.44	-1.44	-1.44
	Max	0.86	0.80	0.86
Panel B: dichotomous variables				
Buyer characteristics				
Central government (1)	Freq	48.9%	55.0%	46.4%
Local authorities (3)	Freq	20.6%	16.7%	22.1%
Water, energy, transportation, and telecommunications sectors (4)	Freq	3.8%	3.1%	4.1%

Body governed by public law (6)	Freq	11.8%	11.6%	11.8%
Other (8)	Freq	11.1%	9.0%	11.9%
National or federal agency (N)	Freq	0.4%	0.2%	0.5%
Regional or local agency (R)	Freq	2.4%	1.4%	2.8%
Not specified (Z)	Freq	1.1%	2.9%	0.4%
Market characteristics				
Austria	Freq	0.5%	1.1%	0.3%
Belgium	Freq	2.4%	5.3%	1.2%
Cyprus	Freq	1.1%	0.3%	1.4%
Germany	Freq	6.3%	10.6%	4.6%
Spain	Freq	26.7%	9.5%	33.7%
Finland	Freq	0.8%	1.7%	0.4%
France	Freq	3.8%	10.7%	1.0%
Greece	Freq	4.9%	2.1%	6.0%
Italy	Freq	33.9%	32.5%	34.4%
Netherlands	Freq	1.5%	3.6%	0.6%
Portugal	Freq	2.7%	3.6%	2.4%
Slovenia	Freq	6.1%	18.2%	1.3%
Slovakia	Freq	9.4%	0.8%	12.9%

Note. This table provides descriptive statistics for the entire data set as well as for the subsets of tenders with and without starting prices. The table does not report statistics for the additional 78 dummy variables that describe additional characteristics of contracts (type and CPV code), markets (publication year), or buyers (main activity).

Table 3: Tenders' starting price frequency by ex-post price estimate cohorts

Cohorts [€]	No. of observations	% with starting price	Starting price std. deviation
0 m to 0.5 m	6,368	69%	0.46
0.5 m to 1.0 m	3,369	74%	0.44
1.0 m to 2.0 m	1,938	72%	0.45
2.0 m to 5.0 m	1,503	77%	0.42
5.0 m to 10.0 m	926	69%	0.46
10.0 m to 15.0 m	303	77%	0.42
15.0 m to 22.5 m	236	70%	0.46
All cohorts	14,643	71%	0.48

Note. This table provides starting price information on tenders published on TED. Since the excluded all below-thresholds tenders for the investigation of anchoring effects yielded by starting prices, the first cohort does not contain any observation with an ex-post price estimate below €130,000.

Table 3 shows that the percentages of tenders with a starting price varied from a high of 77% for tenders with award values between €2.0 million and €5.0 million to a low of 69% for tenders in the lowest cohort, which went up to €0.5 million. However, when we did not control for other variables, the likelihood of starting price disclosure was not linearly correlated with higher contract values.

6.3.3 *Descriptive statistics for tenders with published starting prices*

Table 4 contains the descriptive statistics for the variables in the data set for the tenders with published starting prices (above and below monetary thresholds). We used this data set to investigate the impact that different kinds of starting prices would have on performance.

Table 4: Descriptive statistics for tenders with published starting prices

Variables	Statistic	All starting prices	Precise starting price points	Round starting price points	Starting price ranges
	Observations	12,289	5,675	5,967	647
Panel A: nondichotomous variables					
Award value [€]	Min	1,939	8,412	1,939	2,400
	Max	22,557,062	22,557,062	22,500,000	6,275,000
	M	1,295,404	1,481,875	1,173,944	779,989
	SD	2,439,019	2,763,936	2,184,955	1,122,754
Ex-post price estimate [€]	Min	3,000	7,907	3,000	4,000
	Max	29,145,898	29,145,898	28,500,000	6,400,000
	M	1,647,181	1,959,556	1,434,767	866,258
	SD	3,044,638	3,498,945	2,660,948	1,233,106
Procurement performance (log (award value - ex-post price estimate))	Min	-1.41	-1.41	-1.41	-1.39
	Max	0.81	0.78	0.81	0.80
	M	-0.25	-0.31	-0.21	-0.11
	SD	0.33	0.36	0.30	0.25

Number of offers submitted	Min	1.00	1.00	1.00	1.00
	Max	20.00	20.00	20.00	18.00
	M	4.32	4.60	4.06	4.21
	SD	3.76	4.08	3.47	3.06
Starting price precision	Min	0.10	0.57	0.10	
	Max	1.00	1.00	0.56	
	M	0.59	0.88	0.32	
	SD	0.31	0.14	0.12	
Panel B: dichotomous variables					
Contract refers to services	Freq	55%	60%	51%	41%
Contract refers to supplies	Freq	34%	31%	37%	36%
Contract refers to works	Freq	11%	9%	12%	23%
Contracting authority is based in Austria	Freq	0%	0%	1%	2%
Contracting authority is based in Belgium	Freq	2%	1%	2%	7%
Contracting authority is based in Cyprus	Freq	1%	1%	1%	1%
Contracting authority is based in Germany	Freq	11%	3%	14%	41%
Contracting authority is based in Spain	Freq	29%	43%	19%	2%
Contracting authority is based in Finland	Freq	2%	0%	1%	22%
Contracting authority is based in France	Freq	2%	0%	3%	8%

Contracting authority is based in Greece	Freq	6%	9%	4%	0%
Contracting authority is based in Ireland	Freq	0%	0%	0%	1%
Contracting authority is based in Italy	Freq	30%	29%	35%	3%
Contracting authority is based in Malta	Freq	0%	0%	0%	0%
Contracting authority is based in the Netherlands	Freq	1%	0%	1%	5%
Contracting authority is based in Portugal	Freq	3%	1%	4%	0%
Contracting authority is based in Slovenia	Freq	1%	1%	2%	0%
Contracting authority is based in Slovakia	Freq	13%	12%	14%	5%
Bolstering starting price ranges	Freq				26%
Bracketing starting price ranges	Freq				31%
Back down starting price ranges	Freq				43%

Note. This table shows descriptive statistics for the entire data set and the subsets of tenders with precise starting price points, round starting price points, and starting price ranges. The table does not report statistics for the additional 77 dummy variables that describe additional characteristics of items (contract type and CPV code), markets (year and country of origin), or buyers (type and main activity).

Table 4 shows high heterogeneity within the tenders (with a released starting price) included in the data set. The awarded values ranged from €1,938 to €22.6 million, with a mean price of €1.30 million. The ex-post price estimate of tenders averaged €1.67 million or 127.2% of the mean awarded value. The average tender performance was -0.25, thereby indicating positive performance levels, in general, within the procurement tenders included in the data set. An average tender received 4.32 offers with a high of 20 offers submitted and a low of 1 offer submitted. Of interest, 94.7% (11,642) of the tenders disclosed a round (5,967) or precise (5,675) starting price point, whereas only 5.3% (647) of the tenders published a starting price range. If the buyers published a starting price range, they mostly decided on back down ranges (43%). By contrast, bolstering ranges (26%) and bracketing ranges (31%) were less likely to occur when the buyers used a starting price range.

Panel A shows that the precision level of starting price points was relatively high (at a median value of 0.59). The range and standard deviation indicated high variability in the precision of starting price points. The values awarded at public tenders that released a round (precise) starting price point ranged from €1,938 (€8,412) to €22.6 million (€22.5 million) with a mean awarded value of approximately €1.48 million (€1.17 million). The average tender with a round (precise) starting price point averaged 4.06 (4.60) offers, and the average procurement performance index was -0.21 (-0.31). Compared with tenders without a round starting price point, and when other factors were not controlled for, tenders with a precise starting price point had, on average, a slightly lower value, received more interest from bidders, and were related to improved performance.

For tenders with a starting price range, the awarded values varied from €2,400 to €6.28 million with a mean value of €0.80 million. The corresponding tender received, on average, 4.21 offers and showed an average performance index value of -0.11. Therefore, when other factors were not controlled for, tenders with a starting price range had, on average, smaller values than tenders with a starting price point. Furthermore, tenders with a starting price range enjoyed lower performance levels than tenders with a starting price point. More specifically, compared with all other kinds of starting prices, precise starting price points showed an improved performance level (-0.31).

Panel B shows how observations varied according to the tender's characteristics. For example, 51% (60%) of the tenders with round (precise) starting price points were used to buy services, 37% (31%) to buy supplies, and

12% (9%) to buy works. Contracting authorities were more likely to use starting price ranges when procuring services (41%) than when procuring contracts for supplies (36%) or works (23%).

Furthermore, a tender's likelihood of disclosing a kind of starting price varied according to the buyer's country of origin. Contracting Authorities based in Germany were the most striking example. They accounted for 41% of the tenders that published starting price ranges and represented only 14% (13%) of the tenders with round (precise) starting price points. We assumed that different national market norms and regulations would influence buyers' starting price choices: The Directives only provide the overall legislative framework, but each EU member state implements them into different national regulations. Moreover, implicit market norms (e.g., preferences for specific tender elements) may differ between EU countries.

6.4 Empirical results

6.4.1 Publication of a starting price

To evaluate the disclosure of starting prices in tenders, we first examined the determinants of the likelihood that procurement officials published a starting price in a CN. Second, we analyzed the effect of the publication of starting prices on procurement performance as well as on the number of bidders.

6.4.1.1 How tender characteristics affect the release of a starting price

We assumed that the likelihood of a starting price published in a CN was a function of buyer, market, and contract characteristics. We estimated the probability of a tender publishing a starting price as a probit model specified as:

$$Pr(SPRICE_i = 1 | Z_i) = \Phi(b_i Z_i) + \varepsilon_i \quad (1)$$

where $SPRICE_i = 1$ if a CN contains a starting price and 0 otherwise, and Z_i is a vector of buyer, market, and contract variables. Φ is the standard cumulative normal distribution, b_i is the estimated coefficient, and e_i is the estimation error. $b_i Z_i$ produced a probit score. We used this score to evaluate which variables significantly predicted a tender's likelihood of disclosing a starting price in the CN.

Table 5 reports the estimates of the probit model (Equation 1). To test the research hypothesis H1, we examined four factors within tenders: the type of Contracting Authority, the main field of activity, the country of origin, and the ex-post price estimate. To evaluate the sensitivity of the estimated coefficients, we report the results of four alternative specifications.

Table 5: How tender characteristics affect the release of a starting price

	Dependent variable: Starting price release in a CN							
	Model 1.1		Model 1.2		Model 1.3		Model 1.4	
Independent variables	Probit		Probit		Probit		Probit	
	β (z-stat)		β (z-stat)		β (z-stat)		β (z-stat)	
Contract characteristics								
Log (Ex-post price estimate)	0.038	***					-0.013	
	(4.900)						(-1.424)	
Buyer characteristics								
Central government (1)			-0.184	**			-0.273	***
			(-2.385)				(-3.321)	
Local authorities (3)			0.078				-0.148	*
			(0.964)				(-1.709)	
Body governed by public law (6)			-0.150	*			-0.185	**
			(-1.807)				(-2.077)	
Other (8)			0.039				-0.161	*
			(0.467)				(-1.784)	
National or federal agency (N)			0.105				0.162	
			(0.603)				(0.837)	
Regional or local agency (R)			0.265	***			-0.134	
			(2.584)				(-1.224)	
Not specified (Z)			-1.124	***			-0.286	*
			(-9.492)				(-2.204)	
Market characteristics								
Belgium					-0.132		-0.194	

			(-1.603)	(-1.068)
Cyprus			1.582 ***	1.401 ***
			(8.361)	(9.065)
Germany			0.195	0.178
			-1.608	-1.747
Spain			1.417 ***	1.373 ***
			-12.853	-13.105
Finland			-0.220	-0.17
			(-1.178)	(-1.501)
France			-0.653 ***	-0.718 ***
			(-6.102)	(-5.428)
Greece			1.312 ***	1.228 ***
			-10.623	-11.135
Italy			0.729 ***	0.692 ***
			-6.542	-6.800
Netherlands			-0.322 **	-0.337 **
			(-2.569)	(-2.432)
Portugal			0.474 ***	0.426 ***
			-3.561	-3.916
Slovenia			-0.888 ***	-0.943 ***
			(-8.224)	(-7.644)
Slovakia			2.140 ***	2.041 ***
			-16.214	-16.675
N	14643	14643	14643	14643

Note. This table reports the probit regression results from Equation 1. The z-values are reported in parentheses. Coefficient estimates for 19 additional buyer characteristics (Models 1.2 and 1.4) and the intercept are not reported.
$^*p < .10$. $^{**}p < .05$. $^{***}p < .01$.

Model 1.1 included only the natural logarithm of the ex-post price estimate as an independent variable.[59] The model implied that, when we did not control for other factors, a tender's likelihood of releasing a starting price was positively correlated with the tender's value. In Model 1.2, the estimated coefficients showed that the likelihood of the publication of a starting price varied across buyer characteristics. Compared with the omitted sector authorities, Contracting Authorities belonging to the categories of Central Government, Regional or Local Agency, and Not Specified were

[59] Procurement officials might deliberately decide not to publish starting prices in tenders for valuable contracts. Thus, including the buyers' cost estimate (i.e., the ex-post price estimate) in the econometric specification mirrors the cost expectations of procurement officials better than including the actual outcome of the auction (i.e., the award value).

significantly less likely to publish starting prices in tenders.[60] Model 1.3 included market dummies to control for varying national norms. In line with the discussion of the descriptive statistics, a tender's likelihood of releasing a starting price significantly depended on national market conditions. Relative to the omitted Austrian market, the coefficient estimates for other national markets (besides Belgium, Germany, and Finland) were statistically different from zero. The combined Model 1.4 included all the previously discussed variables. It confirmed that the likelihood of publishing a starting price significantly varied across buyer and market characteristics. However, after controlling for other variations, the likelihood of releasing a starting price was no longer positively correlated with a higher outcome value. Instead, the coefficient was negative but nonsignificant.

6.4.1.2 *How the release of a starting price impacts procurement performance*

To examine the correlation between providing a starting price and procurement performance, we first estimated a standard OLS regression. We used the results as a benchmark to compare the alternative estimates presented in the selection-corrected model. We used the following OLS regression model, specified as:

$$APERF_i = a_0 + \sum_{j=1}^{k} b_j X_{ji} + cSPRICE_i + d\log(OFFERS_i) + e(HET_i * SPRICE_i) + \varepsilon_i \quad (2)$$

where $\mathrm{PERF_i}$ is the natural logarithm of the difference between the ex-post price estimate and the award value; $\mathrm{b_j}$ is a vector of coefficients on contract, buyer, and market characteristics $\mathrm{X_{ji}}$; c is the coefficient of the dummy variable $\mathrm{SPRICE_i}$ with a value of 1 if a starting price is published and 0 otherwise; d is the coefficient of the logarithmized variable $\mathrm{OFFERS_i}$; e is the coefficient of the interaction between $SPRICE_i$ and the variable HET_i, encapsulating the standard deviation in award values in

[60] Moreover, we found that the likelihood of disclosing a starting price similarly depended on the (unreported) main field activity of a contracting authority.

the same CPV class; and ε_i is the random error with mean 0 and variance σ.[61]

Table 6 reports the OLS estimation results from Equation 2. The table presents the results from alternative models to test how sensitive the estimated coefficients are to the specification. Besides a dummy variable indicating whether the tender disclosed a starting price, Model 2.1 includes the interaction of this dummy with an interval-scaled, continuous heterogeneity variable. We used this interaction term to evaluate the impact of starting price heterogeneity in a given CPV class on the relation between a starting price and procurement performance. In Model 2.2, we added the number of offers submitted as another variable to control for the expected positive effect of more bidders on procurement performance.

Table 6: How the release of a starting price impacts procurement performance – OLS results

	Dependent variable: Procurement performance			
	Model 2.1		**Model 2.2**	
Independent variables	**OLS**		**OLS**	
	b (t-stat)		b (t-stat)	
Intercept	-0.204	***	-0.062	***
	(-18.797)		(-5.430)	
Publication of a starting price	-0.053	***	-0.054	***
	(-5.642)		(-5.664)	
Price heterogeneity * publication of a starting price	0.015	*	0.020	**
	(1.586)		(2.238)	
Log (number of submitted offers)			-0.256	***
			(-32.322)	
Contract variables	Yes (46)		Yes (46)	
Market variables	Yes (18)		Yes (17)	
Buyer variables	Yes (28)		Yes (26)	
Observations	14,643		14,643	
Adjusted R-squared	0.219		0.271	
F-statistic	47.689		62.228	

Note. This table reports the regression estimates from Equation 2. The *t* values are displayed in parentheses.
$^{*}p < .10$. $^{**}p < .05$. $^{***}p < .01$.

[61] We used the log variable to reflect the idea that an additional bidder's impact on performance is likely to increase at a decreasing rate.

In Model 2.1, we found that the estimated coefficient for the publication of starting prices was negative and significant. Hence, the publication of a starting price was correlated with a higher level of procurement performance. In Model 2.2, which included the logarithmized number of offers as another variable, the estimated coefficient for the release of a starting price remained negative and significant. Consistent with our initial expectations, the estimated coefficient regarding the number of offers submitted was significant and negative, indicating that the participation of an additional bidder decreased the procurement price relative to the estimated costs. Moreover, both models implied that increased price heterogeneity in tenders for similar contracts decreased the relation between the publication of a starting price and performance levels.

Given the results of the probit model (Table 5), the publication of a starting price might be selective. Tenders with starting prices might be different from others. If these omitted characteristics were related to performance levels, the estimated coefficient for the publication of a starting price would incorporate these effects and suffer from selection bias.[62] To control for the likelihood of selection bias in the starting price publication variable, we estimated a two-stage Heckman selection-corrected model. The inclusion of the inverse Mill's ratio (IMR) corrects for potential bias in the estimates of the coefficients (Heckman, 1979). Accordingly, we defined the second stage outcome regressions as:

$$APERF_i = a_0 + \sum_{j=1}^{k} b_j X_{ji} + cSPRICE_i + d\log(OFFERS_i) + e(HET_i * SPRICE_i) + \varepsilon_i \quad (3)$$

Except for the inclusion of the IMR, the second stage specification in Equation 3 was identical to Equation 2. The selection-corrected model used the probit specification from Model 1.4 to estimate the first stage and construct the IMR. We estimated the second stage by including the IMR in the specifications of Models 3.1 and 3.2. Table 7 reports the results of the second stage estimates of the selection-corrected model.

---

62 The standard selection bias refers to incomplete information in the dependent variable. In the second type of selection bias, full information on the incomplete variable is available, but its distribution is selective. In the present work's data set, procurement performance might be affected by the same factors influencing buyers' decisions to disclose a starting price.

Table 7: How the release of a starting price impacts procurement performance – Selection-corrected results

Independent variables	Dependent variable: Procurement performance Model 3.1 Stage 2 selection-corrected b (t-stat)		Model 3.2 Stage 2 selection-corrected b (t-stat)	
Intercept	-0.204	***	-0.06	***
	(-18.813)		(-5.276)	
Publication of a starting price	-0.038	***	-0.056	***
	(-5.604)		(-6.127)	
Price heterogeneity * publication of a starting price	0.015		0.020	**
	(1.593)		(2.245)	
Inverse Mill's ratio	-0.013		-0.013	
	(-1.470)		(-1.485)	
Log (number of submitted offers)			-0.256	***
			(-32.338)	
Contract variables	Yes (46)		Yes (46)	
Market variables	Yes (18)		Yes (17)	
Buyer variables	Yes (28)		Yes (26)	
Observations	14,643		14,643	
Adjusted R-squared	0.219		0.271	
F-statistic	47.181		61.626	

Note. This table reports the Heckman selection-correction regression results from Equation 3. The *t* values are displayed in parentheses.
$^{*}p < .10$. $^{**}p < .05$. $^{***}p < .01$.

To evaluate the effect of any selection bias on the estimates of the coefficients, we compared the estimation results from Model 3.2 with those from the OLS Model 2.2. Because the effect of the estimated coefficient on the IMR was not statistically significant, we did not reject the null hypothesis of no selectivity. Accordingly, the explanatory powers of the two specifications were similar; the coefficient estimates of the selection-corrected estimates confirmed the results of OLS Model 2.2. In both models, the estimate of the coefficient for predicting the publication of a starting price was negative and significant. The coefficient's magnitude in the selection-corrected model increased slightly (c = -0.056 vs. c = -0.054). However, the effect of the selection-correction on the estimate was not dramatic. Both models suggested that the release of a starting price improved procurement performance. The coefficient for the interaction between the publication dummy and the index for price heterogeneity from similar tenders indicated that greater price heterogeneity significantly decreased the impact of starting prices on procurement performance.

6.4.1.3 *How the release of a starting price impacts the number of bidders*

In public procurement, the potential number of suppliers is enormous compared with the number of bidders. Therefore, we used Poisson regression to control for the impact of starting prices on the number of bidders. Related studies have used similar count data models to examine the determinants of the bidders' entry decisions (Bajari & Hortaçsu, 2003; T. Li & Perrigne, 2003).

We specified the regression model as:

$$OFFERS_i = a_0 + \sum_{j=1}^{k} b_j X_{ji} + cSPRICE_i + d\log(ESTIMATE_i) + \varepsilon_i \quad (4)$$

where $OFFERS_i$ is the number of bids submitted; b_j is a vector of coefficients on contract, buyer, and market characteristics X_{ji}; c is the coefficient for the dummy variable $SPRICE_i$ with a value of 1 if a starting price is published and 0 otherwise; d is the coefficient for the logarithmic value of the ex-post price estimate variable $ESTIMATE_i$; and ε_i is the random error with mean 0 and variance σ.[63]

[63] We added the value of the ex-post price estimate to control for the fact that higher valued procurement auctions attract the interest of more bidders (Onur et al., 2012).

Table 8: How the release of a starting price impacts the number of bidders

Independent variables	Dependent variable: Number of offers submitted Model 4.1 Parameter estimates b (χ2-stat)		Model 4.2 Parameter estimates b (χ2-stat)	
Intercept	2.045 (1.710)		1.939 (1.536)	
Publication of a starting price	0.087 (92.181)	***	0.086 (88.579)	***
Log (Ex-post price estimate)			0.011 (6.758)	***
Contract variables	Yes (46)		Yes (46)	
Market variables	Yes (18)		Yes (18)	
Buyer variables	Yes (28)		Yes (28)	
Observations	14,643		11,642	
LR-statistic	10053.852	***	10060.589	***

Note. This table presents the Poisson parameter estimate from Equation 2. The Wald Chi-Square values are presented in parentheses.
$^{*}p < .10$. $^{**}p < .05$. $^{***}p < .01$.

In Model 4.1, the estimated coefficient for starting price publication was positive and significant: The release of a starting price was correlated with a larger number of submitted bids. This relation remained significant in Model 4.2, which controlled for how the monetary value of the procurement tender affected the number of bids. The estimated coefficient of the ex-post price estimate remained positive and significant. In line with initial expectations, the release of a starting price was correlated with more bidding activity in Model 4.2 as well.

6.4.2 Formulation of published price estimates

6.4.2.1 How starting price precision affects procurement performance

We studied how increased numerical precision in starting prices influenced buyers' performance by using the following regression:

$$PERF_i = a_0 + \sum_{j=1}^{k} b_j X_{ji} + cPREC_i + dPREC^2{}_i + e\log(OFFERS_i) + \varepsilon_i \quad (5)$$

where $PERF_i$ is the natural logarithm of the difference between the ex-post price estimate and the awarded value; b_j is a vector of coefficients representing buyer, item, and market characteristics X_{ji}; and c is the coefficient for the variable $PREC_i$, which measures the level of starting price precision. We included the coefficient *d* from the quadratic variable $PREC^2_i$ to test whether increased precision had a curvilinear inverted-U-shaped effect on procurement performance; e is the coefficient for the logarithmized variable $OFFERS_i$; and ε_i is random error with mean 0 and variance σ.[64]

Past tender studies (Brannman et al., 1987; Paarsch, 1992) have shown that the relation between the number of bidders and final tendered prices is likely to be nonlinear. The prices decrease with the number of bidders as competition intensifies with more bidders. However, the final price does not decrease monotonically with increased competition. From some point on, prices decrease at a slower rate (the likelihood that an additional bidder with a better appreciation of an item will enter the tender decreases constantly). Once a tender has reached its full degree of competitiveness, prices no longer fall (the bidder with the best available appreciation has already entered the tender).

However, some researchers have argued that an increase in the number of bidders may lead to higher final prices in procurement tenders due to a winner's curse that increases in severity (Hong & Shum, 2002). Because increased competition leads to more aggressive bidding, the winner's curse may become disproportionally more severe when competition intensifies. Rationally bidding suppliers would incorporate this winner's curse into their strategy by bidding less aggressively.

However, we argue that the winner's curse will not result in a quadratic relation between the number of bidders and final prices within tenders. First, although the winner's curse might decrease procurement performance from a theoretical point of view, researchers only barely replicated its impact on bidding behavior by investigating transaction data from the field. Second, in the sealed-bid format of public procurement, bidders cannot observe the level of competition before placing their bid. Hence, they

[64] We used the log variable to reflect the idea that an additional bidder's impact on performance was likely to increase at a decreasing rate.

will not incorporate a potentially worse winner's curse into their bidding strategy. Accordingly, we used a log predictor for the number of bids in Equation 5 to reflect that the participation of an additional bidder will improve procurement performance at a decreasing rate.

Table 9 presents the regression results for the alternative models (Equation 5) used to study the sensitivity of the estimated coefficients. In Model 5.1, starting price precision was the primary variable of interest besides the item, market, and buyer characteristics, which were control variables. To extend Model 5.1, we added the quadratic term of starting price precision in Model 5.2 so that we could test whether it was possible to have too much precision. Models 5.3 and 5.4 extended these two specifications by including the logarithmized number of offers submitted. We used this variable to control for the expected positive effect of more bidders on performance.

Table 9: How starting price precision affects procurement performance

	Dependent variable: Procurement performance							
	Model 5.1		Model 5.2		Model 5.3		Model 5.4	
Independent variables	**OLS**		**OLS**		**OLS**		**OLS**	
	b (t-stat)		b (t-stat)		b (t-stat)		b (t-stat)	
Intercept	-0.410	***	-0.400	***	-0.25	***	-0.250	***
	(-30.156)		(-24.107)		(-17.587)		(-14.205)	
Starting price precision index	-0.029	***	-0.079	*	-0.024	**	-0.071	*
	(-3.100)		(-1.701)		(-2.501)		(-1.579)	
Quadratic starting price precision index			0.04				0.045	
			(-1.061)				(-1.239)	
Log (number of submitted offers)					-0.107	***	-0.107	***
					(-29.075)		(-29.074)	
Item variables	Yes (46)		Yes (46)		Yes (46)		Yes (46)	
Market variables	Yes (17)		Yes (17)		Yes (17)		Yes (17)	
Buyer variables	Yes (26)		Yes (26)		Yes (26)		Yes (26)	
Observations	11,642		11,642		11,642		11,642	
Adjusted R-squared	0.24		0.24		0.292		0.292	
F-statistic	49.38		41.917		54.360		53.776	

Note. This table presents the regression estimates according to Equation 1. The t values are shown in parentheses.
$^{*}p < .10$. $^{**}p < .05$. $^{***}p < .01$.

In Model 5.1, we found that the coefficient for starting price precision was negative and significant such that increased starting price precision was related to higher performance.[65] In Model 5.2 (focused on the shape of this relation), the coefficient for starting price precision remained negative and significant. By contrast, the coefficient for quadratic starting price precision was positive but not quite significant. Models 5.3 and 5.4 included the logarithmized number of offers as another variable and replicated the findings. Thus, both models further supported a linear relation between increased starting price precision and higher performance. Consistent with the expectations, the coefficient for the number of offers submitted was significant and negative. In both conditions, the respective coefficients indicated that the participation of an additional bidder decreased the final price relative to the estimated price but at a decreasing rate. Most of the other control variables were also significant.[66]

6.4.2.2 *How starting price precision affects the number of bids submitted*

To measure how starting price precision would affect the number of bids submitted, we computed similar regression models. However, we used the number of offers submitted as the dependent variable. We used Poisson regression to estimate the respective models. We specified the regression model as:

$$OFFERS_i = a_0 + \sum_{j=1}^{k} b_j X_{ji} + cPREC_i + dln(ESTIMATE_i) + \varepsilon_i \qquad (6)$$

where $OFFERS_i$ is the number of bids submitted; b_j is a vector of coefficients representing buyer, item, and market characteristics X_{ji}; c is the coefficient for the variable $PREC_I$, which measures the level of starting price precision; d is the coefficient for the logarithmic ex-post price estimate variable ESTIMATE; and ε_i is random error with mean 0 and variance σ.

Table 3 presents the regression results for alternative models (Equation 6) that were tested to determine the sensitivity of the estimated coefficients. In Model 6.1, starting price precision was the primary variable of interest.

[65] We conducted robustness checks by investigating this relation on a country-specific level (e.g., for Spain, Italy, and Slovakia). The results corroborated the reported relation between starting price precision and performance.

[66] In all conditions, for the collective F-tests for the market, buyer, and item dummy variables, the null hypotheses that the coefficients of these variables were equal to zero was rejected.

We used item, market, and buyer characteristics as control variables. In Model 6.2, we added the value of the ex-post price estimate to Model 6.1 to control for the fact that higher valued procurement tenders attract more bidders' interest (Onur et al., 2012).

In Model 6.1, the coefficient for starting price precision was positive and significant such that increased starting price precision was related to a larger number of submitted bids. This relation remained significant in Model 6.2, which controlled for how the monetary value of the procurement tender affected the number of bids. Consistent with our expectations, the estimated coefficient for the ex-post price estimate was positive and significant. Moreover, increased starting price precision was related to higher bidding activity in this model as well.

Table 10: How starting price precision affects the number of bids submitted

	Dependent variable: Number of submitted offers			
	Model 6.1		Model 6.2	
Independent variables	Parameter estimates		Parameter estimates	
	b (Wald χ2)		b (Wald χ2)	
Intercept	1.775	***	1.438	***
	(0.060)		(0.024)	
Starting price precision index	0.096	***	0.087	***
	(34.182)		(27.699)	
Log (ex-post price estimate)			0.032	***
			(66.840)	
Item variables	Yes (46)		Yes (46)	
Market variables	Yes (17)		Yes (17)	
Buyer variables	Yes (26)		Yes (26)	
Observations	11,642		11,642	
LR-statistic	9091.87		9158.48	

Note. This table presents the Poisson parameter estimate from Equation 2. The Wald Chi-Square values are shown in parentheses.
*$p < .10$. **$p < .05$. ***$p < .01$.

6.4.2.3 *How starting price ranges affect procurement performance*

To study the performance differences between the kinds of starting prices, we computed two types of statistical analyses. First, we computed a one-way Welch ANOVA to determine whether the procurement performance level was different for tenders with different kinds of starting prices. We classified the tenders into three groups: precise point prices ($n = 5{,}675$), imprecise point prices ($n = 5{,}967$), and price ranges ($n = 647$). The performance level differed significantly between the different kinds of starting prices, Welch's F (2, 1913.471) = 218.131, $p < .001$. Performance levels increased, in the following order, from price ranges ($M = -0.11$, $SD = 0.25$) to imprecise point prices ($M = -0.21$, $SD = 0.30$) to precise point prices ($M = -0.31$, $SD = 0.36$). A Games-Howell post hoc analysis revealed that the mean performance level increase from price ranges to precise point prices (-0.20, 95% CI [-0.22, -0.17]) was statistically significant ($p < .001$) and so was the increase from imprecise point prices to precise point prices (-0.10., 95% CI [-0.11, -0.08], $p < .001$). Moreover, the performance level increase from price ranges to imprecise point prices (-0.10, 95% CI [-0.13, -0.08]) was significant ($p < .001$) as well.

Second, we applied a series of Ordinary Least Squares (OLS) regressions to the overall data set and to the subset of tenders with price ranges to further study these differences between performance effects. We distinguish between the effects of starting price ranges, precise starting point prices, and imprecise starting point prices. We define the following three different regression specifications in more detail:

$$PERF_i = a_0 + \sum_{j=1}^{k} b_j X_{ji} + cPOINTROUND_i + d\log(OFFERS_i) + \varepsilon_i \tag{7}$$

$$PERF_i = a_0 + \sum_{j=1}^{k} b_j X_{ji} + cPOINTPREC_i + d\log(OFFERS_i) + \varepsilon_i \tag{8}$$

$$PERF_i = a_0 + \sum_{j=1}^{k} b_j X_{ji} + cRANGE_i + d\log(OFFERS_i) + \varepsilon_i \tag{9}$$

where $PERF_i$ is the dependent variable; b_j is a vector of coefficients for tender, buyer, item, and market characteristics X_{ji}; *c* indicates the influence of the starting price type that was utilized in each tender; *d* is the coefficient of the logarithmized variable $OFFERS_i$; and ε_i is random error with mean 0 and variance σ. If a starting price was used, the dummy variables were set to 1; otherwise, they were set to 0. The regression specifications in Equations 7, 8, and 9 enabled us to observe the effect of each starting price type in isolation while controlling for other factors that could affect the awarded value in relation to the ex-post price estimate.

In addition to these equations, we studied the effect of all the starting price types jointly by using the following equation:

$$APERF_i = a_0 + \sum_{j=1}^{k} b_j X_{ji} + cPOINTROUND_i + dPOINTPREC_i + eRANGE_i + f\log(OFFERS_i) + \varepsilon_i \quad (10)$$

Table 11: Effects of different kinds of starting prices on procurement performance

Independent variables	**Dependent variable: Procurement performance**							
	Model 7		**Model 8**		**Model 9**		**Model 10**	
	b (t-stat)		b (t-stat)		b (t-stat)		b (t-stat)	
Constant	-0.327	***	-0.165	***	-0.158	***	-0.346	***
	(-14.038)		(-7.090)		(-6.809)		(-15.067)	
Precise starting price points	-0.02	***						
	(-3.450)							
Round starting price points			0.015	***			0.019	***
			(2.699)				(3.327)	
Starting price ranges					0.020		0.034	**
					(1.471)		(2.438)	
Log (number of submitted offers)	-0.106	***	-0.106	***	-0.106	***	-0.106	***
	(-29.742)		(-29.739)		(-29.808)		(-29.755)	
Item variables	Yes (46)		Yes (46)		Yes (46)		Yes (46)	
Market variables	Yes (17)		Yes (17)		Yes (17)		Yes (17)	
Buyer variables	Yes (26)		Yes (26)		Yes (26)		Yes (26)	
Observations	12,289		12,289		12,289		12,289	
F-statistic	55.578		55.597		55.427		54.99	
Adjusted R^2	0.288		0.288		0.287		0.288	

Note. This table presents the regression results for the OLS specifications defined in Equations 3 to 6. The t values are displayed in parentheses.
$^{*}p < .10$. $^{**}p < .05$. $^{***}p < .01$.

The tested models confirmed the results of the previously computed ANOVA.[67] Model 7 showed that precise starting price points were related to higher levels of procurement performance. Round starting price points

[67] We tested leaner models without the number of offers submitted as a variable. These models yielded the same significant coefficients.

showed a lower level of performance (Model 8). However, we found no significant relation between starting price ranges and performance (Model 9). Whereas the coefficients implied that price ranges were related to lower performance, this relation was not significant. The combined specification (Model 10) confirmed the above results: Compared with precise starting price points, round price points and price ranges were significantly related to decreased performance. As expected, Table 11 confirms that the bidding activity was crucial for performance. Prices decreased with the number of bidders until the tender reached its full degree of competitiveness.

Although the regression results presented above imply that starting price ranges do not increase buyers' performance in tenders, we probed further for any performance differences within different types of starting price ranges. We analyzed the subset of price ranges more closely. A one-way Welch ANOVA was computed to determine whether performance level was different for tenders with different types of starting price ranges. We divided the tenders into three groups: bolstering price ranges ($n = 171$), bracketing price ranges ($n = 199$), and back down price ranges ($n = 277$). Performance levels increased—in the following order—from bracketing price ranges ($M = -0.13$, $SD = 0.28$) to back down price ranges ($M = -0.11$, $SD = 0.23$) to bolstering price ranges ($M = -0.10$, $SD = 0.24$). However, the differences between these tender groups were not significant; Welch's $F(2, 379.143) = 0.409$, $p = .665$. Accordingly, bolstering, bracketing, and back down starting price ranges did not differ in their impact on buyers' performance.

7. Discussion of empirical results

7.1 Publication of a starting price

7.1.1 How tender characteristics affect the release of a starting price

The results of Table 5 partially confirmed our initial research hypothesis H1 that the likelihood of a starting price publication would depend on whether buyer, market, and contract conditions varied between different tenders. First, for buyer conditions, the empirical results for Models 1.1 and 1.4 largely corresponded with our initial expectations. We proposed that the increased (approximated) procurement expertise of officials that manage tenders within Contracting Authorities would increase the likelihood that a starting price would be released. Compared with procurement officials in sectoral authorities that arguably possess the highest professionalism as a reaction to increased market pressure, officials in other kinds of Contracting Authorities were significantly less likely to publish starting prices.

Second, Table 5 shows that the variation in the likelihood of publication depended on market characteristics as well. In Models 1.2 and 1.4, most coefficients on the country level were significant. We argue that differences in national market norms and procurement regulations might primarily drive such variations. Compared with the omitted variable "Austria," the coefficient for the variable "Germany" was one of the few that were not significant. Compared with other EU economies, the Austrian and German markets are homogenous and unified; their legal systems are similar and are even based on each other to some extent. The low cultural and linguistic barriers allow suppliers to participate in both markets. Thus, we found additional arguments that heterogeneity in market norms and legal requirements cause differences in the likelihood of starting price disclosure.

A. Rhode, *Public Procurement in the European Union*, Schriften zum europäischen Management, https://doi.org/10.1007/978-3-658-28073-4_7

Third, we found no evidence that the likelihood of publishing a starting price depended on the complexity of a contract. In high-value tenders, procurement officials did not seem to conceal starting prices to maintain an information advantage. The increased cost uncertainty for potential suppliers in high-value tenders did not motivate procurement officials to publish starting prices more frequently. Gatzlaff and Liu (2013) argued that the value of potential offers might vary more in complex transactions. Given the significant information asymmetries in public procurement, we found no reason to believe that this statement should not apply to tenders. However, Contracting Authorities cannot reject all offers without obstruction compared with sellers in housing transactions. They will not conceal starting prices to avoid preventing very inexpensive offers.

Instead, Contracting Authorities might not want to receive very low offers at all. The Directives imply that procurement officials must award one of the interested suppliers – nearly independently of the tender's economic outcome. As stated in Section 4.4, the Directives require procurement officials to award a contract based on the supplier selection criteria published in the CN. Thus, they might be downright forced to award a low-priced "too good to be true" offer despite the potentially low quality of that offer, thus resulting in a poor value-for-money award decision.

Section 4.4 likewise explained that the Directives contain provisions that enable procurement officials to exclude abnormally low offers, but they do not clearly define abnormally low offers, nor do they provide any specific methods for identifying them. Even significantly undercutting other bids might not automatically justify the exclusion of an offer. Instead, Contracting Authorities cannot exclude an offer without previously asking the supplier for detailed information about the nature of the offer's value.

7.1.2 *How the release of a starting price impacts procurement performance*

The results presented in Table 6 confirm research hypothesis H2, which proposed that Contracting Authorities should enjoy a first-mover advantage by releasing a starting price: Tenders that released a starting price enjoyed higher performance levels. This finding remained valid in Model 2.2, which controlled for the influence of the number of bidders on performance levels. Neither model implied that starting prices created entry barriers, resulting in lower performance. The results refuted our initial belief that the release of a starting price in CNs harmed performance levels. Finally, the results corresponded with already existing research evidence (Kamins et al., 2004; Kristensen & Gärling, 2000) that less extreme anchors can yield a first-mover advantage in economic transactions.

Moreover, we found that increased price heterogeneity in similar tenders significantly decreased the relation between starting prices and procurement performance. This pattern corresponds with an interpretation of anchoring that relies on the availability of anchor-consistent information (Strack & Mussweiler, 1997). In CPV classes with high heterogeneity, the presence of tenders of similar contracts for different prices provided suppliers with salient anchor-disconfirming evidence. Furthermore, if unobserved tender qualities were the primary drivers of the results, we would expect them to play a more significant role in more heterogeneous CPV classes, amplifying the impact of the performance. Still, the results of table 6 demonstrate the opposite – further increasing the trust in the validity of the chosen econometric models.

Because buyer, market, and contract conditions significantly affected the likelihood that a starting price would be published in Model 1.4, the distribution of the kinds of tenders with starting prices might be nonrandom. However, Table 5 shows that such conditions did not affect the relation between starting prices and performance. Instead, the coefficients for the publication of a starting price in the OLS model and the alternative selection-corrected model agreed. In both models, releasing a starting price positively impacted procurement performance, and the size of this impact depended on the availability of anchor-consistent information. Moreover, the coefficient for the number of submitted offers remained significantly negative in Model 3.2 as well.[68]

[68] Although the empirical results did not imply that the starting price effect varied by price cohort, we examined the effect separately by price cohort. We used the same selection-correction models for the tests within the subsets. The results consistently replicated the findings reported above. Again, the first-mover advantage persisted, even for starting prices in auctions involving more valuable and complicated contracts with arguably higher information asymmetries.

7.1.3 How the release of a starting price impacts the number of bidders

The results in Table 11 refute research hypothesis H4, which proposed that the publication of a starting price in a CN would lower the number of bids. Instead, the publication of a starting price was correlated with a larger number of submitted offers in Models 4.1 and 4.2. For public tenders, we could not replicate the findings from prior negotiation research on the potential downsides of a starting price release (Galinsky et al., 2009; Lee et al., 2018; Schweinsberg et al., 2012). In tenders, starting prices might fail to create entry barriers due to the structural particularities of public procurement. First, starting prices in public tenders may lack the necessary degree of aggressiveness – unlike first offers in negotiations. Past research has advised first movers in negotiations to formulate starting prices that are as extreme as reasonably possible to anchor counterparties effectively (Thompson, 2015). However, the extremity of first offers might reverse the first-mover advantage in some negotiations, either by producing impasses (Yip & Schweinsberg, 2017) or creating entry barriers (Lee et al., 2018). The legal requirement for procurement officials to publish realistic nonaggressive starting prices in a CN may mitigate the danger that the release of a starting price will offend potential suppliers and motivate them to refrain from entering the tender. Thus, released starting prices in tenders created no entry barriers.

Second, different from negotiations, demand auctions, or housing sales, starting prices in public tenders are missing any first-mover commitment. In negotiations, first movers are expected to close the deal when recipients accept their starting price. Because negotiators can never get a better deal than their first offer, starting prices usually exceed the first-mover's reservation price. Recipients believe that a starting price indicates the value of the first mover's reservation price (Lee et al., 2018). The reservation price acts as the indifference point between accepting an offer and ending the negotiation. Negotiators will only accept an outcome that improves their reservation price (van Poucke & Buelens, 2002). Thus, recipients will refrain from entering a negotiation if they believe that their reservation price (e.g., their production costs) does not overlap with the reservation point of the counterparty.

In demand auctions, a starting price (effectively working as a reservation price or minimum bid) increases the risk that no transaction takes place at all if the reservation price exceeds any bidder's maximum willingness to pay (Galinsky et al., 2009). By contrast, potential suppliers in public procurement may still enter a tender with a starting price below their estimated costs in case of a contract award: They still have the chance to win the contract award at a final price that exceeds the starting price (e.g., in tenders with low competition).

Therefore, starting prices in tenders better resemble list prices in housing sales where final prices can lie below (or above) starting prices. The starting price of a property signals a partial commitment (Beracha & Seiler, 2014). The seller agrees to sell the house at the starting price if one buyer agrees to pay at least this price. On the other hand, buyers will try to push to get a final price of a house that lies below the starting price. If two or more submit bids for a property, the seller conducts a first-price auction and sells the house to the highest bidder. However, if the highest bid undercuts the seller's reservation price, the homeowner can always decide to reject all bids and wait for new interest. Accordingly, counterparties might refrain from entering a tender if the seller's starting price far exceeds what they are willing to pay.

In public procurement, starting prices might fail to create similar barriers because Contracting Authorities do not possess the discretion to restart a tender and wait for additional bidders due to regulatory burdens and budgetary constraints.

As stated in Section 4.2.3.1, the Directives define the unequivocal minimum (15 days) and maximum (52 days) deadlines for the duration of an open procedure, which Contracting Authorities must specify in a binding manner in the CN. Moreover, the Directives imply that Contracting Authorities must award a supplier almost independently of the tender's economic outcome. Only in severe cases do the Directives allow a tender to be reissued if the first procurement auction achieved an economically undesirable outcome. However, retendering is not automatically justified if the award value exceeds the starting price. The Directives remain silent on the degree of excess necessary for a termination—in absolute amounts or percentages. Regulation still implies that Contracting Authorities must refer to an objective market price to deny the economic viability of the contract award. Even when the final price excessively exceeds the starting price, the Directives require the Contracting Authority to demonstrate why a new tender would yield an improved outcome. If procurement officials still cancel a tender, they must restart the procedure from scratch by issuing a new CN, resulting in significant transaction costs for the Contracting Authority and potential suppliers.

From a budgetary perspective, procurement officials have a strong incentive to award tenders promptly to utilize their allocated budget and avoid future budget cuts. Procurement officials typically must apply in advance for budget approval for planned tenders. If their projects get approval, the estimated costs go into their annual budget. The Contracting Authorities strive, therefore, to carry out approved tenders in the fiscal year provided for them. Besides, Contracting Authorities risk future budget cuts if they fail to award the project within the given fiscal year. In public finance, underutilizing an allocated budget might lower the monetary value of future budget allocations.

However, Table 8 implies that the release of a starting price increased the number of submitted bids. We found that past anchoring research has failed to provide satisfactory explanations for why tenders with starting prices should attract the interest of even more bidders. Instead, we referred to auction theory to explain why starting prices facilitated bidders' entry decisions. Procurement officials typically award contracts on a fixed price basis – usually without the possibility of further renegotiations. Fixed-price contracts bind suppliers to complete the project independent of the incurred costs (Bajari & Tadelis, 2001). Due to this cost uncertainty, the winner's curse may arise (Kagel & Levin, 1986). The Contracting Authority likely possesses more information about the costs of the contract than the potential suppliers (Laffont & Tirole, 1993). The EU Directives provide specific calculation methods for the realistic estimation of starting prices, which thereby express the buyer's estimation of the contract costs. Moreover, stakeholders expect Contracting Authorities to act with integrity (Telgen et al., 2007).

Accordingly, the publication of a starting price might reduce a supplier's entry risks by lowering information asymmetry and cost uncertainty. If a starting price reduces information asymmetries in the costs of a contract, suppliers may be more likely to enter a tender because their perceived risk level decreases. In addition to reducing the overall risk of entry, publishing a starting price can simplify suppliers' entry process. The better predictability of the final costs for rendering the contract decreases the transaction costs that incur when suppliers calculate adequate offers, which enable them to both win contracts and minimize the risk of cost overruns.

7.2 Formulation of a published starting price

7.2.1 How starting price precision affects procurement performance

The results in Table 9 imply that increased precision in starting price points improves buyers' performance in tenders. These results confirm research hypothesis H5. Besides, Table 9 refutes research hypothesis H6 about the possibility of a U-shaped relation between starting price precision and performance. However, we believe that the findings on precision effects in public tenders still correspond to the attribution of competence explanation. According to the attribution of competence explanation, recipients view more precise anchors as more credible – if they ascribe a high level of expertise to the first-moving party (Loschelder et al., 2016). We believe that this expertise-based precision effect plays an active role in public procurement, where regulation limits the exchange of information between parties. In such a rigid transactional environment, counterparties face difficulties when scrutinizing the first mover's competence. Informational asymmetries prevent suppliers from ascribing low competence to procurement officials who give precise starting prices. In public tenders, highly precise anchors will not backfire as counterparties have no chance to question the first mover's competence. Moreover, suppliers expect public procurement officials to act with integrity (Telgen et al., 2007). Thus, recipients may believe that increased precision entails a better description of the contract's value.

First, the results demystify initial reservations about the efficacy of increased anchor precision in tenders. Findings from prior negotiation research initially inspired this skeptical attitude. Loschelder et al. (2017) found that increased anchor precision backfired for high-value contracts for which a precise anchor (to the cent) might signal low competence in procurement officials. The tender transactions analyzed in the current data set had relatively high monetary values. Table 7 shows that the average award value of the tenders was €2.4 million and that (without controlling for other factors) procurement officials disclosed (on average) more precise starting prices for higher valued tenders. However, the empirical results imply that increased starting price precision improves outcomes – even for tenders involving valuable (and thus complex) contracts. Independent of the contract complexity, counterparties assume high first-mover competence in public tenders.

Second, the results show that precision can improve the anchor potency of less aggressive starting prices as well. Loschelder, Stuppi et al. (2014) claimed that increased precision should prove particularly advantageous for more extreme anchors. Extremity reduces an anchor's plausibility because recipients think the anchor needs to be adjusted (Schweinsberg et al., 2012). Therefore, precision might increase the plausibility of an extreme and rather incredible anchor. We wondered whether potential suppliers in public procurement might interpret starting prices as plausible, independent of their precision. Whereas recipients usually interpret starting prices in negotiations as unacceptable, starting prices in tenders are less extreme. Instead, EU directives stipulate that organizations should estimate the starting price of a contract based on a realistic calculation. However, the results in Table 9 imply that precision boosted the plausibility of reasonable starting prices in tenders as well.

7.2.2 How starting price precision affects the number of bids submitted

The results of Table 10 refute the initial research hypothesis H7, which proposed that increased precision in starting price points would decrease the number of offers submitted in tenders. Instead, increased starting price precision was related to a larger number of bids submitted in both models 6.1 and 6.2. For public tenders, we could not replicate the findings from prior negotiation research on the potential downsides of increased anchor precision. In public procurement, precise starting price points do not create barriers to entry. The potential signal that precise starting prices lie close to the buyer's reservation price leaves the entry decision of potential suppliers unaffected. The EU Directives enable procurement officials to reissue a tender if the initial procurement auction yields an economically poor outcome. However, procurement officials cancel their procedures only in exceptional cases because retendering brings about additional and significant transaction costs.

As already stated in Section 7.1.3, procurement officials must adhere to strict regulations if they annul a tender. If the awarded contract value merely exceeds the starting price, this does not justify a cancellation. Regulation remains silent on the degree (stated in monetary amounts or as percentages) of overshooting that is necessary for a cancellation of a tender. It merely implies that procurement officials must refer to a market price to deny the economic viability of a tendered outcome. In practice, the awarded value must greatly exceed the starting price before procurement officials can consider retendering. Even in this case, procurement officials must demonstrate why a new tender (e.g., a different procedure) would obtain a more reasonable price. As a result, Contracting Authorities only rarely possess the discretion to retender a contract award. Since procurement officials likely must accept the result of a procedure independent of the outcome in relation to their reservation price, potential bidders can neglect to determine how far a Contracting Authority's reservation price is away from the starting price. Similarly, based on a decrease in starting price precision, bidders will not infer that procurement officials will accept higher prices to shorten their transaction times (Backus et al., 2016). Instead, tenders run for a fixed period as the EU directives stipulate uniform minimum timespans and deadlines.

Moreover, existing negotiation studies have failed to explain why increased anchor precision decreases the number of bids and increases potential suppliers' interest in public procurement. The scale-granularity explanation (Janiszewski & Uy, 2008), the attribution of competence explanation (Mason et al., 2013), and the potential roundness advantage (Yan & Pena-Marin, 2017) all fail to offer an appropriate explanatory approach. In public tenders, precise starting prices as a signal of increased first-mover knowledge seem to facilitate bidders' entry decisions. In public procurement, regulations allocate risk mainly on the suppliers' side (Tadelis, 2012). Procurement officials award most contracts on a fixed-price basis without the possibility of further renegotiations. Therefore, fixed-price contracts bind suppliers to complete the project independent of the incurred costs (Bajari & Tadelis, 2001).[69]

The winner's curse may thereby arise as the winning supplier tends to have optimistic assumptions about the contract's costs (Kagel & Levin, 1986). Potential suppliers must evaluate their entry decisions and carefully calculate bids if they want to minimize the risk of a loss when they win the contract. Because increased precision enhances the credibility of starting prices, potential bidders believe that the value of a more precise starting price lies closer to the costs that are incurred when a contract is awarded. Since the suppliers' perceived risk level decreases, they are more likely to submit a bid and enter a tender. Likewise, the increase in the attributed expertise of more precise starting prices lowers the entry barriers of tenders by simplifying the entry decision as well. Typically, due to substantial information asymmetries, interested bidders put significant effort into calculating bids that enable them to both win contracts and minimize the risk of cost overruns. This task becomes less cumbersome than usual if public procurement officials publish more reliable starting price information. Naturally, decreases in potential suppliers' entry costs lead to increased bidding activity.

7.2.3 How starting price ranges affect procurement performance

7.2.3.1 Comparing starting price ranges with other kinds of starting prices

The regression results in Table 11 confirm the prior results regarding the positive influence of increased precision in starting price points on performance. However, the results for Models 9 and 10 contradict the initial expectation that (compared with other kinds of starting prices) starting price ranges lead to improved performance (H7). Compared with negotiations, starting price ranges in public tenders do not induce potential suppliers to react with less extreme counteroffers. The econometric set-up of the empirical investigation does not allow for the refutation of the idea that suppliers interpret price ranges as politer than equally extreme starting price

[69] This conclusion is still valid after the 2014 reform of the Directives that allowed renegotiations under specific circumstances. Due to significant transaction costs and strict preconditions, renegotiations vastly remain the exception in public tenders.

points. However, the results show that potential differences in perceived politeness do not affect bidding behavior. The missing significance of this result likely stems from the low degree of interparty dynamics in public procurement: Compared with negotiations, the impersonal determination of prices in tenders leaves less room for interpersonal exchange. The exchange of written messages in tenders mainly concerns the determination of the final price. In public procurement, regulations further restrict the exchange of information between parties. During a tender, potential suppliers can submit only one offer and cannot alter this offer after it is submitted. Since the Directives forbid renegotiations of offers, the first offer of a supplier is typically also the last in a tender.

Regulations prohibit procurement officials from engaging in private talks with suppliers. In open procedures, the directives permit any further (even public) informational exchange after the submission of offers until the contract award. Consequently, parties do not interact during the supplier selection phase. In such a rigid setting, the politeness-inducing aspects of starting price ranges remain ineffective. In negotiations, recipients may care how the first mover interprets an assertive counteroffer in response to a range. However, in public procurement, potential suppliers can ignore the buyer's interpretation. The regulation's high transparency demands require procurement officials to award contracts on the terms published in the CN and restrict them from discriminating against any potential supplier.

7.2.3.2 Comparing different types of starting price ranges

The results of the one-way Welch ANOVA do not support the research hypotheses on performance differences between types of starting price ranges (H8a, H8b, and H8c). The results contradict the initial belief that bolstering price ranges, compared with other types of starting price ranges, lead to improved performance in tenders (H8a). Ames and Mason's (2015) findings implied that starting price ranges exert both a relational and an informative effect on bidders' behavior in economic transactions. The results refute the presence of both effects in public tenders. Regarding the first effect, the politeness-inducing aspects of starting price ranges played a subordinate role in tenders. Due to low behavioral discretion of procurement officials during the supplier selection, variances in their characteristics, signaled via different types of published starting price ranges, did not influence suppliers' beliefs and reactions.

The results of the one-way Welch ANOVA imply that starting price ranges have no informational influence in public tenders as well. Compared with back down or bracketing starting price ranges, more ambitious bolstering starting price ranges did not significantly affect performance levels. In public procurement, bolstering starting price ranges might not shape the counterparties' beliefs about possible outcomes. Accordingly, the selection attention hypothesis fails to encapsulate the impact of bolstering price ranges in tenders. In negotiations, counterparties may concentrate on the more attractive value of a range as an indication of the first mover's bargaining limits. Recipients use this value to identify the first mover's reservation price. As stated in section 7.1.3, compared with negotiations and housing transactions, procurement officials' reservation prices in public tenders are nonbinding. Therefore, bidders can neglect to identify reservation prices. When preparing their offers in response to a CN, potential suppliers do not focus their attention on the more appealing end of a starting price range. Thereby, bolstering price ranges forfeit their informational effect in tenders.

8. Managerial implications and practical recommendations

This chapter develops managerial recommendations for procurement officials on how to design their tenders to ensure a high level of procurement performance in practice. We base these recommendations primarily on the findings generated in Chapters 5 and 7. In contrast to the more descriptive analyses in the previous chapters, the present chapter is rather prescriptive. It contains concrete recommendations that procurement officials can use in practice when designing public tenders.

For this purpose, Section 8.1 consists of three subsections that follow the standard tender stages identified in Chapter 4. In the beginning, we will develop a framework that captures the dimension of public tenders and the decision-making of procurement officials. In Section 8.1, we will complement the managerial recommendation by presenting regulatory implications of the present work for public procurement.

Since procurement officials conduct most tenders as auctioned procedures, the discussed recommendations will assume that tenders work like procurement auctions – if not explicitly stated otherwise. The last section (Section 8.3) acknowledges that procurement auctions have gained popularity in private sector purchasing as well. Thus, this section will discuss the validity and practicability of the results of the present work for purchasers in the private sector.

8.1 Managerial implications for public tenders

Figure 9 in Chapter 4 shows that stipulations of the Directives entail six standardized tender stages that procurement officials must follow. The analyses in Chapter 4 yield that they possess several options for designing a tender that might influence procurement performance in three of these

A. Rhode, *Public Procurement in the European Union*, Schriften zum europäischen Management, https://doi.org/10.1007/978-3-658-28073-4_8

stages: During the determination of specifications, the choice of award procedure, and the supplier selection.

In theory, tenders may simply serve the task to identify the economic costs of potential suppliers associated with the contract award (Carpineti, Piga, & Zanza, 2006). In practice, however, the challenge for procurement officials in managing tenders expands above identifying suppliers' cost functions. First, procurement officials must decide what contract to acquire and how to communicate their procurement needs to potential suppliers. Second, they must establish appropriate specifications and details about the respective remuneration. Third, they must run an award procedure that assigns the tendered contract to the best supplier. Fourth, they must correctly analyze the content and the value of the offers that were submitted. Chapter 4 identified eight performance-oriented measures for procurement officials during these different tender phases. Figure 13 in chapter 5 summarizes those measures.

In practice, procurement officials need to distinguish between two kinds of performance-oriented measures.

> **Optional measures**: Procurement officials can decide whether to implement a measure because the Directives allow them the necessary discretion. Thus, they can either decide to implement them or not to implement such measures. They can even entirely fail to consider the choice at all. The best example of such a performance-oriented measure is the release of a starting price. Section 7.1 showed that officials might deliberately decide to publish a starting price in a Contract Notice to influence the behavior of potential suppliers. However, officials can also conduct and complete tenders without even considering the publication of a starting price.

> **Obligatory measures**: In contrast to optional performance-oriented measures, procurement officials must decide between the implementation of different measures in any tender. The Directives require them to choose one of the provided measures. The selection of an award procedure perfectly illustrates an obligatory measure. The Directives demand to choose one of the established procedures. Without such a choice, procurement officials cannot continue with the tender and cannot even initiate the tender by publishing a CN. Instead, at the beginning of the

tender, they must publicly define their choice of an award procedure in the CN.

The difference between optional and obligatory measures is not the only relevant distinction for discussing their impact on procurement performance. Depending on the type of tender, a specific measure can increase or decrease procurement performance. In accordance, we must develop a classification system for tenders that allows differentiating the impact of the identified measures on performance.

To classify different kinds of tenders, we took the classic procurement portfolio approach by Kraljic (1983) and adapted it to public procurement. The author's approach relies on the notion that suppliers pursue different interests in each procurement project. Thus, depending on the procurement project, purchasers need to develop different strategies. Accordingly, a decisive starting point for performance management in tenders is the question of whether measures can affect the balance of power between the Contracting Authority and potential suppliers. In line with the research questions, we mainly focus on how those decisions may shift the balance in favor of the buying side. While Contracting Authorities typically enjoy more bargaining power in public tenders, they may be excessively dependent upon a certain supplier to meet some of their acquisition needs (i.e., in the case of monopolistic or oligopolistic market structures). In such tenders, procurement officials may undertake the measures necessary to rebalance the power distribution.

The procurement portfolio approach by Kraljic (1983) implies two variables for the classification of public tenders that affect the power balance of between buyer and supplier in a procurement project:

- **Economic importance:** Different input variables such as material costs, volumes, the share of wallet, or influence on organizational goals may determine the importance of a single tender. As a rule of thumb, the following applies: The higher the budgetary volume, the more significant the economic impact of a tender.
- **Supply market risk:** The availability of the item, the number of potential suppliers, the switching costs, inventory risks, and potential substitutes all may indicate the risks affecting the supply market. If Contracting Authorities need to procure an item from a supplier without

any available alternatives, they face a high supply market risk. Alternatively, the supply market risk is low if a Contracting Authority can source a (standardized) item from many suppliers without high switching costs. The number of available suppliers may act as an adequate rule of thumb for this classification.

Figure 16: Criteria for classifying a tender

Economic importance	Supply market risk
> Relative procurement volume (specific procurement volume in relation to total procurement volume) > The share of the contract (merchandise group) in the cost of goods sold > Impact of the contract on the overall degree of organizational performance > Cost reduction potential through (for example, due to supplier competition or contract pooling) > Price elasticity > Discount and bonus rules	> Branded product or standardized product > Patent/licensed product > Availability of substitutes > Special requirements concerning quality and logistics > Tradition of supplier relationship > Supplier's share of procurement volume > Contribution of authority's spend to the total supplier's business > Market structure (e.g., monopoly) > Market situation (i.e., buyer's or seller's market) > Supplier's capacity utilization > Supplier's financial stability > Financial situation of the supplier > -Supplier-related switching costs

Source: Own illustration based on Van Weele and Eßig (2017)

Figure 16 shows that, in practice, procurement officials can assess many criteria to gain an adequate understanding of economic importance and supply market risk, thus defining the kind of tender at hand.

Figure 17: Four different tender archetypes

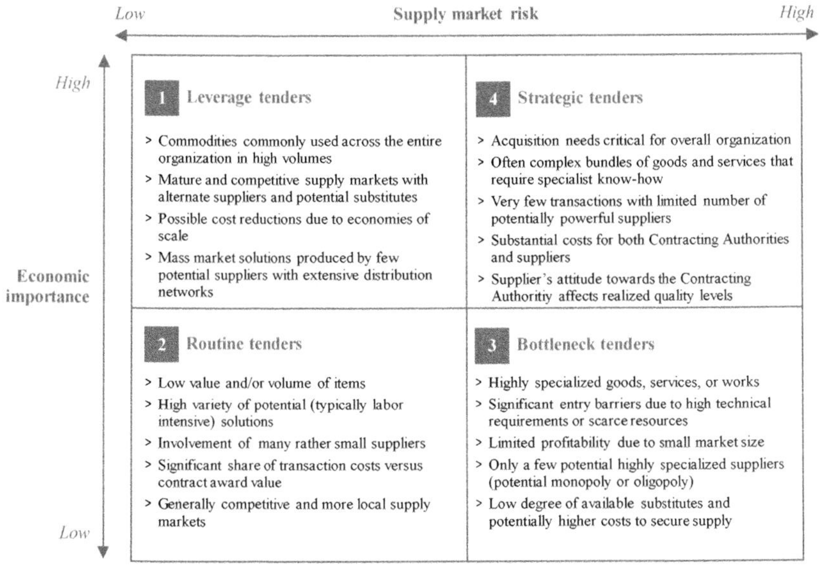

Source: Own illustration based on Kraljic (1983)

Figure 17 shows how the combination of these variables results in a two-by-two matrix with four quadrants, each of which classifies a tender archetype. We will discuss the four quadrants in more detail.

1. Leverage tenders

In leverage tenders, contracting Authorities can source from various suppliers on largely standardized quality levels (Kraljic, 1983). These tenders may account for a relatively large proportion of the total budget of a Contracting Authority. Hence, a small price change might already be economically significant. Thus, procurement officials might be motivated to engage in an aggressive sourcing policy. Since leverage tenders commonly refer to commodities used across the entire organization with high volume, typical examples of leverage tenders do not exist but rather depend on the organizational goals and the respective activities by the organizational members. For the example of public hospitals, often used and continuously needed pharmaceuticals (e.g., antibiotics or painkillers) would classify as leverage tenders. Typically, the contracting authority can freely choose from among a group of several homogeneous suppliers without high switching costs in leverage tenders. However, the homogeneity of the solution increases the risk of collusion and price-fixing cartels.[70]

2. Routine tenders

Routine tenders are typically less of a concern for the Contracting Authority (Kraljic, 1983). They usually refer to low-value contracts and many potential suppliers. The procurement of office supplies provides a perfect example of this type of tender in public administrative bodies. Typically, (indirect) transaction costs account for a large share of the overall costs. Particularly in public procurement, they might even surpass the directly attributable acquisition costs as regulations entail significant transaction costs (both for Contracting Authorities and potential suppliers) in any tender.

3. Bottleneck tenders

Bottleneck tenders cover contract awards, which are characterized by a comparatively low monetary value and yet limited availability of potential suppliers (Kraljic, 1983). Sometimes, only a single supplier might be able to provide a solution that provides a match for the acquisition needs. Bottleneck tenders often arise when demanded items (e.g., natural resources) are rare or scarce. In public healthcare, such items would include some catalysts, pigments, or vitamins. Typically, the dominant position of the supplier may result in relatively high costs, long delivery times, and a reduced level of after-sales services.

4. Strategic tenders

Strategic tenders include technically complex, often tailor-made contracts of considerable economic significance. Typically, a Contracting Authority cannot replace a single existing supplier in the short term or only at substantial cost in strategic tenders. As a rule, these tenders account for a large share of the overall procurement budget. Good examples might include holistic IT, software, or telecommunications systems. Ideally, the interactions between the Contracting Authority and the supplier are usually intensive

[70] However, with active collusion among suppliers, the contract would fail to meet the definition of leverage tender and would instead be classified as a strategic tender due to increased supply market risks.

and dynamic – typically one of the main obstacles in public procurement. Regarding the power balance between the two parties, either the supplier (e.g., in the acquisition of ERP software) or the Contracting Authority (e.g., for defense contracts) may play the dominant role in the market.

If the Contracting Authorities enjoy high bargaining power, they can impose their contract conditions on the suppliers. Suppliers will likely perceive the relationship as rather one-sided and not as a stable and robust partnership. The relationship between the suppliers and the Contracting Authorities remains uneven: Contracting Authorities dictate their requirements, and the supplier must cover them. When the suppliers have greater dominance, the power balance reverses: Due to exclusive technologies or unique market access, suppliers have created a market position that puts Contracting Authorities in (absolute) dependence on them. Accordingly, the supplier can charge relatively high prices for their solutions. In general, a Contracting Authority has little choice but to tailor the contract specifications to the available suppliers.

Uyarra and Flanagan (2010) argued that a purchasing portfolio model applies to public procurement as well because the decisions of procurement officials and private-sector purchasers dovetail in their considerations of supply market risk and economic importance.[71] In public procurement, officials may act in a risk-averse manner in response to some of their additional challenges (see Section 2.4). However, similar to their private-sector counterparts, they may pursue the tasks of minimizing the supply risk and utilizing their purchasing power while managing supplier relationships (Gelderman & Van Weele, 2005). Since the effect of performance-oriented measures in tenders heavily depends on the given buyer-supplier relationship, procurement officials may require differentiated measures for each of

[71] We acknowledge that Uyarra and Flanagan (2010) established their fourfold typology of public procurement: efficient procurement, adapted procurement, technical procurement, and experimental procurement. However, we do not use their typology because it is more oriented toward innovation than performance management. For discussing performance management in tenders, its four dimensions are fully congruent with those by Kraljic (1983). Thus, we stick to the common portfolio matrix typology to ensure better comprehensibility of the developed performance-oriented recommendations. Since procurement officials, in practice, are likely familiar with the terms defined by Kraljic (1983), they can more easily understand and profit from the performance implications of a directly linked framework from tender classification.

the four tender archetypes. Likewise, procurement officials need to understand not only which performance-oriented measures to use in each category but also which measure can enable them to escape the category and move to a more attractive position in the matrix (Gelderman & Van Weele, 2002).

Chapter 5 showed that the effect of performance-oriented measures depends on the classification of a tender as Common Value or Private Value. Thus, we aim to link this auction-theory-based classification to the procurement portfolio approach by Kraljic (1983). Previous studies have failed to establish this link (to our best knowledge) despite the outstanding importance and popularity of both classifications in their respective stream of research.

We refer to the difference in suppliers' uncertainty on the valuation of the awarded contract by other suppliers to establish this link. In a nutshell, the degree of supply market risk for the Contracting Authority approximately reflects the cost uncertainty (being indicative of Common Values) of suppliers. We acknowledge that, in practice, most contract awards will do not fully meet the requirements of the Private Value model or the Common Value model and will instead combine aspects of both models. Procurement officials will need to determine which aspect is most likely to dominate the other in a given tender.

For tenders with low supply market risks (e.g., abundant raw materials or office supplies), the Common Value model is likely to play a dominant role because the input costs of potential suppliers are similar. Since suppliers still do not know the objective value of the contract award, the winner's curse might arise in such tenders. For tenders with high supply market risks (e.g., scarce raw materials or ERP systems), Private Value aspects are likely to prevail. Due to the natural scarcity of inputs or individualized production processes, each supplier is likely to face an idiosyncratic cost function. Thus, they know their individual valuation of the contract award. Since they will not change their offers, if they learn about the cost estimates of other suppliers, the winner's curse will not be likely to arise in such tenders.

8.1.1 Determination of specifications

8.1.1.1 Publishing a Prior Notice

Section 5.1.1 confirmed working hypothesis W1, which proposed that an increase in the number of submitted bids due to a publication of a PN would improve procurement performance in tenders. Accordingly, Contracting Authorities may strive to publish a PN before initiating the tender.[72] The publication of a PN allows (additional) potential suppliers to prepare themselves to participate in the tender. An extended preparation period may reduce the costs of participating in a (complex) tender, thus leading to an increase in the number of offers that are submitted. Similarly, the PN could enable potential suppliers to join their efforts. However, the publication of a PN remains the exception for EU tenders (PwC et al., 2011). We employ practice-oriented classification of tenders inspired by Kraljic (1983) to reconcile this mismatch between the likely positive influence on performance and low prevalence in the field of publishing a PN.

1. Leverage tenders

Due to the low supply market risk, Contracting Authorities may refrain from publishing a PN in leverage tenders. Since a Common Value component may prevail, the increase in competition enabled by a PN might backfire: The negative effect of the winner's curse may outweigh the positive impact of increased competition. Since competition is already quite high in most leverage tenders, Contracting Authorities should publish a PN only if they suspect collusion among incumbent suppliers. In such a case, a PN could attract new entrants and help to break up collusive agreements.

2. Routine tenders

Due to the same degree of supply market risks, the recommendations for leverage tenders remain valid for routine tenders: Due to potentially dominant Common Value aspects, Contracting Authorities might better refrain from publishing a PN. Moreover, the release of a PN prolongs the lead time of a tender. Since procurement officials already face relatively high

[72] So far, past empirical research has missed validating the claim that tenders with a published PN profit from more bidders' interest. However, we have found no reason to assume that a provisional notice will lower the number of potential suppliers. From a competition perspective, no past study has indicated that publishing a PN will cause harm.

transaction costs in routine tenders, they should abstain from the release of a PN and instead focus on reducing lead times to keep transaction costs in check.

3. Bottleneck tenders

A lack of availability of potential suppliers characterizes bottleneck tenders, i.e., an oligopolistic or even monopolistic market structure can occur. Due to high supply market risks, the publication of a PN might improve procurement performance by enabling new entrants to practice in bottleneck tenders. Typically, high entry barriers characterize bottleneck tenders. By publishing a PN, a Contracting Authority provides suppliers with more time to overcome these barriers. A more extended preparation period allows more suppliers to build up the required know-how – either internally or by joining efforts with others. Both opportunities will stimulate bidders' participation. Likewise, the omnipresent danger of collusion will significantly decrease – notably, if the publication of a PN encourages the market participation of new entrants. Moreover, the winner's curse will not be likely to be significant with fewer bidders involved in bottleneck tenders.

4. Strategic tenders

Due to the same high degree of supply market risk, the recommendations for bottleneck tenders remain valid for strategic tenders: Contracting Authorities may profit from publishing a PN. The prolonged preparation might be particularly useful in high value and thus potentially complex strategic tenders. More bidders will be likely to participate by using the information entailed in a PN to prepare their offers and join their efforts.

8.1.1.2 Formulation of contract specifications

Section 5.1.2 concluded that Contracting Authorities, whenever possible, should opt for a functional specification in a CN. Since technical specifications may burden suppliers with increased transaction costs, procurement officials can use functional specifications to lower bidders' entry barriers.

1. Leverage tenders

In leverage tenders, procurement officials can profit from formulating functional specifications. Potential suppliers usually offer a variety of suitable solutions on comparable quality levels. While technical specifications may restrict the scope of the contract, functional specifications take full advantage of the full range of suitable solutions. Functional specifications enable the participation of alternate suppliers and even allow for substitutes that the procurement officials do not consider before initiating a tender. Moreover, suppliers might be able to submit lower offers because functional specifications allow them to adapt proposed solutions to individual cost functions.

2. Routine tenders

Due to similar supply market risks, procurement officials may prefer functional specifications in routine tenders as well. Functional specifications could significantly lower the relatively high transaction costs. Functional specifications could antagonize potential entry barriers of technical specifications by motivating bidders who would have otherwise been offended by disproportionately high transaction costs to participate in a routine tender.

3. Bottleneck tenders

Functional specifications provide potential suppliers with more discretion for the formulation of submitted offers. Potential suppliers may reflect this increased flexibility in the fulfillment stage by estimating lower costs. Thus, functional specifications should result in lower offers. Moreover, functional specifications might be especially beneficial for tendering contracts for innovative solutions. Typically, solutions sourced in bottleneck tenders (and strategic tenders) demand more specialized production processes and higher levels of supplier expertise. Functional specifications allow potential suppliers to submit offers that are less dependent on the expertise of the procurement officials. Thereby, functional specifications may widen the range of potential suppliers. Procurement officials may source alternative (and possibly more innovative) solutions than they would ever have considered.

In bottleneck tenders, the typically small number of potential suppliers create the risks of collusion and corruption. The widening of the supply market induced by publishing a PN might also act as an effective remedy against these risks. By lowering the supply market risk, functional specifications might even allow Contracting Authorities to move left in the portfolio matrix from bottleneck tenders to routine tenders.

4. Strategic tenders

The arguments for why functional specifications are useful for the acquisition of innovative solutions apply to strategic tenders as well. They often demand specialized know-how that the procurement officials not possess. In such a case, the technical specification would increase the risk of misspecifications. Like in bottleneck tenders, technical specifications might be inappropriately detailed and limit the number of interested suppliers in strategic tenders.

8.1.1.3 Division into lots

Section 5.1.3 discussed tradeoff in awarding lots between the benefits of increased competition and the downsides of lower economies of scale and higher transaction costs. On the one hand, smaller lots lower the economic risks entailed in high-value contracts that otherwise may prevent (primarily small and medium-sized) potential suppliers from participating. On the other hand, splitting a single contract increases the relative share of entry costs and prevents economies of scale for the winning supplier. Accordingly, the following practical recommendations for the division into lots heavily depends on the type of tender.

1. Leverage tenders

For leverage tenders, the division of a contract into smaller lots may cause adverse performance effects that outshine positive competition effects. Typically, procurement officials aim to aggregate the demands of different organizational units to allow lower winning bids due to economies of scale. The division of a (potentially valuable and complicated) leverage tender into smaller lots may lower economies of scale, thus disproportionately increasing suppliers' cost (estimates). Particularly in leverage tenders, economies of scale determine the costs of supplying abundantly available items such as certain raw materials (Silberston, 1972).[73]

2. Routine tenders

[73] The potential downsizes of awarding a massive contract in lots causing diseconomies of scale will likely not arise given the nature of contracts in leverage procurement.

Procurement officials should usually avoid awarding a contract in several lots in routine tenders. On the one hand, splitting a single contract into several independent lots increases the already high share of transaction costs, further lowering the extent to which the tender will attract potential suppliers. On the other hand, the average contract values are rather low. Thus, further splitting them into smaller parts might not enable the participation of additional suppliers as the economic risks entailed are generally manageable in routine tenders. Like leverage tenders, the pooling of contracts seems more sensible. The thereby enabled economies of scale and the lowered significance of transaction costs should attract more suppliers and allow for potentially lower bids.

3. Bottleneck tenders

The division of contracts into smaller lots might widen the supply market by encouraging bidders' participation. Theoretically, awarding smaller lots may work as a remedy for the highly limited number of potential suppliers in bottleneck tenders. However, splitting a contract into several lots is not likely to be an effective countermeasure in bottleneck tenders. Since no additional potential suppliers may exist at all, smaller lots may completely fail to stimulate bidders' interest in bottleneck tenders. In the case of a monopoly, for example, the division into lots will not encourage more bidder participation but might cause higher transaction costs. As with routine tenders, splitting a low-value bottleneck tender might not yield any competitive benefits but might only disproportionally increase transaction costs.

4. Strategic tenders

For strategic tenders, the division of a contract into smaller lots may yield different performance effects. We must distinguish between tenders where the Contracting Authority enjoys a dominant market position and the opposite case in which the suppliers have higher bargaining power.

On the one hand, if the power balance is in favor of Contracting Authorities, they can dictate the terms of the contract award. In such a case, they should choose to aggregate demand to foster supplier's economies of scale. Due to the high level of competition among suppliers, lower costs due to economies of scale will result in lower bids. By contrast, the division of contracts into smaller lots would impede the procurement performance by lowering economies of scale.

On the other hand, a supplier or a group of suppliers might hold a dominant market position. Under such circumstances, suppliers usually charge high prices for their solutions, and procurement officials have no choice but to accept these prices. In the software industry, for example, a handful of big players (e.g., SAP, Oracle, or Microsoft) possess very comfortable bargaining situations and can charge high prices for their solutions. With such dominant suppliers, a division of a contract into smaller lots might generate cost savings for a Contracting Authority. It might enable the participation of new (smaller) entrants who otherwise would refrain from bidding because they only offer parts but not the entire solution.

New entrants also may be willing to offer better value-for-money solutions. Since the contract award is financially more significant for them than for the typically larger incumbents, they will strive to win the contract award and try to establish a long-term supplier relationship; both improve the procurement performance for the Contracting Authority. Moreover, even if new entrants do not win the contract award, their participation might stimulate competition. By breaking up the oligopolistic market structure that usually allows for implicit or explicit collusion, their participation may drive down the bids of the incumbents as well.

8.1.1.4 Publication of a starting price

Section 7.1 argues that Contracting Authorities should publish starting prices in CNs to improve their procurement performance in tenders. In any case, because procurement officials are legally required to estimate the contract costs before a tender begins, the publication of this estimate will cause almost no additional transaction costs. Moreover, the recommendation to publish starting prices remains valid across all kinds of tenders. Section 7.1 shows that the release of a starting price drives performance-enhancing intrapsychic processes that arise independently of the transactional characteristics of a tender.

In all four tender archetypes, starting prices will anchor the behavior and cognition of potential suppliers. The cognitive mechanisms of insufficient adjustment and selective accessibility that explain how starting prices positively influence outcomes always remain in force. First, potential suppliers might not move far from a starting price published in a CN. Suppliers exposed to a low starting price correct up when preparing the bid but stop adjusting when they encounter the lowest amount they would accept. Second, individuals may generate more arguments that are consistent with the anchor in all kinds of tenders. For example, a supplier exposed to a rather low-priced contract might attend more to cost-savings potential than to inherent cost risks. Regardless of which explanation better describes the phenomenon, the starting price will yield these anchoring effects regardless of the supply market risk and the economic importance of a tender.[74]

Likewise, the alternative explanation of the positive performance influence of starting prices provided by auction theory may also apply to all the dimensions of the matrix. Auction theory argues that the release of private information is responsible for the positive impact of the release of a starting price on procurement performance. The release of a starting price intensifies competition among bidders by making values more predictable and lowering the winner's curse. Likewise, the publication of a starting price may reduce a supplier's entry risks by lowering information asymmetry and cost uncertainty.

As stated in Section 5.1.4, the validity of these considerations depends on the influence of Common Value aspects in the given tender. With a robust Private Model dominance, the release of a starting price may remain ineffective as potential suppliers face no uncertainty about their costs. In practice, however, dominant Private Value aspects may only seldom arise in tenders. Even in leverage tenders and routine tenders, valuations of potential suppliers will still be affiliated to at least some extent. For example, even in the sourcing of raw materials such as heating oil, the necessary logistics services will cause Affiliated Values. Thus, the release of a starting price may improve outcomes for Contracting Authorities in all kinds of tenders even if an anchoring-based notion entirely fails to explain to the relation between starting prices and procurement performance.[75]

---

[74] The strength of this anchoring effect may vary across tenders. The results of Chapter 6 imply that the strength of the assimilative anchors decreases if bidders have access to anchor-disconfirming evidence. Thus, the anchoring effect of starting prices might be particularly influential in bottleneck tenders that typically occur less frequently. Without the mere existence of similar tenders, anchor-disconfirming evidence does not exist as well.
[75] The results of section 6.4 strongly imply that anchoring effects at least partially explain the reported first-mover advantage. Auction-theory-based determinations cannot explain

8.1.1.5 *Formulation of a published starting price*

A similar line of thought explains why, independent of the kind of tender, the implications of section 7.2 on the precision effects of starting prices still apply. This section recommends that procurement professionals should always formulate their starting prices as precisely as possible and that they should abstain from formulating starting prices as ranges. Starting price precision affects outcomes in tenders because they shape intrapsychic processes. We argue that these processes work independently of the type of tender.

The attribution-of-competence account might best explain why precise starting prices improve outcomes. Potential suppliers consider more precise anchors to be more credible – if they ascribe a high level of expertise to the first-moving procurement officials. These expertise-based precision effects prevail in tenders where regulation severely limits the exchange of information between parties. In such an environment, counterparties face difficulties when scrutinizing the first mover's competence. Informational asymmetries prevent suppliers from referring low competence from precise starting prices. Potential suppliers confronted with precise starting prices do not have access to enough information to question the competence of the procurement officials who formulated the starting price. Instead, recipients believe that increased precision entails a better description of the contract's actual value. Thus, suppliers are likely to interpret (even highly) precise starting prices as more credible.

In all the four tender archetypes, this increased credibility reduces entry risks for potential suppliers. Thereby, increased precision does not create any entry barriers but even lowers them. Since the regulation heavily limits procurement officials' discretion in all kinds of tenders, a possible reservation price of the Contracting Authorities loses its relevance, causing potential suppliers to fail to ascribe increased inflexibility to procurement officials who offer precise opening values.

---

why more considerable price heterogeneity in similar auctions significantly reduces the performance impact of starting prices. Besides, the (anchoring) effect of starting prices remained significant after controlling for the impact of increases in bidders' interest on procurement performance.

Likewise, the explanation for why starting price ranges do not exert significant relational or information effects remain valid independent of the supply market risk or economic importance involved in the tender: For the procurement of raw materials and highly specialized consulting services alike, starting price ranges do not induce politeness due to lower first-mover discretion. Suppliers are likely to ignore potentially signaled first-mover's characteristics and procurement officials' interpretations of their bids. Also, the informational effect of starting price ranges will remain ineffective across the matrix's dimensions. Because potential suppliers can neglect to identify the procurement official's (nonbinding) reservation price, they will not focus their attention on the upper end of a published price range.

The validity of the results concerning the ineffective anchoring effects of starting price ranges depends on the informational and relational provisions of the Directives but not on any transactional characteristics of tenders. Whereas the politeness mechanism seems to require a sufficient degree of interpersonal exchange between parties, the informational effects seem to depend on the relevance of a first mover's reservation price. Due to the restrictions imposed by the Directives, both the conditions are not met in all types of tenders.

8.1.2 Choice of the award procedure

In this section, we assume that the open procedure remains procurement officials' standard choice of award procedure. Thus, we interpret the implementation of a negotiated procedure or a restricted procedure as a deviation from the standard. Thereby, we mirror the idea of past Directives that procurement officials can use open procedures for all tenders but can employ the auctioned and restricted procedure only if certain conditions apply (see Section 4.4).

Since, after the reform of the Directives in 2014, only negotiated procedures need to fulfill certain requirements, procurement officials go through the same two-stage decision process in each tender:

> They must decide whether they should employ an auctioned or a negotiated procedure.

> If they have neglected the negotiated procedure, they must assess whether to design the tender as an open or restricted procedure.

We aim to provide procurement officials with practical recommendations regarding the different kinds of tenders defined by portfolio matrix dimensions. Accordingly, we assume that procurement officials can opt for a negotiated procedure in each dimension.[76] In accordance with Section 5.2, we stipulate that performance-oriented procurement officials will not exploit their increased discretion in negotiated and restricted procedures to engage in unlawful relationships with suppliers. Instead, they may refrain from engaging in an open procedure solely to potentially improve their procurement performance.

8.1.2.1 *Auctioned vs. negotiated procedures*

On the surface, Section 5.2 implies that procurement officials should stick to auctioned procedures for more simple tenders while opting for negotiations for more complex tenders. Procurement officials may use an auctioned procedure only for the procurement of standardized and straightforward works, supplies, or services that show a low supply market risk and low added value.[77] Due to stifled communication in auctioned procedures, procurement officials may fail to include relevant supplier's information when drafting the contract specifications. Incomplete specifications increase the likelihood of later stage adaptations and their corresponding ex-post transaction costs.

However, we argue that, in practice, this decision not only depends on the economic importance of tenders but also supply market risk. Thus, different implications may arise across the dimensions of the portfolio matrix.

---

[76] However, a co-dependence between the kind of tender and procurement officials' scope of action may arise. For example, the Directives imply that Contracting Authorities should refrain from negotiations for contracts that various potential suppliers can provide on acceptable quality levels. Hence, procurement officials should not use negotiated procedures for largely standardized contracts that are likely to be classified as leverage tenders and routine tenders.

[77] In accordance, Manelli and Vincent (1995) argued that open procedures become inefficient as soon as Contracting Authorities pursue value-for-money objectives. Because they can never precisely determine the scope of the contract, procurement officials always face the risk of ending with a lower quality supplier in standardized and rigid open procedures.

1. Leverage tenders

For leverage tenders, auctioned procedures may allow procurement officials to capitalize on their high market power against the suppliers and to enforce lower final prices. An auctioned procedure can exploit the sufficient degree of competition between the suppliers by incentivizing them to reveal the real costs. These positive competition effects prevail in leverage tenders as transaction costs for changing a supplier remain nonsignificant: Procurement officials can easily switch between several suppliers that provide similar solutions at comparable quality levels.

Low switching costs enable procurement officials to improve their procurement performance by exchanging a more expensive supplier for a cheaper one. Otherwise, in practice, such a change in suppliers often backfires. Switching costs include more than (simple-to-measure) financial aspects. Instead, any organizational and processual dependencies on the current supplier may yield high switching costs. Those costs will be particularly high if a supplier is actively involved in design and development phases or takes over essential tasks in life cycle management (e.g., repair or maintenance). In such situations, procurement officials must check whether the alternate suppliers can provide the same services at no additional cost and at comparable quality levels.

2. Routine tenders

Due to the comparable (low) supply market risks, an auctioned procedure may yield positive competition effects in routine tenders as well. Procurement officials may profit from competition between suppliers in auctioned procedures for typical non-critical contracts. Moreover, the potential increase in ex-ante transaction costs further lowers the attractiveness of negotiations in routine tenders. Given the reduced monetary volumes of routine tenders, Contracting Authorities should keep transaction costs low to avoid suffering from low interest from suppliers.

3. Bottleneck tenders

For bottleneck tenders, auctioned procedures may be unsuitable because of the low degree of competition between potential suppliers and the increased complexity of the supply market. The natural scarcity of some needed solutions (e.g., in the case of rare or specialized materials) may significantly standardize suppliers' costs (and corresponding valuations of the contract award). If the same input prices determine the better part of the suppliers' cost base, an auctioned procedure will not foster more competitive bidding. Since the differences between suppliers' costs remain nonsignificant, the revelation of suppliers' actual costs will not result in lower final prices.

By contrast, procurement officials might prefer negotiations for the specialized works, supplies, or services in bottleneck tenders. With such contracts, procurement officials may struggle to define matching specifications. As discussed in Section 5.3, procurement officials should enter negotiations with suppliers if they face the risk of contract misspecifications. Negotiations allow for the joint development of contingency plans with suppliers to prevent potential supply disruptions that are likely to arise with bottleneck tenders.

However, Contracting Authorities should be aware that they might risk collusion among suppliers in a negotiated procedure. Since smaller, more complete, and more developed supply markets characterize bottleneck tenders, the risk of supplier collusion is particularly high. Potential suppliers know each other, can anticipate each other's economic situations, and may jointly agree on their submitted offers. Compared with negotiations, an auctioned procedure may motivate other (new) competitors to enter the tender. New entrants can reduce the risk of price agreements, cartels, and other collusive behavior.[78]

Procurement officials can try to attract new entrants in a negotiated procedure by issuing a previous call for competition. Without a call for competition, new entrants do not have any chance to catch the procurement official's attention.[79] After the call for competition, procurement officials should permit as many as possible capable suppliers to the subsequent

---

[78] For bottleneck tenders, such new entrants might not exist because only some suppliers will have the necessary specialized know-how or the access to scarce resources.

[79] For bottleneck tenders, procurement officials might only enjoy a short market overview and might not know alternate suppliers who can potentially deliver better value for money. A prior call for competition would allow them to attain a better market overview. If procurement officials can identify previously unknown suppliers, they will effectively lower the supply market risk: Bottleneck tenders might transform into more desirable routine tenders.

negotiation stage. The Directives require procurement officials to admit a minimum of three participants to a negotiation. However, this number is not likely to be sufficient for preventing collusion among suppliers (see Section 5.1). Notably, if procurement officials are used to award contract via auctioned procedures, they might formulate unnecessarily strict eligibility criteria in a negotiated procedure and risk contracting the supply market. In auctioned procedures, strict eligibility criteria allow procurement officials to exclude less reliable suppliers from supplier selection. In negotiations, the procurement official enjoys more discretion in handling and identifying unreliable contractors during the supplier selection phase. Thus, they can use more flexible eligibility criteria without significantly increasing the risks of awarding a low-quality offer.

4. Strategic tenders

Like bottleneck tenders, the complexity of the supply market makes auctioned procedures less attractive for strategic tenders. While procurement volumes might be attractive enough for suppliers, the apparent complexity of the awarded contract is not suitable for auctioned procedures. Since strategic tenders (as already implied by the literal sense of the term) matter for achieving organizational goals, procurement officials typically initiate them quickly after budget approval. Thus, misspecifications and contractual incompleteness are particularly likely to occur in the case of auctioned procedures.

By contrast, negotiations ease the correct understanding of supplier needs and the definition of contract specifications that allow better value-for-money offers. Likewise, procurement officials can profit from the competence of suppliers – particularly for development and design purposes that are likely in strategic tenders. Engaging in negotiations may enable potential innovation and quality improvements.

Like bottleneck tenders, negotiated procedures may suffer from collusion among suppliers in strategic tenders. Thus, we recommend the same remedies: Procurement officials should avoid negotiated procedures without a prior call for competition and should employ slightly relaxed eligibility criteria to maximize competition among suppliers during the negotiation stage.

8.1.2.2 Open vs. restricted procedures

In general, Section 5.2 implies that procurement officials should opt for a restricted procedure for high-value contracts. However, in practice, the chosen award procedure will impact outcomes depending on both the monetary scope and the supply market risk of tenders. We argue that the choice between an open and a restricted procedure depends on three factors that this section will discuss in detail:

> Economic effects of high competition
> Advantages of restricting competition
> Risk of collusion among suppliers

1. Leverage tenders

Procurement officials may significantly profit from using restricted procedures in leverage tenders. Theoretically, due to low supply market risk, an open procedure might suit the acquisition of straightforward and commodity-type acquisitions typical for leverage tenders. However, restricting competition will yield substantial benefits for leverage tenders in practice.

First, open procedures will maximize competition between suppliers, thus harming Contracting Authorities' outcomes. The relation between increased competition and performance depends on the dominance of Common Values or Private Values and existing entry barriers. While suppliers generally face low entry barriers for leverage tenders, a prevailing Common Value might cause a steady winner's curse (see Section 8.1.1.1). Thus, the downsides of increased competition may outweigh its potential benefits in leverage tenders.

Second, restricting competition will lower Contracting Authorities' transaction costs in screening offers. In leverage tenders awarded via an open procedure, procurement officials will typically receive many offers as award values are attractive, and many suppliers can deliver the required solution. Thus, checking all submitted offers is particularly costly, and a limited procedure might allow considerable savings in transaction costs.

Moreover, restricting the competition may improve the quality of the submitted offers by facilitating long-term relationships with reputable suppliers. Due to low switching costs, supplier relationships are typically short-term oriented in leverage tenders. Restricting the competition may allow the preferred supplier to achieve higher economies of scale, resulting in increased procurement performance. Theoretically, such a preferred supplier selection risks a gradually tightening supply market: Contracting Authorities may become increasingly dependent on a specific supplier. Thereby, a leverage tender may transform into an economically less desirable strategic tender. However, the Directives legally require Contracting Authorities not always to invite the same group of suppliers to submit bids. Thereby, regulations mitigate this risk in leverage tenders: Bids of alternative suppliers providing possible substitutions for the archetypal mass-market products will prevent the perpetuation of collusive agreements among incumbent suppliers.

Third, restricted procedures may not significantly increase the risk of collusion among bidders. Although this risk increases with restricted competition in leverage tenders as well, procurement officials mitigate this if they do not always pre-select the same group of suppliers. While the homogeneity of solutions may theoretically allow for price-fixing cartels in leverage tenders, new entrants that can be invited to submit bids phase are abundantly available.

2. Routine tenders

Although the significance of the three evaluation criteria differs slightly in routine tenders compared with leverage tenders, we derive the same recommendation for Contracting Authorities: They should opt for a restricted procedure even though the open procedure might theoretically be particularly suitable for routine, straightforward, and commodity-type tenders.

First, Common Value aspects might also be dominant for routine tenders: Further increasing the number of bidders might backfire as low entry barriers already ensure a high degree of competition. Second, lower transaction costs arising within a restricted procedure particularly matter in routine tenders whose performance levels usually suffer from significant transaction costs. Third, routine tenders are characterized by a low risk of active collusion among suppliers. Procurement officials can easily mitigate collusion by varying the bidders when calling to submit offers in the second stage of a restricted procedure.

3. Bottleneck tenders

Superficially, some of the empirical findings discussed in Chapter 5 may imply that restricted procedures are better suited to non-routine tenders. However, we argue that, unlike negotiations, the potential upsides of increased discretion in restricted procedures remain ineffective for bottleneck tenders. Restricted procedures and negotiated procedures yield distinctively different discretionary upsides: Negotiation fosters the exchange of information with suppliers, while restricted procedures accentuate the significance of supplier reputation. However, reputable suppliers do not face much competition in bottleneck tenders. Thus, their entry incentives will not increase significantly by restricting competition.

For bottleneck tenders, restricting competition will not work as an effective remedy for potentially incomplete contractual designs. Instead, procurement officials should focus on widening the supply market in bottleneck tenders. However, open procedures do not offer any respective performance advantages over the restricted procedures as both allow the procurement officials to get a better market overview. Comparable to the open procedure, the restricted procedure allows all potential suppliers to submit an expression of their interest during the pre-qualification phase. If the pre-qualification does not adversely discriminate against potential new entrants, a restricted procedure does not unnecessarily further restrict the supply market. Likewise, an open procedure will not maximize competition in bottleneck procurements as the number of potential suppliers is not sufficient for a high degree of competition. Accordingly, collusion may arise with both kinds of award procedures.[80]

4. Strategic tenders

Given the complexity of the supply market and contractual specifications, open procedures might not be suitable for strategic tenders. Thus, procurement officials may consider restricting competition. However, we argue that the advantages of restricting competition depend on the Contracting Authority's bargaining power. Since transaction costs are less high in strategic tenders, procurement officials should focus on the impact of a

[80] We doubt that auctioned procedures are generally suitable for bottleneck tenders. From a performance perspective, the 2014 reform of the Directives fortunately unrestricted the use of negotiated procedures for non-standardized contracts. Thus, in practice, procurement officials must no longer rely on auctioned procedures in bottleneck tenders that typically qualify as non-standardized contracts.

restricted procedure, that is, they should not focus on the transaction costs but on the final prices.

Contract award values affect the tender entry decision of suppliers. Therefore, (both reputable and less reliable) suppliers will be motivated to participate in typically valuable strategic tenders. Thus, the increased discretion in a restricted procedure may make it easier to award the contract to a more reputable supplier. If Contracting Authorities enjoy a high level of bargaining power, their relationship with suppliers will not be balanced. With such power balance, procurement officials may strive to minimize final prices in each tender. Thus, suppliers may perceive the relationship as unstable and focused on only the short term. As stated in Section 5.2.2, procurement officials thus face a moral hazard as the winning supplier has no interest in building a good reputation. Restricted procedures might incentivize appropriate supplier behavior by signaling interest in building more stable relationships and emphasizing the importance of reputation.

However, this restriction may hurt performance if Contracting Authorities depend on some suppliers in strategic tenders. By restricting competition, the already low level of competition among suppliers diminishes even further. Thus, procurement officials should refrain from applying restricted procedures when suppliers have a dominant market position. Instead, they should apply open procedures to increase competition among suppliers and potentially lower bids.

8.1.3 Selection of suppliers

8.1.3.1 Designing a scoring rule

Section 5.3 implied that procurement officials should assign significant weights to quality characteristics when designing a scoring rule. To check the validity of this recommendation in practice, we do not need to distinguish between the different kinds of tenders because the price is never the sole decision criterion in any of the four quadrants in the portfolio matrix. Focusing the scoring rule on the lowest price criterion might backfire in each kind of tender.

On the one hand, the advantages of qualitative criteria are particularly pronounced for high-value and thus more complex contract awards. On the other hand, the disadvantages of lowest price tenders become even more significant in the oversupplied market (i.e., with low supply market risk due to many potential suppliers). Therefore, procurement officials should always put considerable weight on non-price criteria.

For lowest price auctions to profit in comparison with scoring auctions, findings discussed in section 5.3 claimed that Contracting Authorities must know the cost of increased quality, be knowledgeable enough to formulate complete specifications, and be able to choose from several suppliers who can fulfill the required quality levels. We argue that even for tenders with low supply market risks, these prerequisites are seldom fulfilled in practice. For routine tenders, procurement officials will likely struggle to capture the large variety of potential solutions in their contract specifications. For leverage tenders, high-volume acquisitions of commodities from a mass market might fulfill the above requirements. However, the additional aggressiveness induced by an increased focus on the price in the award decision will be likely to backfire. Since the dominance of Common Value aspects characterizes most leverage tenders, increased competition between suppliers will increase prices due to a strong winner's curse (see Section 8.1.1.1).

8.2 Managerial pathways in practice

In sum, the theoretical and empirical investigations of the present work allow concrete recommendations to be derived for procurement officials in tenders. Depending on the kind of tender, we provide procurement officials with scientifically validated recommendations for how to improve their outcomes in tenders. Figure 18 summarizes these recommendations on performance-oriented measures regarding the kind of tender at hand.

Figure 18: Managerial recommendations for performance-oriented measures in tenders

	1 Leverage tenders	2 Routine tenders	3 Bottleneck tenders	4 Strategic tenders
Publish a Provisional Notice	X	X	√	√
Formulate functional contract specifications	√	√	√	√
Divide contract into smaller lots	X	X	X	√ / X
Publish a starting price	√	√	√	√
Formulate a precise starting price	√	√	√	√
Choose negotiated instead of open procedure	X	X	√ / X	√
Choose restricted instead of open procedure	√	√	N.A.	√ / X
Focus on quality in scoring rules	√	√	√	√

√ Implementation recommended   X Implementation not recommended

Source: Own illustration

Because we were able to derive unequivocal recommendations for most of the combinations of performance measures and tenders, we can translate the upper matrix into a concrete manual that procurement officials can use while managing a tender in practice. Only for strategic tenders, we did not always define unambiguous recommendations. In strategic tenders, Contracting Authorities must not only define the kind of tender, but they must also consider the given power balance. Since relationships with suppliers vary according to the (perceived) balance of power, their incentive to deliver on quality promises depends on the power balance as well. Thus, procurement officials might strive to install reputation-based mechanisms that motivate the winning supplier to realize higher quality levels if the Contracting Authority enjoys a low bargaining power. Figure 19 summarizes the findings in the form of a step-by-step manual for Contracting Authorities.

Figure 19: Recommended performance-oriented measures for different kinds of tenders

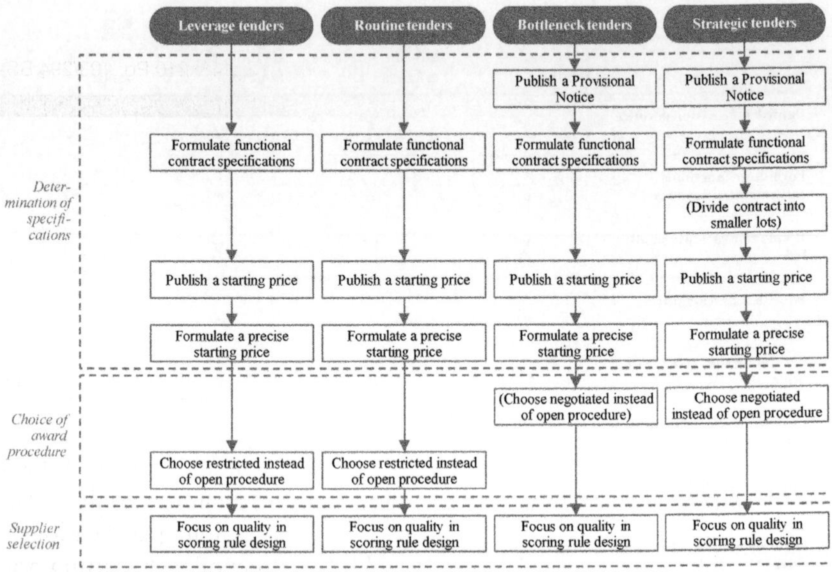

Source: Own illustration

First, we notice that the present work does not recommend that procurement officials should use the open procedure in tenders. This recommendation seems at least puzzling, given that the Directives still define open procedures as standard. The chosen research perspective of the present work can explain this derived recommendation. We formulated the research questions not from a regulatory perspective but from a managerial perspective. We aimed to investigate how Contracting Authorities could improve their procurement performance in public tenders – given the rigid boundaries set by regulation and by other transactional particularities.

The open procedure is the most strictly formalized and predictable award procedure (Leinemann et al., 2016). Accordingly, an open procedure ensures compliance with the Directives and the procurement principles (equal treatment and non-discrimination of potential suppliers) at the cost of restricting the procurement officials' discretion. In this light, the finding that an open procedure is the least performance-oriented award procedure is not surprising but seems virtually compulsory. Given the heterogeneity of tenders, the most standardized and uniform procedure is likely to yield worse outcomes than more discretionary procedures (e.g., restricted or negotiated procedures).

However, this argument implicitly assumes that procurement officials will not exploit their increased discretion in the less formalized procedures to engage in illegal behavior. Thus, by no means do the managerial implications yielded by the present work imply that regulators should abolish open procedures. Even from a purely performance-oriented perspective of legislators, an open procedure may ensure that, in practice, procurement officials consistently behave according to both organizational goals and regulatory stipulations.

Typically, this assumption might not hold in practice for several reasons. First, the interface of the public and private sector, as well as the stronger separation of ownership and control in the public sector, naturally create incentives for corruption (Coppier & Piga, 2006). Second, principal-agent issues that are typically for any purchasing organizations arise in public tenders as well. Like their private-sector counterparts, public procurement officials might follow hidden agenda goals. The particularities of public procurement may even further increase the likelihood of principal-agent problems in tenders (see Section 2.3). Third, recent empirical research has reported that European procurement officials in weak institutional environments indeed exploited the increased discretion in less restrictive award procedures (Chong et al., 2016). Since open procedures enjoy transparency advantages that can prevent corruption and collusion, they might produce more economic upsides than any other award procedure in practice.

We argue that it makes sense for the Directives to favor the open procedure: Only its unique combination, which diminishes illegal behavior but maximizes competition among bidders, may allow for the minimization of waste in public procurement. Since the reduction of waste is the flip side of increased procurement performance, the present work would have developed totally different practical recommendations if we had defined the research questions from a regulatory perspective.

Second, the managerial recommendations argue that procurement officials should not divide a contract into smaller lots to ensure high tender performance. The nature of this recommendation also depends on the research perspective of the present work. This recommendation relies on the definition of performance in tenders used in the present work, which defined performance as economic efficiency (in terms of value for money).

This definition allowed the best practices to be identified and transferred from private purchasing to public procurement. Moreover, it enabled us to clearly assess the impact of these performance-oriented measures on tender outcomes. However, the goals of public procurement include more than primary performance objectives. As stated in Section 2.2, public procurement differs from private purchasing in the existence of secondary interests (i.e., issues that go beyond the contract itself). The present work primarily neglected secondary interests in the current analysis because Contracting Authorities' procurement performance is part of their primary interests. However, secondary interests still exist in practice and may even govern the award decisions of procurement officials (see Section 2.4). In 2004, the Directives allowed for the division of a contract into smaller lots to enable the pursuit of a secondary and not a primary procurement goal: namely, to foster the increased inclusion of SMEs in public tenders.

Smaller lots attract more SMEs that would otherwise be discouraged by the financial and economic risks involved in a large tender. SMEs might neglect expensive tenders as they entail too many economic risks that (at worst) could even jeopardize their economic viability. Particularly in Europe, SMEs play a significant economic role and act as the backbone of the economy (Lukács, 2005). By facilitating the access of SMEs to public tenders, the Directives thus also strengthen the goals of the Maastricht Treaty to foster cross-border economic integration. The reform of the Directives pursued the political objective that the public sector should lead by example to foster the creation of a single internal market within the EU.

Accordingly, the integration of SEMs into public procurements is a secondary policy goal with considerable social and economic impacts. Thus, the managerial opportunity to award a contract in smaller lots is very desirable from the perspective of society. However, when procurement officials heavily restrict their managerial perspective to a single tender at hand, they should refrain from dividing the lots to avoid lower procurement performance and increased transaction costs.

8.3 Regulatory implications for public tenders

Next, we discuss how regulators might incorporate the performance-related insights of the present work. Therefore, we must distinguish between the regulatory implications of the two kinds of managerial recommendations: unconditional and conditional performance-oriented measures.

8.3.1 Conditional measures

For conditional measures (i.e., measures that will improve procurement performance only in some kinds of tenders), the role of the regulators is straightforward: The underlying regulations should provide procurement officials with the scope of actions necessary to implement the respective measures. Since the research questions of the present work only focused on measures within the scope of actions granted by the Directives, all the measures that we previously discussed fulfill this condition. Accordingly, the current version of the Directives already allows Contracting Authorities to implement all the identified performance-oriented measures.[81]

To make a choice between an auctioned and a negotiated procedure, the Directives contain rules that procurement officials must comply with. Despite taking a more relaxed stance on this managerial choice, the 2014 version of the Directives still stipulates that Contracting Authorities can opt for a negotiated procedure only for the acquisition of non-standardized items. However, this restriction dovetails with managerial recommendations of the present work that procurement officials should not rely on negotiations for routine and leverage tenders. Both kinds of tenders refer to less individualized (usually mass market) items whose acquisition via negotiation is likely to suffer from the decreased competition (particularly valid for leverage tenders) or unnecessary high transaction costs (particularly valid for routine tenders).

---

[81] Still, Contracting Authorities must comply with the general principles of public procurement when implementing those measures. For example, procurement officials should not divide a contract into smaller lots to deliberately avoid the regulatory umbrella of the Directives. Among other things, such behavior would contradict the principle of non-discrimination because only tenders that adhere to the Directives ensure the fair treatment of all potential suppliers across EU member states' borders (e.g., by publishing the tender on TED).

Even if leverage or routine tenders qualify as non-standardized items according to the Directives, we would not recommend that Contracting Authorities use negotiations. While an open procedure might indeed be unsuitable for acquiring more individualized items, the upper discussion implies that procurement officials should use restricted auctions as the intermediate form between open and negotiated procedures in such tenders. Thus, we argue that the reformed Directives no longer unnecessarily restrict the Contracting authorities' scope of actions in choosing the most appropriate award procedure. Accordingly, regulators were right to increase the discretion of Contracting Authorities. In the future, however, regulators should avoid restricting them again. Otherwise, they might endanger current levels of performance in public procurement across EU member states.

8.3.2 Unconditional measures

For unconditional measures (i.e., measures that will improve procurement performance regardless of the kind of tender), different policy implications arise. While regulators were entirely correct to provide procurement officials with sufficient managerial discretion to implement conditional performance-oriented measures, they may consider limiting the scope of actions to foster the implementation of unconditional measures.

The case for further tender standardization may seem at odds with a lot of other arguments that were previously discussed and presented. Is the heterogeneity of tenders not the main reason why more standardized regulatory systems are likely to harm average performance levels in public procurement (Schapper et al., 2006)? Typically, increased regulatory standardization aims to curb corruption but may prevent procurement officials from managing tenders more efficiently. For example, Tadelis (2012) showed that the risk of lower value for money increases with stricter and more detailed regulatory rules in public procurement.

However, we argue that by enforcing qualitative criteria in the supplier selection, the latest reform of the Directives already provides an example of how restricting managerial discretion may improve procurement performance. Before the 2014 reform, Contracting Authorities could choose between a scoring rule or the lowest price for awarding a contract. The reform enforced using scoring rules for supplier selection. In public tenders, even such (potentially sub-optimally designed) scoring rules that include quality-oriented award criteria will outperform the lowest price rules (Lewis & Bajari, 2011). Since, even after the 2014 reform, procurement officials can still focus on the lowest price in their scoring rules, one may even recommend that regulators should further restrict the managerial discretion of procurement officials by introducing minimum weights for quality criteria. At least, one should not assume that regulatory standardization always worsens outcomes.

8.3.2.1 Publication of a starting price

Besides recommending an increased focus on quality criteria in scoring rules, we also identified three further unconditional performance-oriented measures:

> the formulation of functional contract specifications,
> the publication of a starting price,
> and increased numerical precision in starting prices.

While one may construct extreme examples (e.g., tenders for raw materials without any potential substitutes such as certain rare minerals) when the formulation of functional specifications might – not only theoretically – unnecessarily increase transaction costs, no such examples exist given the publication and formulation of precise starting prices.[82] Thus, we recommend that regulators should continue to provide procurement officials with the choice between technical and functional specifications, but they should question the currently provided scope of action regarding the publication of the starting price.

The opportunity to conceal starting prices may harm procurement performance in tenders. Since the Directives already require estimating the costs of a contract before the tenders begin, the publication of this estimate results in almost no additional transaction costs. However, section 6.3 showed that procurement officials sometimes decided not to publish a

[82] Moreover, empirical research so far has admittedly failed to compare the performance effects of functional versus technical contract specifications in tenders. While past research has not provided any caveats for why the publication of functional specifications might lower competition, we refrain from providing hasty recommendations to regulators.

starting price. This non-disclosure could hail from economic considerations, managerial inertia, or commercial ignorance.

Independent of the actual reason, the present work advises regulators to restrict procurement officials' discretion by enforcing the publication of starting prices. In the first case, procurement officials might believe that they will improve their performance by concealing starting prices from suppliers. For example, they might anticipate that the release of a starting price will backfire by lowering the number of offers. However, the empirical results of Section 6.3 imply that such well-intentioned considerations will backfire in practice. In procurement, the beliefs of practitioners and the findings of researchers often contradict each other. The on-going discussion about using starting prices (i.e., making the first offer) in negotiations perfectly illustrates this conflict. Traditionally (and even nowadays, despite the plethora of studies that disprove them), a lot of highly experienced practitioners argue that one should never make the first offer because one will risk showing one's cards. Instead, negotiators should let the counterparty go first. Previous research has shown that this practitioner belief stems from an increased satisfaction with the negotiation process (because making the first offer entails anxiety) and not from their actual performance (Rosette, Kopelman, & Abbott, 2014).

However, at least some research-based arguments imply that moving first may backfire under some exceptional circumstances in negotiations (Loschelder, Swaab, et al., 2014). The present work implies that comparable first-mover disadvantages do not exist in tenders. Instead, the particularities of public procurement prevent that publishing starting prices might backfire. Compared with negotiations, potential entry barriers may not arise in tenders because starting prices lack aggressiveness and missed any first-mover commitment. On the contrary, starting prices may even increase bidders' interest by lowering information asymmetries concerning the actual costs of the contract.

Since the present work did not report any limitations or conditions for the positive relation between the release of a starting price and increased procurement performance, regulators should consider requiring that starting prices be published. Such a legal requirement would not only overcome potentially faulty economic beliefs of practitioners but would counteract the other two potential sources behind non-disclosure: managerial inertia and commercial ignorance. On the one hand, prior research (see Section 7.1.1) showed that, in practice, procurement officials' managerial decisions in tenders are highly dependent upon organizational or regulatory traditions and thus suffer from inertia. On the other hand, procurement officials often still lack the necessary commercial education and the sensitivity for economic performance. Thus, they remain focused on legal compliance and might simply not care about utilizing their managerial discretion to improve their procurement performance (see Section 2.2.2).

8.3.2.2 Formulation of a starting price

Regarding the formulation (i.e., the definition of numerical precision) of published starting prices, the empirical results from Section 6.2 provide some policy implications as well. Whereas we found that increased numerical precision increased the anchor potency of starting point prices and attracted more interest from bidders, we found that starting price ranges did not exert significant relational or information effects.[83] Due to low first-mover discretion in public tenders, starting price ranges did not induce politeness. Suppliers most likely ignored the potential signals of procurement officials' characteristics and first mover's interpretations of their bids. Moreover, starting price ranges did not exert an informational effect. Because suppliers did not strive to identify the procurement official's (non-binding) reservation price, they did not focus their attention on the upper end of the published price range.

These empirical results imply that (more precise) starting price points are superior to starting price ranges from a performance perspective in tenders. Accordingly, regulators should consider forbidding their use and should instead require the publication of starting price points.[84] As shown in

[83] Readers should treat these implications with a healthy degree of caution. Compared with starting price points (N = 11,350), starting price ranges had a limited prevalence (N = 647). This prevalence lowers confidence when interpreting the missing significance of price ranges.

[84] Still, the results did not allow any regulatory recommendations about the precision of starting point prices to be derived. A regulation that would prescribe a minimum degree of numerical precision in starting prices would not only be odd but would also – at least partly – contradict the notion that starting prices are based on truthfully and realistically calculated internal cost estimates.

Section 6.3.3, starting price ranges were unpopular in most EU member states. Germany (41% of the observations), Finland (22% of the observations), and Italy (8% of the observations) were the only countries where starting price ranges enjoyed some popularity with Contracting Authorities. In the rest of the EU member states, hardly any tenders disclosed starting price ranges. Therefore, procurement officials do not seem to use starting price ranges out of economic considerations but due to implicit market norms (primarily driven by past regulatory differences). As argued above in Section 8.2.2.2, in response to such managerial inertia, the Directives would do well to restrict procurement officials' scope of actions in steering the implementation of performance-oriented measures.

8.4 Managerial implications for the private sector

This section discusses the implications of the present work for purchasing managers in the private sector. We will pay close attention to the nature of the chosen research design and the differences between public procurement and private purchasing: Both limit the scope of the potential transfer of findings from the present work.

The research design of the present work relies on the observation that previous researchers have largely failed to investigate performance in public procurement and have instead focused on private purchasing. Performance management in public tenders lags far behind in terms of empirical analysis and scientific knowledge (Flynn & Davis, 2014). In practice, public procurement officials typically achieve lower performance levels than their private-sector counterparts (Afonso et al., 2005). While legal compliance and secondary goals heavily restrict procurement performance management in tenders, omnipresent profitability pressures incentivize purchasing managers in private-sector organizations to identify, develop, and implement performance-oriented measures.

Accordingly, private purchasing practitioners might not learn a lot from performance management in the public sector. Contracting Authorities have probably failed to develop best practices that will allow their private-sector counterparts to improve their performance levels further. Historically, the public sector has gained more experience only with a single performance-oriented measure discussed in the present work: The use of procurement auctions for selecting suppliers. In the private sector, agents have been using auctions since the 16th century – but nearly exclusively for selling items to interesting bidders (Kaufmann & Carter, 2004). The use of (electronic) auctions in private-sector purchasing has significantly increased only since the 1990s – driven mainly by developments in information and communication technology. However, the private sector still overwhelmingly relies on negotiations when sourcing from suppliers (Bajari et al., 2009). By contrast, US public-sector authorities have regularly been using procurement auctions to source from suppliers since the beginning of the 19th century (McAfee & McMillan, 1989).

Historically, economic research – mainly based on the perspective of the private sector –has comprehensively investigated demand auctions but has remained rather silent about procurement auctions. In purchasing research, authors have been more focused on "face-to-face" negotiations.

However, since the boom of digital business models and purchasing solutions (eBay being the most famous example), several studies (Beall, 2003; Carter et al., 2004; Jap, 2002, 2003) have empirically investigated procurement auctions in private purchasing. Some authors have even comprehensively investigated how purchasers can improve their outcomes by strategically designing private-sector B2B procurement auctions (Eichstädt, 2008; Mithas & Jones, 2007; Schnabel, 2016; Subramanian, 2009).

Since procurement officials in the public sector enjoy considerably less freedom in designing tenders, a transfer of the present work's managerial recommendations to the private sector seems only partly sensible – particularly given the adequate level of available scientific research on private purchasing. However, past investigations of private-sector procurement auctions share one blind spot: They have largely remained within the classic economic research perspectives (i.e., within game theory and auction theory). Accordingly, they have neglected to study the anchoring effects that could arise due to the publication of starting prices. Even when authors have mentioned the potential influence of anchoring effects on outcomes, they have mostly referred to the empirical study by Ku et al. (2006) on the potential reversal of the first-mover advantage in auctions. However, this perspective has insufficiently included the intrapsychic and relational differences between demand auctions and procurement auctions as well as different transaction formats (e.g., anchoring effects in sealed vs. open bid auctions).

Thus, the empirical results of the present work on the anchoring effects of starting prices may yield valuable insights for the management of private-sector procurement auctions as well. However, we must consider the particularities of public procurement for the transfer of such insights to prevent potentially misguided recommendations. From a practical perspective, an application of performance-oriented measures on private-sector procurement auctions is particularly relevant. First movers in the private sector face competitive pressures that are absent from the public sector. They employ procurement auctions not to comply with regulations but to lower their procurement costs significantly. Thus, they will be especially interested in how starting prices affect their procurement performance.

8.4.1 Publication of a starting price

The present work recommends that Contracting Authorities in public tenders should publish starting prices in their CNs to improve performance. However, we cannot give the same advice to practitioners in the private sector because our results were highly dependent upon the transactional and regulatory particularities of public procurement. Notably, the potential barriers to entry could increase in private sector procurement auctions because of the use of typically more extreme and binding types of starting prices.

Private sector managers have more discretion in designing rules and allocation mechanisms in procurement auctions. Due to increased managerial discretion, first movers can choose from different types of starting prices (e.g., price estimates, minimum bids, and reference prices). These kinds of starting prices differ in their extremity. The results of past research imply that extreme anchors are more potent, but they increase the risk of lower bidder participation in procurement auctions. Since the number of bidders determines performance in procurement auctions to a large extent, private sector procurement managers could particularly benefit from their discretion by publishing more flexible and less extreme starting prices.

However, such starting prices are not common in the practice of the private sector (e.g., first movers in art auctions, housing sales, or online marketplaces employ more rigid starting prices). It remains a mystery why higher numbers of auctioneers do not use nonbinding, less extreme starting prices to benefit from the combined forces of amplified anchoring power and increases in bidders' interest. Future research might investigate the effects of different kinds of starting prices in private-sector procurement auctions to potentially replicate the implications of the present work.

8.4.2 *Formulation of a starting price*

In Section 6.4, we found that increased numerical precision increases the anchor potency of starting price points and attracts higher interest from bidders. Moreover, we reported that starting price ranges do not exert significant relational or information effects in tenders. Thus, we could not replicate the implications identified by Ames and Mason (2015) for range anchors. Still, the validity of the results concerning the (tandem) anchoring effects of starting price ranges depends on the informational and relational provisions of public procurement regulation. Whereas the politeness mechanism seems to require a sufficient degree of interpersonal exchange between parties, the informational effects seem to depend on the relevance of a first mover's reservation price.

However, the particularities of public procurement prevent us from providing private-sector auctioneers with a clear research-based recommendation on how to formulate starting prices in procurement auctions to increase their performance. Due to limiting regulations for awarding a contract and selecting suppliers in public procurement, tenders differ from other kinds of transactions. Whereas regulation typically prohibits any renegotiation of submitted offers, purchasing transactions in the private sector are often more flexible because they combine elements of an (up-front) auctioned mechanism and a (subsequent) negotiation phase. Thus, they increase the room for informational exchange of information and allocate more discretion to the first mover. Thus, we cannot provide any managerial recommendations regarding the use of starting price ranges to first movers in private-sector procurement auctions. Future research might fill the gap provided by existing studies that have failed to investigate effects of precision in some of the most prominent auctioned settings (e.g., open cry auctions for art and antiques, sealed-bid and mixed-format housing sales, or electronic reverse auctions with automotive suppliers).

Accordingly, the present work cannot recommend that private-sector practitioners should formulate their starting prices as precisely as possible or that they should abstain from formulating starting prices as ranges. The potential disadvantages of increased anchor precision could become more potent in more flexible award procedures with more first-mover discretion. Increased barriers to entry caused by precise anchors will certainly harm outcomes levels in such procurement auctions typical to private-sector purchasing.

Instead, we still believe that first movers in the private sector (particularly in negotiations) can significantly improve their procurement performance by using bolstering range anchors. Private-sector organizations typically rely on other economic transactions such as negotiations to source from suppliers. Negotiations show a more personal exchange between parties and pronounce the relevance of a first mover's reservation price. Since most real-life negotiations combine value-creating and value-claiming components (Thompson, 2015), bolstering range offers should mainly occur in practice as they can positively affect the perceived location of the first-mover's reservation price without damaging the relationship with the counterparty.

Several studies have argued that procurement auctions in private purchasing may bring about more favorable purchase prices (Gattiker et al., 2007; Jap, 2002; Mithas & Jones, 2007). As a result, private sector organizations have employed auctions to purchase works, supplies, or services. However, particularly in the industrial sector, suppliers have widely criticized procurement auctions as a measure solely targeted toward exploiting them. Because this criticism has deteriorated supplier relationships and caused economic setbacks, many companies have discontinued the use of procurement auctions. Nevertheless, competition induced by procurement auctions may yield positive effects for purchasers and suppliers (e.g., increased transparency, fairness, and comparability). If suppliers interpret starting price ranges as friendly and conciliatory, range anchors will allow procurement officials to claim more value while increasing the acceptance of procurement auctions and maintaining good supplier relationships.

9. Conclusion

9.1 Summary

The present work was aimed at investigating how Contracting Authorities can improve their procurement performance in public tenders. To pursue this overarching goal, we covered five sequential yet distinct research questions.

1. **Research question: What scope of action do Contracting Authorities have in the design of public tenders?**

After introducing tenders and performance management in public procurement in Chapters 2 and 3, we investigated Contracting Authorities' scopes of actions in tenders. By applying a processual procurement model by Van Weele and Eßig (2017) on public tenders, we identified four standard tender stages that procurement officials have to manage in tenders. In these stages, we found that regulation in the EU grants eight scopes of action (i.e., tender design options) from the first determination of specifications to the final selection of suppliers. Figure 20 shows that Contracting Authorities can design a tender (potentially influencing the award decision) before the publication of a CN. In contrast to private-sector purchasing, the EU Directives that enforce prohibitive standardization and high predictability heavily limit the extent to which first movers can influence the outcome once they have publicly announced a procurement auction.

A. Rhode, *Public Procurement in the European Union*, Schriften zum europäischen Management, https://doi.org/10.1007/978-3-658-28073-4_9

Figure 20: Fundamental regulatory structure of a tender

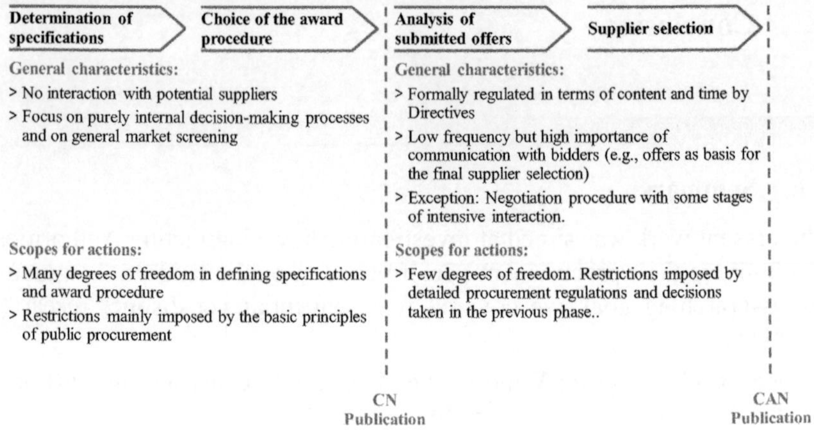

Source: Own illustration based on Glas (2012)

2. Research question: Given their scope of action, how can Contracting Authorities improve their procurement performance in public tenders?

We hypothesized that Contracting Authorities could exploit the scopes of actions granted by the Directives to implement various performance-oriented measures. Past research has largely failed to analyze performance management in public tenders. Thus, chapter 5 relied on findings from closely related streams of research to build working hypotheses on performance-oriented measures in tenders. In sum, past research findings allowed us to derive eight working hypotheses on how Contracting Authorities could improve their procurement performance in tenders, given their regulated scope of actions.

3. Research question: How do past empirical studies evaluate the impact of these identified measures on procurement performance in public tenders?

After defining working hypotheses concerning performance-oriented measures, we turned to the scattered research findings on tenders (and procurement auctions) to look for empirical support. For six working hypotheses, we found sufficient empirical evidence to conclude (with the necessary degree of caution) that the implementation of the respective measure will likely yield beneficial performance effects for Contracting Authorities. In a nutshell, previous research has provided vital insights for performance management in tenders.

First, we reported that most identified performance-oriented measures rely on the notion that increased competition between potential suppliers will lower final prices in tenders. Most of past empirical studies have implied that attracting more suppliers is a somewhat dominant strategy to improve procurement performance in auctioned procedures. Likewise, sufficient competition may prevent collusive behavior. Particularly if Contracting Authorities expect only a low level of interest from suppliers, they should try to attract more bidders. Previous research has reported that, on average, a procurement auction requires six to eight participating bidders to achieve a fully competitive level.

Most authors have reported an inversely proportional relation between competitiveness and final prices in tenders. However, under the status of full competitiveness, performance-enhancing effects due to the entry of additional bidders may become nonsignificant (i.e., when the outcome of the imperfectly competitive tender setting gets close to the outcome of a perfectly efficient competitive market). In some tenders, too much competition may even backfire because of the winner's curse and its anticipation by rational suppliers. However, bidders have only rarely adjusted their behavior to the winner's curse in past field studies. Thus, we argue that Contracting Authorities should strive to attract more bidders by implementing the corresponding performance-oriented measures in practice: In most tenders, the risks induced by low competition significantly outweigh the potential drawbacks of higher competition.

Second, we argued that policymakers in the EU had made regulatory progress in improving the performance of Contracting Authorities in tenders. The latest reform of the Directives in 2014 allowed procurement officials to implement the award procedure that best suits their acquisition needs. Before this reform, the Directives strongly advocated the use of open procedures and allowed for other procedures only under exceptional circumstances. The 2014 reform established restricted procedures as an equivalent alternative to open procedures and allowed negotiated procedures to be applied for the procurement of non-standard contracts. The results of Chapter

5 (as well as the managerial recommendation in Chapter 8) show that Contracting Authorities' outcomes will likely profit from the significantly widened scopes of action – if procurement officials use their increased discretion in the desired manner and not to engage in unlawful behavior. Thus, we believe that the 2014 reform of the Directives reflects a high degree of trust in procurement officials: Regulators probably ascertained a high degree of compliance with the Directives. Otherwise, they would not have drastically increased the transactional discretion of procurement officials in awarding contracts. In comparison with other procurement regulations across developed countries with similar high-quality institutional environments (e.g., the United States or Singapore), the current version of the EU Directives provides Contracting Authorities with a high degree of discretion to potentially implement performance-oriented measures.

Third, we found that past research almost entirely neglected to investigate starting price effects in public tenders. The existence of this research gap was surprising as a plethora of studies have demonstrated how starting prices affect outcomes in economic transactions such as buyer-supplier negotiations, demand auctions, and housing sales. The empirical investigations of the present work took the rich, yet also diverse and sometimes even contradictory findings of past research on starting price effects as the starting point. With these investigations, we aimed to answer the last two research questions.

4. **Research question: Can Contracting Authorities improve their procurement performance by publishing a starting price in public tenders?**

In Chapter 6, we first investigated Contracting Authorities' decision to disclose a starting price in a CN and its impact on procurement performance. Although the Directives require Contracting Authorities to assess the value of contracts before the tender starts, many transactions (about 30% in the final data set) concealed their starting prices. Given that previous studies on negotiations and auctions indicated that starting prices may serve as anchors in tenders to enhance procurement performance, the nonpublication of starting prices has remained a mystery. We speculated that starting prices in public tenders might not always yield a first-mover advantage but could instead backfire by lowering the number of offers and preventing lower than expected bids.

Chapter 6 showed that the disclosure of starting prices depends on tender characteristics. Because Contracting Authorities do not conceal starting prices at public tenders for more complex and more expensive contracts, we speculate that they enjoy no information advantage on the actual contract costs—or at least do not make use of it. Instead, market norms shape procurement officials' decisions to publish starting prices more than economic considerations, which typically play a subordinate role in public procurement. Accordingly, we argued that increased procurement professionalism might correlate with an increase in the likelihood of publishing a starting price in a CN.

With the help of a two-stage selection-correction model, we found that auctions that disclosed a starting price showed better outcomes for the Contracting Authority. Whereas this correlation does not necessarily imply causality, we found no contradictory evidence that the release of starting prices might reverse a first-mover advantage in tenders. Instead, the performance-enhancing implications of an anchoring-based interpretation of the empirical results corresponded to the auction theory notion that Contracting Authorities can use starting prices to improve procurement performance in public tenders. The positive influence of starting prices on the number of bids implies that the first-mover advantage somewhat depended on the reduced information asymmetries caused by disclosing starting prices. Nevertheless, the empirical results suggest that anchoring effects at least partially explain the first-mover advantage in public tenders. Auction-theory-based determinations cannot explain why more considerable price heterogeneity in similar tenders significantly reduces the impact of starting prices on performance. Besides, the (anchoring) effect of starting prices remained significant after we controlled for the impact of increased bidders' interest on procurement performance.

Contrary to our preliminary beliefs, we replicated some of the previous empirical findings by Silva et al. (2008). Initially, we doubted whether the publication of a starting price would reduce information asymmetries in tenders. First, inspired by Bajari and Tadelis (2001), we assumed that neither the procurement officials nor the suppliers would possess significant private information at the beginning of a tender. Second, we took into consideration the fact that previous field studies have hardly been able to replicate the theoretical effects of Common Value uncertainty on auctioneers' performance (Haile, 2001; Hong & Shum, 2002; Paarsch, 1992). We also speculated that—given the high average complexity and monetary value of public procurement contracts—procurement officials could deliberately conceal starting prices to improve results (Gatzlaff & Liu, 2013). Instead, our empirical results implied that procurement officials did not refrain from publishing starting prices due to economic considerations, but rather because they did not take sufficient account of performance aspects in their tender design.

5. Research question: How should Contracting Authorities formulate a starting price to improve their procurement performance?

In Chapter 6, we also investigated the impact of different kinds of starting prices in public tenders. We explored how starting prices (formulated as (imprecise) ranges or as (precise) point values) affected procurement performance and bidders' interest. We reported that increases in the precision of published starting prices were linearly correlated with better performance levels and a larger number of bids. These starting price effects depended on the informational and relational provisions of public procurement regulation. In the regulated environment created by the Directives, potential suppliers confronted with precise starting prices could not question the competence of procurement officials. Thus, suppliers interpreted (even extremely) precise starting prices as more credible. This increased credibility reduced (anticipated) entry risks for suppliers as well. Besides, increased precision did not create entry barriers. Since the Directives heavily limited the discretion of Contracting Authorities, any possible reservation price of procurement officials lost its relevance and caused potential suppliers to fail to ascribe increased inflexibility to first movers who released precise starting prices.

Whereas we found that increased numerical precision increased the anchor potency of starting point prices and attracted greater interest from potential suppliers, we found that starting price ranges did not exert significant relational or information effects. We could not replicate the implications identified by Ames and Mason (2015) on range anchors. We found no empirical evidence for the initial assumption that the relational benefits of range anchors might prevail in public procurement where Contracting Authorities need to spark the interest of possible suppliers in a marketplace.

The limited discretion of procurement officials likewise prevented the informational and relational effects of price ranges from becoming effective: Potential suppliers are likely to ignore potentially signaled first-mover characteristics and procurement officials' interpretations of their bids. Moreover, starting price ranges do not exert an informational effect. Because suppliers neglect to identify the first-mover's (nonbinding) reservation price,

9.2 Contribution to the literature and research outlook

9.2.1 A practical framework for procurement officials

Public procurement is a primary function of government. As such, it massively impacts welfare, public organizations, taxpayers, and private businesses (Grandia, 2018). Recently, policymakers and Contracting Authorities alike have focused a great deal of attention on improving their public procurement efforts. Nevertheless, past academic authors have not recognized public procurement as an essential policy instrument and have failed to establish a respective research field. For a long time, researchers have treated public procurement activities as a minor subset of private-sector purchasing. Although the Journal of Public Procurement specifically caters to practitioners and academics who are active in public procurement, it is not listed in the ISI International Citation Index (Allen, Hemming, & Potter, 2013). Studies on public procurement outside of this journal are scattered, and a holistic literature review is missing. In an extensive literature review on purchasing and supply management, Spina, Caniato, Luzzini, and Ronchi (2013) identified public procurement as a relevant field for future review studies.

Managing public tenders is closely related to other classical questions of business administration. Still, researches have so far largely neglected tenders. Instead, business research (as well as education) has been more focused on the management of private sector purchasing. Despite this historic underexposure, studies on performance management in tenders nowadays do exist – even if they are profoundly scattered. Most of the performance-oriented studies on tenders have focused on investigating a single specific legal, administrative, or transactional aspect. The works edited by Eßig (2013) or Thai (2017a) discuss several examples of such studies.

A few authors have investigated performance management in public tenders more holistically (Berndt, 1988; Blome, 2007; Glas, 2012; Ilius, 2004; Schapper et al., 2006). However, these studies have been primarily conceptual, prescriptive, or descriptive in nature. If past studies on tenders followed an empirical set-up, they mostly relied on qualitative interviews or case studies. Typically, the scope of their research was holistic, covering all stages within public procurement – usually defined from the initial make-or-buy-decision to the final evaluation of the contract award. Due to their holistic research questions, these studies have provided procurement officials with only negligible and vague practical recommendations.

The study by Glas (2012), as the most recent in this line of studies, nicely illustrated the difference in the research focus between past tender studies and the present work. Similar to the present work, Glas (2012) defined the design of a tender as the management of measures given the scope of actions provided by public procurement regulation. However, the author did not focus on procurement officials' operational tasks that arose from this definition but instead covered the strategic development of public procurement as a managerial function within Contracting Authorities. Thus, the author catered more to the perspective of high-ranking officials or policymakers on how to introduce performance management to Contracting Authorities. However, his work remained mostly silent about providing any concrete managerial recommendations for procurement officials. To the best of our knowledge, the present work remains the only one so far to develop well-founded recommendations – based on past and own empirical research – that help procurement officials to manage tenders in a performance-oriented way.

9.2.2 An empirical investigation of performance determinants in tenders

A lack of transactional field studies also characterizes past research on public procurement. Some factors have been responsible for this lack of empirical research. First, researchers have struggled to get access to comprehensive transaction data on public tenders (Onur et al., 2012). Second, high variation and heterogeneity in public procurement have resulted in low comparability of typically atomic empirical results (Soudek & Skuhro, 2013). Third, performance-oriented research has suffered in particular as public procurement outcomes have often lacked a benchmark against which they could be compared (Ohashi, 2009). Public tenders tend to rely on a specific set of regulatory rules; there is not much experimentation with alternative designs as well.

In the last couple of years, regulators have improved public access to tender transaction data. Some authors have empirically examined the determinants of performance in public tenders. However, they have mostly focused on the number of bidders as the primary variable of interest. We argue that the still heavily limited access to holistic and reliable field data in public procurement is responsible for this limited scope of past research. The data situation in Europe illustrates this problem: Even though TED was established by the 2004 Directives, it is still not fully available in an open data format.

Since the EU only publishes part of TED in open data formats, the present work relied on manual and very labor-intensive data entry efforts to investigate the research hypotheses in the empirical investigation. While the prior studies could employ simpler econometric set-ups to investigate competition effects, the empirical analysis of other (potentially weaker and less prominent) performance determinants in tenders needs to be more finely structured. Thus, it comes as no surprise that the present work's empirical investigation of starting price effects in public tenders is without comparison. As such, it can serve as a starting point for future empirical research on performance management in tenders.

While we argued in Chapter 5 that the present empirical research is sufficient to support our working hypotheses, we also reported that additional empirical research would not only increase our confidence in the reliability of the conclusions that we drew but would also expand and deepen the current understanding of tender performance.

First, we found only indirect support for two working hypotheses. An actual empirical investigation of the performance effects of the publication of a PN and of the formulation of functional specifications is still outstanding. We only could derive well-grounded recommendations for procurement officials because of the lack of any theoretical arguments or empirical evidence that both measures might have a negative impact on bidders' interest as the antecedent of procurement performance.

Still, the publication of a PN could potentially harm performance in case of mismanagement: When procurement officials have previously published a PN, the minimum deadline for the submission of offers shrinks to 36 days. If officials employ other shortening measures such as allowing the electronic submission of bids (minus 5 days) and online response to bidder inquiries (minus 12 days), they can shrink the deadline to a minimum of 15 days. Although shortening the deadline can decrease transaction costs, it entails the risks of few and possibly poorly prepared offers. Thus, future research should investigate whether the publication of a PN can backfire in case of mismanagement.

Regarding the relation between starting prices and procurement performance, the present work did not identify any need for further research given the current regulatory umbrella of the Directives. Instead, future research should examine the effects of starting prices in other kinds of public tenders (and private-sector procurement auctions). As discussed in section 8.4, researchers may choose to investigate procedures where auctioneers have more discretion in designing rules and mechanisms. With increased discretion or within other transactional settings, first movers may choose to publish different types of starting prices. We believe that different starting prices (e.g., price estimates, minimum bids, and market reference prices) could be most effective in different transactional settings. While more extreme anchors should be more potent, they should also increase the risk of lower bidder participation.

Due to the crucial role of the number of bidders for procurement performance, auctioneers in the private sector could particularly benefit from publishing nonbinding, less extreme starting prices. However, section 8.4 also noted that such starting prices do not appear to be very common in practice – which remains a mystery given the implications of the present work-

A similar argument applies to the future investigation of starting price ranges in private-sector procurement auctions. The validity of the present work's results concerning the (tandem) anchoring effects of starting price ranges depends on the informational and relational provisions of public procurement regulation. Whereas the politeness mechanism seems to require a sufficient degree of interpersonal exchange between parties, the informational effects seem to depend on the relevance of a first mover's reservation price. Procurement auctions in other transactional settings (outside the public sector) may fulfill both requirements.

Particularly in the private industrial sector, suppliers have widely criticized procurement auctions as a measure that is solely targeted toward exploiting them. Because this criticism deteriorated supplier relationships and caused economic setbacks, many companies discontinued the use of auctions. Nevertheless, competition induced by auctions may yield positive effects for buyers and suppliers (e.g., increased transparency, fairness, and comparability). If suppliers interpret starting price ranges as friendly and conciliatory, range anchors will allow buyers to claim more value while increasing the acceptance of procurement auctions and maintaining good supplier relationships.

9.2.3 An extension of the behavioral perspective

Typically, past research has analyzed public tenders from an auction theory perspective. Historically, other authors have tried to develop (sub)-optimal strategies in public tenders – assuming fully rational agents (Bulow & Roberts, 1989; Maskin & Riley, 2000; McAfee & McMillan, 1987). These strategies have usually focused on the Contracting Authorities' task to identify the cost functions of suppliers. However, the present work shows that the performance-oriented management of tenders involves more than revealing suppliers' actual costs. While procurement officials should still contemplate on standard economic concerns when designing a tender, the present work suggests that behavioral considerations at least partially govern how prices are determined in tenders. Contracting Authorities award contracts in a market place setting where they must spark the interest of suppliers. Given the high entry costs and the crucial role of bidders' interest for procurement performance in tenders, it would be odd not to assume that behavioral factors that influence the buyer-seller relationship heavily determine outcomes as well. While research has long recognized this behavioral notion for negotiations used in private-sector purchasing (Thompson, 2015), other authors seem to have forgotten that psychological and cognitive factors may influence outcomes in public procurement as well. To the best of our knowledge, the present study is the first one to investigate outcomes in tenders from a behavioral perspective empirically.

Currently, the present work stands out by attempting to replicate starting price effects in tenders that have previously been reported for other economic transactions – particularly for negations. Given the current replication crisis in the social sciences where many findings are difficult (and sometimes even impossible) to replicate or reproduce, the transfer of practical recommendations from negotiations to tenders is exceptional. The present work left the artificial environment of an experimental laboratory and turned to real-world transactions involving actual money. Due to its application-oriented nature, the empirical investigation of the present work has thus not only expanded the present scope of anchoring research by looking at starting prices in tenders, but it has also improved the practical understanding of performance management in tenders.

Therefore, we argue that the present work can inspire future research on additional behavioral aspects that might influence the buyer-seller relationship in tenders. An empirical investigation of further performance-oriented measures that rely on cognitive mechanisms could be all the more promising as research on psychological influence in negotiations is still in its infancy as well (Malhotra & Bazerman, 2008). The access to transactional data with real monetary consequences for agents usually represents one of the main obstacles for research on negotiations. By contrast, as a reaction to efforts of open data and open government advocates, governments all around the globe have increasingly made data on public tenders publicly available. Although the present work implied that data-entry quality and comprehensive continue to exist as obstacles, future research might employ transaction data from tenders to validate further behavioral insights generated in the field of negotiations. Thereby, the authors of future research could aim to achieve the same goals as the present work: on the one hand, to go outside the laboratory setting to replicate previously generated behavioral insights, and on the other hand, to transfer insights from negotiations to other economic transactions to better understand the requirements for their replication – given the investigated transactional particularities.

References

Afonso, A., Schuknecht, L., & Tanzi, V. (2005). Public sector efficiency: An international comparison. *Public Choice, 123*(3), 321–347. https://doi.org/10.1007/s11127-005-7165-2

Allen, R., Hemming, R., & Potter, B. H. (Eds.). (2013). *The International Handbook of Public Financial Management*. London: Palgrave Macmillan.

Ames, D. R., & Mason, M. F. (2015). Tandem anchoring: Informational and politeness effects of range offers in social exchange. *Journal of Personality and Social Psychology, 108*(2), 254–274. https://doi.org/10.1037/pspi0000016

Ariely, D., & Simonson, I. (2003). Buying, bidding, playing, or competing? Value assessment and decision dynamics in online auctions. *Journal of Consumer psychology, 13*(1), 113–123. https://doi.org/10.1207/S15327663JCP13-1&2_10

Arlbjørn, J. S., & Freytag, P. V. (2012). Public procurement vs private purchasing. *International Journal of Public Sector Management, 25*(3), 203–220. https://doi.org/10.1108/09513551211226539

Arrowsmith, S. (2006). The Past and Future Evolution of EC Procurement Law: From Framework to Common Code? *Public Contract Law Journal, 35*(3), 337–384.

Arrowsmith, S. (2008). EC Regime on Public Procurement. In K. V. Thai (Ed.), *International handbook of public procurement* (pp. 252–284). CRC Press.

A. Rhode, *Public Procurement in the European Union*, Schriften zum europäischen Management, https://doi.org/10.1007/978-3-658-28073-4

Asker, J., & Cantillon, E. (2008). Properties of scoring auctions. *The RAND Journal of Economics*, *39*(1), 69–85. https://doi.org/10.1111/j.1756-2171.2008.00004.x

Ax, T., & Schneider, M. (2005). *Rechtshandbuch der Weg zum öffentlichen Auftrag: Vergabemanagement für Unternehmer. Bau und Vergabe*. Berlin: Lexxion Der Juristische Verl.

Backus, M., Blake, T., & Tadelis, S. (2016). On the empirical content of cheap-talk signaling: An application to bargaining. *NBER working paper*, *21285*.

Bajari, P., & Hortaçsu, A. (2003). The Winner's Curse, Reserve Prices, and Endogenous Entry: Empirical Insights from eBay Auctions. *The RAND Journal of Economics*, *34*(2), 329–355. https://doi.org/10.2307/1593721

Bajari, P., Houghton, S., & Tadelis, S. (2014). Bidding for Incomplete Contracts: An Empirical Analysis of Adaptation Costs. *American Economic Review*, *104*(4), 1288–1319. https://doi.org/10.1257/aer.104.4.1288

Bajari, P., McMillan, R., & Tadelis, S. (2009). Auctions Versus Negotiations in Procurement: An Empirical Analysis. *Journal of Law, Economics, and Organization*, *25*(2), 372–399. https://doi.org/10.1093/jleo/ewn002

Bajari, P., & Tadelis, S. (2001). Incentives versus Transaction Costs: A Theory of Procurement Contracts. *The RAND Journal of Economics*, *32*(3), 387–407. https://doi.org/10.2307/2696361

Baker, G., Gibbons, R., & Murphy, K. J. (2002). Relational Contracts and the Theory of the Firm. *The Quarterly Journal of Economics*, *117*(1), 39–84. https://doi.org/10.1162/003355302753399445

Ballesteros-Pérez, P., González-Cruz, M. C., Pastor-Ferrando, J. P., & Fernández-Diego, M. (2012). The iso-Score Curve Graph. A new tool for competitive bidding. *Automation in Construction*, *22*, 481–490. https://doi.org/10.1016/j.autcon.2011.11.007

Ballesteros-Pérez, P., Skitmore, M., Pellicer, E., & González-Cruz, M. C. (2015). Scoring rules and abnormally low bids criteria in construction tenders: A taxonomic review. *Construction Management and Economics, 33*(4), 259–278. https://doi.org/10.1080/01446193.2015.1059951

Banerjee, A. V., & Duflo, E. (2000). Reputation Effects and the Limits of Contracting: A Study of the Indian Software Industry *The Quarterly Journal of Economics, 115*(3), 989–1017. https://doi.org/10.1162/003355300554962

Beall, S. (2003). *The role of reverse auctions in strategic sourcing. Focus study*. Tempe AZ: W.P. Carey School of Business Arizona State University; CAPS Research.

Beamon, B. M. (1999). Measuring supply chain performance. *International Journal of Operations & Production Management, 19*(3), 275–292. https://doi.org/10.1108/01443579910249714

Beracha, E., & Seiler, M. J. (2014). The Effect of Listing Price Strategy on Transaction Selling Prices. *The Journal of Real Estate Finance and Economics, 49*(2), 237–255. https://doi.org/10.1007/s11146-013-9424-1

Bergman, M. A., & Lundberg, S. (2013). Tender evaluation and supplier selection methods in public procurement. *Journal of Purchasing and Supply Management, 19*(2), 73–83. https://doi.org/10.1016/j.pursup.2013.02.003

Berndt, R. (1988). *Marketing für öffentliche Aufträge*. München: Vahlen.

Berndt, R., & Fantapié Altobelli, C. (Eds.). (1998). *Springers Handbuch der Betriebswirtschaftslehre*. Berlin: Springer.

Bertrand, M., Duflo, E., & Mullainathan, S. (2002). *How Much Should We Trust Differences-in-Differences Estimates?* Cambridge, MA: National Bureau of Economic Research. https://doi.org/10.3386/w8841

Besley, T., & Case, A. (2000). Unnatural Experiments?: Estimating the Incidence of Endogenous Policies. *The Economic Journal, 110*(467), 672–694. https://doi.org/10.1111/1468-0297.00578

Blome, C. (2007). *Öffentliches Beschaffungsmarketing: Ein Kennzahlensystem für das Vergabemanagement*. Wiesbaden: DUV. https://doi.org/10.1007/978-3-8350-9470-3

Bovis, C. (2012). *EU public procurement law* (Second edition). *Elgar European law*. Cheltenham, UK, Northampton, MA, USA: Edward Elgar.

Boyne, G. A. (2002). Concepts and Indicators of Local Authority Performance: An Evaluation of the Statutory Frameworks in England and Wales. *Public Money and Management*, *22*(2), 17–24. https://doi.org/10.1111/1467-9302.00303

Brannman, L., Klein, J. D., & Weiss, L. W. (1987). The Price Effects of Increased Competition in Auction Markets. *The Review of Economics and Statistics*, *69*(1), 24. https://doi.org/10.2307/1937897

Brint, A. T. (2003). Investigating Buyer and Seller Strategies in Online Auctions. *The Journal of the Operational Research Society*, *54*(11), 1177–1188. https://doi.org/10.1057/palgrave.jors.2601629

Bucchianeri, G. W., & Minson, J. A. (2013). A homeowner's dilemma: Anchoring in residential real estate transactions. *Journal of Economic Behavior & Organization*, *89*, 76–92. https://doi.org/10.1016/j.jebo.2013.01.010

Bulow, J., & Klemperer, P. (1996). Auctions Versus Negotiations. *The American Economic Review*, *86*(1), 180–194. https://doi.org/10.3386/w4608

Bulow, J., & Roberts, J. (1989). The Simple Economies of Optimal Auctions. *Journal of Political Economy*, *97*(5), 1060.

Caldwell, N., & Bakker, E. (2008). Procurement process in the public sector: an international perspective. In K. V. Thai (Ed.), *International handbook of public procurement* (pp. 427–441). CRC Press.

Callender, G., & Matthews, D. (2002). The economic context of government procurement: New challenges and new opportunities. *Journal of Public Procurement*, *2*(2), 216–236. https://doi.org/10.1108/JOPP-02-02-2002-B003

Carayannis, E. G., & Popescu, D. (2005). Profiling a methodology for economic growth and convergence: Learning from the EU e-procurement experience for central and eastern European countries. *Technovation*, *25*(1), 1–14. https://doi.org/10.1016/S0166-4972(03)00071-3

Cardella, E., & Seiler, M. J. (2016). The effect of listing price strategy on real estate negotiations: An experimental study. *Journal of Economic Psychology*, *52*, 71–90. https://doi.org/10.1016/j.joep.2015.11.001

Carpineti, L., Piga, G., & Zanza, M. (2006). The variety of procurement practice: Evidence from public procurement. In N. Dimitri, G. Piga, & G. Spagnolo (Eds.), *Handbook of procurement.* Cambridge: Cambridge University Press.

Carter, C. R., Kaufmann, L., Beall, S., Carter, P. L., Hendrick, T. E., & Petersen, K. J. (2004). Reverse auctions—grounded theory from the buyer and supplier perspective. *Transportation Research Part E: Logistics and Transportation Review*, *40*(3), 229–254. https://doi.org/10.1016/j.tre.2003.08.004

Case, K. E., & Shiller, R. J. (2003). Is There a Bubble in the Housing Market? *Brookings Papers on Economic Activity*, *2003*(2), 299–362. https://doi.org/10.1353/eca.2004.0004

Chalmers, A. F., & Bergemann, N. (Eds.). (2007). *Wege der Wissenschaft: Einführung in die Wissenschaftstheorie* (6., verbesserte Auflage). Berlin, Heidelberg: Springer-Verlag Berlin Heidelberg. Retrieved from http://dx.doi.org/10.1007/978-3-540-49491-1 https://doi.org/10.1007/978-3-540-49491-1

Che, Y.-K. (1993). Design Competition Through Multidimensional Auctions. *The RAND Journal of Economics*, *24*(4), 668. https://doi.org/10.2307/2555752

Che, Y.-K., & Kim, J. (2006). Robustly Collusion-Proof Implementation. *Econometrica*, *74*(4), 1063–1107. https://doi.org/10.1111/j.1468-0262.2006.00694.x

Chever, L., Saussier, S., & Yvrande-Billon, A. (2017). The law of small numbers: Investigating the benefits of restricted auctions for public procurement. *Applied Economics*, *49*(42), 4241–4260. https://doi.org/10.1080/00036846.2017.1279270

Chong, E., Klien, M., & Saussier, S. (2016). The use and abuse of discretionary procurement procedures: Evidence from the European Union. *Working Paper Chaire EPPP*.

Christensen, T., & Lægreid, P. (2002). *New public management: The transformation of ideas and practice / edited by Tom Christensen and Per Lægreid*. Aldershot: Ashgate.

Coppier, R., & Piga, G. (2006). Why Do Transparent Public Procurement and Corruption Go Hand in Hand? *Rivista di Politica Economica, 96*(1), 185–206.

Coviello, D., Guglielmo, A., & Spagnolo, G. (2018). The Effect of Discretion on Procurement Performance. *Management Science*, *64*(2), 715–738. https://doi.org/10.1287/mnsc.2016.2628

Decarolis, F. (2014). Awarding Price, Contract Performance, and Bids Screening: Evidence from Procurement Auctions. *American Economic Journal: Applied Economics*, *6*(1), 108–132.

Dimitri, N. (2013). "Best value for money" in procurement. *Journal of Public Procurement, 13*(2), 149–175. https://doi.org/10.1108/JOPP-13-02-2013-B001

Dini, F., Pacini, R., & Valletti, T. (2006). Scoring rules. In N. Dimitri, G. Piga, & G. Spagnolo (Eds.), *Handbook of procurement* (pp. 293–321). Cambridge: Cambridge University Press.

Domberger, S., Hall, C., & Li, E. A. L. (1995). The Determinants of Price and Quality in Competitively Tendered Contracts. *The Economic Journal*, *105*(433), 1454. https://doi.org/10.2307/2235110

Drolet, A. L., & Morris, M. W. (2000). Rapport in conflict resolution: Accounting for how face-to-face contact fosters mutual cooperation in mixed-motive conflicts. *Journal of Experimental Social Psychology*, *36*(1), 26–50.

Edler, J., & Georghiou, L. (2007). Public procurement and innovation—Resurrecting the demand side. *Research Policy*, *36*(7), 949–963. https://doi.org/10.1016/j.respol.2007.03.003

Eichhorn, P. (2001). Öffentliche Betriebswirtschaftslehre als eine Spezielle BWL. *Wirtschaftswissenschaftliches Studium : WiSt*, *30*(8), 409–416. Retrieved from http://ub-madoc.bib.uni-mannheim.de/9991/

Eichstädt, T. (2008). *Einsatz von Auktionen im Beschaffungsmanagement: Erfahrungen aus der Einkaufspraxis und die Verbreitung auktionstheoretischer Konzepte*. Wiesbaden: Betriebswirtschaftlicher

Verlag Dr. Th. Gabler / GWV Fachverlage GmbH Wiesbaden. Retrieved from http://dx.doi.org/10.1007/978-3-8349-9744-9

Engelbrecht-Wiggans, R., Shubik, M., & Stark, R. M. (1983). *Auctions, bidding, and contracting: Uses and theory / edited by Richard Engelbrecht-Wiggans, Martin Shubik, Robert M. Stark. Studies in game theory and mathematical economics*. New York: New York University Press.

Epley, N., & Gilovich, T. (2006). The anchoring-and-adjustment heuristic Why the adjustments are insufficient. *Psychological science*, *17*(4), 311–318. https://doi.org/10.1111/j.1467-9280.2006.01704.x

Erridge, A. (2007). Public Procurement, Public Value and The Northern Ireland Unemployment Pilot Project. *Public Administration*, *85*(4), 1023–1043. https://doi.org/10.1111/j.1467-9299.2007.00674.x

Erridge, A., & McIlroy, J. (2002). Public Procurement and Supply Management Strategies. *Public Policy and Administration*, *17*(1), 52–71. https://doi.org/10.1177/095207670201700105

Erridge, A., & Nondi, R. (1994). Public procurement, competition and partnership. *European Journal of Purchasing & Supply Management*, *1*(3), 169–179. https://doi.org/10.1016/0969-7012(94)90006-X

Eßig, M. (2013). *Exzellente öffentliche Beschaffung*. Wiesbaden: Springer Fachmedien Wiesbaden. https://doi.org/10.1007/978-3-658-00567-2

Estache, A., & Iimi, A. (2008). *Procurement efficiency for infrastructure development and financial needs reassessed* (No. 4662).

European Commission. TED csv dataset (2012-2015): Tenders Electronic Daily, supplement to the Official Journal of the European Union. Retrieved from https://open-data.europa.eu/cs/data/dataset/ted-csv

European Commission. (2016). *Public procurement indicators 2015: DG GROW G4 - Innovative and e-Procurement*. Brussels: European Comission.

European Commission. (2018). *Public procurement guidance for practitioners: on avoiding the most common errors in projects funded by the European Structural and Investment Funds*. Brussels.

Directive 2004/17/EC of the European Parliament and of the Council of 31 March 2004 coordinating the procurement procedures of entities operating in the water, energy, transport and postal services sectorsOfficial Journal of the European Union 1 (European Union 2004).

Directive 2004/18/EC of the European Parliament and of the Council of 31 March 2004 on the coordination of procedures for the award of public works contracts, public supply contracts and public service contractsOfficial Journal of the European Union 114 (European Union 2004).

Directive 2014/24/EU of the European Parliament and of the Council of 26 February 2014 on public procurement and repealing Directive 2004/18/ECOfficial Journal of the European Union 65 (European Union 2014).

Directive 2014/25/EU on procurement by entities operating in the water, energy, transport, and postal services sectors and repealing Directive 2004/17/ECOfficial Journal of the European Union 243 (European Union 2014).

Flammer, C. (2018). Competing for government procurement contracts: The role of corporate social responsibility. *Strategic Management Journal*, *39*(5), 1299–1324. https://doi.org/10.1002/smj.2767

Flynn, A., & Davis, P. (2014). Theory in public procurement research. *Journal of Public Procurement*, *14*(2), 139–180. https://doi.org/10.1108/JOPP-14-02-2014-B001

Galinsky, A. D., Ku, G., & Mussweiler, T. (2009). To Start Low or To Start High?: The Case of Auctions Versus Negotiations. *Current Directions in Psychological Science*, *18*(6), 357–361. https://doi.org/10.1111/j.1467-8721.2009.01667.x

Galinsky, A. D., & Mussweiler, T. (2001). First offers as anchors: The role of perspective-taking and negotiator focus. *Journal of Personality and Social Psychology*, *81*(4), 657. https://doi.org/10.1037/0022-3514.81.4.657

Gattiker, T. F., Huang, X., & Schwarz, J. L. (2007). Negotiation, email, and Internet reverse auctions: How sourcing mechanisms deployed by buyers affect suppliers' trust. *Journal of Operations Management*, *25*(1), 184–202. https://doi.org/10.1016/j.jom.2006.02.007

Gatzlaff, D., & Liu, P. (2013). List Price Information in the Negotiation of Commercial Real Estate Transactions: Is Silence Golden? *The Journal of Real Estate Finance and Economics*, *47*(4), 760–786. https://doi.org/10.1007/s11146-013-9435-y

Gelderman, C. J., & Van Weele, A. J. (2002). Strategic Direction through Purchasing Portfolio Management: A Case Study. *The Journal of Supply Chain Management*, *38*(2), 30–37. https://doi.org/10.1111/j.1745-493X.2002.tb00127.x

Gelderman, C. J., & Van Weele, A. J. (2005). Purchasing Portfolio Models: A Critique and Update. *The Journal of Supply Chain Management*, *41*(3), 19–28. https://doi.org/10.1111/j.1055-6001.2005.04103003.x

Glas, A. H. (2012). *Public Performance-based Contracting: Ergebnisorientierte Beschaffung und leistungsabhängige Preise im öffentlichen Sektor. Supply Chain Management, Beiträge zu Beschaffung und Logistik*. Wiesbaden: Springer Fachmedien Wiesbaden. Retrieved from http://dx.doi.org/10.1007/978-3-8349-4521-1

Goeree, J. K., & Offerman, T. (2003). Competitive bidding in auctions with private and common values. *The Economic Journal*, *113*(489), 598–613.

Goldberg, V. P. (1977). Competitive Bidding and the Production of Precontract Information. *The Bell Journal of Economics*, *8*(1), 250. https://doi.org/10.2307/3003497

Gómez-Lobo, A., & Szymanski, S. (2001). A Law of Large Numbers: Bidding and Compulsory Competitive Tendering for Refuse Collection Contracts. *Review of Industrial Organization*, *18*(1), 105–113.

Gragan, D. P. (2005). Harnessing procurement transformation in the public sector. *Government Procurement*, *13*(1), 18–19.

Grandia, J. (2018). Public Procurement in Europe. In E. Ongaro (Ed.), *Palgrave handbooks. The Palgrave handbook of public administration and management in Europe* (pp. 363–380). London United Kingdom: Palgrave Macmillan.

Grega, M., & Nemec, J. (2015). Factors Influencing Final Price of Public Procurement: Evidence from Slovakia. *Procedia Economics and*

Finance, *25*, 543–551. https://doi.org/10.1016/S2212-5671(15)00768-6

Gupta, S. (2002). Competition and collusion in a government procurement auction market. *Atlantic Economic Journal*, *30*(1), 13–25. https://doi.org/10.1007/BF02299143

Haile, P. A. (2001). Auctions with Resale Markets: An Application to U.S. Forest Service Timber Sales. *American Economic Review*, *91*(3), 399–427. https://doi.org/10.1257/aer.91.3.399

Hallwood, P. C. (1996). A market in action. *Journal of Economic Studies*, *23*(3), 34–43. https://doi.org/10.1108/01443589610124381

Hausch, D. B., & Li, L. (1993). A common value auction model with endogenous entry and information acquisition. *Economic Theory*, *3*(2), 315–334. https://doi.org/10.1007/BF01212920

Heckman, J. J. (1979). Sample Selection Bias as a Specification Error. *Econometrica*, *47*(1), 153–161. https://doi.org/10.2307/1912352

Heinrich, C. J. (1999). Do government bureaucrats make effective use of performance management information? *Journal of Public Administration Research and Theory*, *9*(3), 363–394. https://doi.org/10.1093/oxfordjournals.jpart.a024415

Hertwig, S. (2014). *Praxis der öffentlichen Auftragsvergabe: Systematik, Verfahren und Rechtsschutz* (5., neubearb. Aufl.). *NJW-Praxis: Vol. 65*. München: Beck.

Hong, H., & Shum, M. (2002). Increasing Competition and the Winner's Curse: Evidence from Procurement. *Review of Economic Studies*, *69*(4), 871–898. https://doi.org/10.1111/1467-937X.00229

Hood, C. (1991). A Public Management For All Seasons? *Public Administration*, *69*(1), 3–19. https://doi.org/10.1111/j.1467-9299.1991.tb00779.x

Hoppe, T., & Sadrieh, A. (2007). *An Experimental Assessment of Confederate Reserve Price Bids in Online Auction* (No. 07011).

Hossain, T., & Morgan, J. (2005). A Test of the Revenue Equivalence Theorem using Field Experiments on eBay. *SSRN Electronic Journal*. Advance online publication. https://doi.org/10.2139/ssrn.655449

Hyytinen, A., Lundberg, S., & Toivanen, O. (2018). Design of public procurement auctions: Evidence from cleaning contracts. *The RAND Journal of Economics*, *49*(2), 398–426. https://doi.org/10.1111/1756-2171.12232

Ilius, L. (2004). *Öffentliches Beschaffungsmarketing: Handlungsempfehlungen zur Ziel-, Strategie- und Massnahmenoptimierung in der öffentlich regulierten Beschaffung. Dissertation: Vol. 976*. Berlin: Winter Industries.

Janiszewski, C., & Uy, D. (2008). Precision of the anchor influences the amount of adjustment. *Psychological Science*, *19*(2), 121–127. https://doi.org/10.1111/j.1467-9280.2008.02057.x

Janssen, W. A. (2014). The institutionalised and non-institutionalised exemptions from EU public procurement law: Towards a more coherent approach. *Utrecht L. Rev.*, *10*, 168.

Jap, S. D. (2002). Online Reverse Auctions: Issues, Themes, and Prospects for the Future. *Journal of the Academy of Marketing Science*, *30*(4), 506–525. https://doi.org/10.1177/009207002236925

Jap, S. D. (2003). An Exploratory Study of the Introduction of Online Reverse Auctions. *Journal of Marketing*, *67*(3), 96–107. https://doi.org/10.1509/jmkg.67.3.96.18651

Jasper, U., & Marx, F. (2018). *Vergaberecht: Textausgabe mit Sachverzeichnis und einer Einführung* (20. Aufl., Stand, Feb. 2018). München, München: Deutscher Taschenbuch-Verlag; Beck.

Jensen, M. C. (2002). Value Maximization, Stakeholder Theory, and the Corporate Objective Function. *Business Ethics Quarterly*, *12*(2), 235. https://doi.org/10.2307/3857812

Johnson, P. F., Leenders, M. R., & McCue, C. P. (2003). A comparison of purchasing's organizational roles and responsibilities in the public and private sector. *Journal of Public Procurement*, *3*(1), 57–74. https://doi.org/10.1108/JOPP-03-01-2003-B003

Kagel, J. H., Harstad, R. M., & Levin, D. (1987). Information Impact and Allocation Rules in Auctions with Affiliated Private Values: A Laboratory Study. *Econometrica*, *55*(6), 1275. https://doi.org/10.2307/1913557

Kagel, J. H., & Levin, D. (1986). The Winner's Curse and Public Information in Common Value Auctions. *American Economic Review*, *76*(5), 894–920. https://doi.org/10.1257/aer.89.1.325

Kamins, M. A., Drèze, X., & Folkes, V. S. (2004). Effects of Seller-Supplied Prices on Buyers' Product Evaluations: Reference Prices in an Internet Auction Context. *Journal of Consumer Research*, *30*(4), 622–628. https://doi.org/10.1086/380294

Kaufmann, L., & Carter, C. R. (2004). Deciding on the Mode of Negotiation: To Auction or Not to Auction Electronically. *The Journal of Supply Chain Management*, *40*(2), 15–26. https://doi.org/10.1111/j.1745-493X.2004.tb00166.x

Kelman, S. (2002). Remaking Federal Procurement. *Public Contract Law Journal*, *31*.

Keuth, H. (Ed.). (2013). *Klassiker auslegen: Bd. 12. Karl Popper, Logik der Forschung* (4., bearb. Aufl.). Berlin: Akad.-Verl.

Kim, I.-G. (1998). A model of selective tendering: Does bidding competition deter opportunism by contractors? *The Quarterly Review of Economics and Finance*, *38*(4), 907–925. https://doi.org/10.1016/S1062-9769(99)80139-2

Kolchin, M. G. (1990). *Purchasing in the industrial, institutional, governmental, and retail sectors: A comparative study*: Center for Advanced Purchasing Studies.

Kosilek, F., & Uhr, W. (2002). *Public electronic procurement. Eine empirische Untersuchung. Reihe: Electronic Commerce: Bd. 17*. Lohmar, Köln: Eul.

Kraljic, P. (1983). Purchasing must become supply management. *Harvard Business Review.*, *61*(5), 109–117.

Krishna, V. (2010). *Auction theory* (2nd ed.). Amsterdam: Academic.

Kristensen, H., & Gärling, T. (1997). The Effects of Anchor Points and Reference Points on Negotiation Process and Outcome. *Organizational Behavior and Human Decision Processes*, *71*(1), 85–94. https://doi.org/10.1006/obhd.1997.2713

Kristensen, H., & Gärling, T. (2000). Anchor Points, Reference Points, and Counteroffers in Negotiations. *Group Decision and Negotiation, 9*(6), 493–505. https://doi.org/10.1023/A:1008722223618

Ku, G., Galinsky, A. D., & Murnighan, J. K. (2006). Starting low but ending high: A reversal of the anchoring effect in auctions. *Journal of Personality and Social Psychology, 90*(6), 975–986. https://doi.org/10.1037/0022-3514.90.6.975

Laffont, J.-J., & Tirole, J. (1993). *A theory of incentives in procurement and regulation*. Cambridge, Mass.: MIT Press.

Lalive, R., & Schmutzler, A. (2011). Auctions vs Negotiations in Public Procurement: Which Works Better? *SSRN Electronic Journal*. Advance online publication. https://doi.org/10.2139/ssrn.1919531

Lane, J.-E. (2002). *New public management: An introduction*: Routledge.

Larson, P. D. (2009). Public vs. private sector perspectives on supply chain management. *Journal of Public Procurement, 9*(2), 222–247. https://doi.org/10.1108/JOPP-09-02-2009-B003

Lee, A. J., Loschelder, D. D., Schweinsberg, M., Mason, M. F., & Galinsky, A. D. (2018). Too precise to pursue: How precise first offers create barriers-to-entry in negotiations and markets. *Organizational Behavior and Human Decision Processes, 148*, 87–100. https://doi.org/10.1016/j.obhdp.2018.03.001

Leinemann, R., Ebert, E.-D., & Kirch, T. (Eds.). (2016). *Die Vergabe öffentlicher Aufträge: GWB Vergaberecht, VgV, KonzVgV, SektVO, VSVgV, VOBA, VOLA-Erläuterungen aller Vergabeordnungen-Nachprüfung von Vergabeverfahren-Vergabestrafrecht-Compliance* (6., völlig neu bearbeitete Auflage). Köln: Bundesanzeiger Verlag.

Levin, D., & Smith, J. L. (1994). Equilibrium in Auctions with Entry. *American Economic Review, 84*(3), 585–599.

Lewis, G., & Bajari, P. (2011). Procurement Contracting With Time Incentives: Theory and Evidence *The Quarterly Journal of Economics, 126*(3), 1173–1211. https://doi.org/10.1093/qje/qjr026

Li, H., & Riley, J. G. (2007). Auction choice. *International Journal of Industrial Organization*, *25*(6), 1269–1298. https://doi.org/10.1016/j.ijindorg.2006.10.003

Li, T., & Perrigne, I. (2003). Timber Sale Auctions with Random Reserve Prices. *The Review of Economics and Statistics*, *85*(1), 189–200. https://doi.org/10.1162/003465303762687802

Lin, C.-H., Huang, W.-H., & Zeelenberg, M. (2006). Multiple reference points in investor regret. *Journal of Economic Psychology*, *27*(6), 781–792. https://doi.org/10.1016/j.joep.2006.03.004

Loschelder, D. D., Friese, M., Schaerer, M., & Galinsky, A. D. (2016). The Too-Much-Precision Effect: When and Why Precise Anchors Backfire With Experts. *Psychological Science.* Advance online publication. https://doi.org/10.1177/0956797616666074

Loschelder, D. D., Friese, M., & Trötschel, R. (2017). How and why precise anchors distinctly affect anchor recipients and senders. *Journal of Experimental Social Psychology*, *70*, 164–176. https://doi.org/10.1016/j.jesp.2016.11.001

Loschelder, D. D., Stuppi, J., & Trötschel, R. (2014). "€14,875?!": Precision Boosts the Anchoring Potency of First Offers. *Social Psychological and Personality Science*, *5*(4), 491–499. https://doi.org/10.1177/1948550613499942

Loschelder, D. D., Swaab, R. I., Trötschel, R., & Galinsky, A. D. (2014). The first-mover disadvantage: The folly of revealing compatible preferences. *Psychological Science*, *25*(4), 954–962. https://doi.org/10.1177/0956797613520168

Lucking-Reiley, D., Bryan, D., Prasad, N., & Reeves, D. (2007). Pennies from eBay: The Determinants of Price in Online Auctions. *The Journal of Industrial Economics*, *55*(2), 223–233. https://doi.org/10.1111/j.1467-6451.2007.00309.x

Lukács, E. (2005). The economic role of SMEs in world economy, especially in Europe. *European integration studies*, *4*(1), 3–12.

Lundberg, S., & Bergman, M. A. (2017). Tendering design when price and quality is uncertain. *International Journal of Public Sector Management*, *30*(4), 310–327. https://doi.org/10.1108/IJPSM-04-2016-0063

Maaravi, Y., Ganzach, Y., & Pazy, A. (2011). Negotiation as a form of persuasion: Arguments in first offers. *Journal of Personality and Social Psychology*, *101*(2), 245–255. https://doi.org/10.1037/a0023331

Malhotra, D., & Bazerman, M. H. (2008). Psychological Influence in Negotiation: An Introduction Long Overdue. *Journal of Management*, *34*(3), 509–531. https://doi.org/10.1177/0149206308316060

Manelli, A. M., & Vincent, D. R. (1995). Optimal Procurement Mechanisms. *Econometrica*, *63*(3), 591. https://doi.org/10.2307/2171909

Manso, P. F., & Nikas, A. (2015). Examining the Effects of Post Tender Negotiation in UK's Public Sector Procurements: An Empirical Study. *Procedia Computer Science*, *64*, 457–465. https://doi.org/10.1016/j.procs.2015.08.543

Maskin, E., & Riley, J. G. (2000). Asymmetric Auctions. *The Review of Economic Studies*, *67*(3), 413–438.

Mason, M. F., Lee, A. J., Wiley, E. A., & Ames, D. R. (2013). Precise offers are potent anchors: Conciliatory counteroffers and attributions of knowledge in negotiations. *Journal of Experimental Social Psychology*, *49*(4), 759–763. https://doi.org/10.1016/j.jesp.2013.02.012

McAfee, R. P., & McMillan, J. (1987). Auctions and Bidding. *Journal of Economic Literature*, *25*(2), 699–738. Retrieved from https://www.jstor.org/stable/2726107

McAfee, R. P., & McMillan, J. (1989). Government procurement and international trade. *Journal of International Economics*, *26*(3-4), 291–308. https://doi.org/10.1016/0022-1996(89)90005-6

McCue, C. P. (2000). The Risk-Return Paradox in Local Government Investing. *Public Budgeting & Finance*, *20*(3), 80–101. https://doi.org/10.1111/0275-1100.00021

McCue, C. P., Prier, E., & Swanson, D. (2015). Five dilemmas in public procurement. *Journal of Public Procurement*, *15*(2), 177–207.

Milgrom, P. R. (1979). A Convergence Theorem for Competitive Bidding with Differential Information. *Econometrica*, *47*(3), 679. https://doi.org/10.2307/1910414

Milgrom, P. R., & Weber, R. J. (1982). A Theory of Auctions and Competitive Bidding. *Econometrica, 50*(5), 1089. https://doi.org/10.2307/1911865

Millet, I., Parente, D. H., Fizel, J. L., & Venkataraman, R. R. (2004). Metrics for Managing Online Procurement Auctions. *Interfaces, 34*(3), 171–179. https://doi.org/10.1287/inte.1040.0073

Minchuk, Y., & Mizrahi, S. (2016). The (in) effectiveness of procurement auctions in the public sector. *Applied Economics Letters, 24*(4), 247–249. https://doi.org/10.1080/13504851.2016.1181704

Mithas, S., & Jones, J. L. (2007). Do Auction Parameters Affect Buyer Surplus in E-Auctions for Procurement? *Production and Operations Management, 16*(4), 455–470. https://doi.org/10.1111/j.1937-5956.2007.tb00272.x

Molander, P. (2014). Public procurement in the european union: The case for national threshold values. *Journal of Public Procurement, 14*(2), 181–214. https://doi.org/10.1108/JOPP-14-02-2014-B002

Molenaar, K. R., & Johnson, D. E. (2003). Engineering the Procurement Phase to Achieve Best Value. *Leadership and Management in Engineering, 3*(3), 137–141. https://doi.org/10.1061/(ASCE)1532-6748(2003)3:3(137)

Murray, G. J. (1999). Local government demands more from purchasing. *European Journal of Purchasing & Supply Management, 5*(1), 33–42. https://doi.org/10.1016/S0969-7012(98)00021-5

Murray, G. J. (2009). Improving the validity of public procurement research. *International Journal of Public Sector Management, 22*(2), 91–103. https://doi.org/10.1108/09513550910934501

Neale, M. A. [Margaret Ann], & Lys, T. (2015). *Getting (more of) what you want: How the secrets of economics and psychology can help you negotiate anything, in business and in life*. New York: Basic Books a member of the Perseus Books Group.

Noch, R. (2016). *Vergaberecht kompakt: Handbuch für die Praxis* (7. Auflage). Köln: Werner Verlag.

Northcraft, G. B., & Neale, M. A. [Margaret A.] (1987). Experts, amateurs, and real estate: An anchoring-and-adjustment perspective on property pricing decisions. *Organizational Behavior and Human Decision Processes*, *39*(1), 84–97. https://doi.org/10.1016/0749-5978(87)90046-X

OECD. (2015). *Government at a Glance 2015*: OECD Publishing. https://doi.org/10.1787/gov_glance-2015-en

OECD. (2017). *Government at a Glance 2017*: OECD Publishing. https://doi.org/10.1787/gov_glance-2017-en

Ohashi, H. (2009). Effects of Transparency in Procurement Practices on Government Expenditure: A Case Study of Municipal Public Works. *Review of Industrial Organization*, *34*(3), 267–285. https://doi.org/10.1007/s11151-009-9208-1

Onur, İ., Özcan, R., & Taş, B. K. O. (2012). Public Procurement Auctions and Competition in Turkey. *Review of Industrial Organization*, *40*(3), 207–223. https://doi.org/10.1007/s11151-011-9299-3

Orr, D., & Guthrie, C. (2005). Anchoring, information, expertise, and negotiation: New insights from meta-analysis. *Ohio St. J. on Disp. Resol.*, *21*, 597.

Paarsch, H. J. (1992). Deciding between the common and private value paradigms in empirical models of auctions. *Journal of Econometrics*, *51*(1-2), 191–215. https://doi.org/10.1016/0304-4076(92)90035-P

Parikka-Alhola, K. (2008). Promoting environmentally sound furniture by green public procurement. *Ecological Economics*, *68*(1-2), 472–485. https://doi.org/10.1016/j.ecolecon.2008.05.004

Pavel, J., & Sičáková-Beblavá, E. (2013). Do E-Auctions Realy Improve the Efficiency of Public Procurement?: The Case of the Slovak Municipalities. *Prague Economic Papers*, *22*(1), 111–124. https://doi.org/10.18267/j.pep.443

Pinker, E. J., Seidmann, A., & Vakrat, Y. (2003). Managing Online Auctions: Current Business and Research Issues. *Management Science*, *49*(11), 1457–1484. https://doi.org/10.1287/mnsc.49.11.1457.20584

PwC, London Economics, & Ecorys (2011). Public procurement in Europe: Cost and effectiveness. Retrieved from http://ec.europa.eu/internal_market/publicprocurement/docs/modernising_rules/cost-effectiveness_en.pdf

Ramsay, J. (2001). Purchasing's strategic irrelevance. *European Journal of Purchasing & Supply Management*, *7*(4), 257–263. https://doi.org/10.1016/S0969-7012(01)00007-7

Reiley, D. H. (2006). Field Experiments on the Effects of Reserve Prices in Auctions: More Magic on the Internet. *The RAND Journal of Economics*, *37*(1), 195–211.

Rezende, L. (2009). Biased procurement auctions. *Economic Theory*, *38*(1), 169–185. https://doi.org/10.1007/s00199-008-0346-8

Rose-Ackerman, S. (1999). *Corruption and government: Causes, consequences, and reform / Susan Rose-Ackerman*. Cambridge: Cambridge University Press.

Rosette, A. S., Kopelman, S., & Abbott, J. L. (2014). Good Grief!: Anxiety Sours the Economic Benefits of First Offers. *Group Decision and Negotiation*, *23*(3), 629–647. https://doi.org/10.1007/s10726-013-9348-4

Samuelson, W. F. (1985). Competitive bidding with entry costs. *Economics Letters*, *17*(1-2), 53–57. https://doi.org/10.1016/0165-1765(85)90126-0

Saussier, S., & Tirole, J. (2015). Renforcer l'efficacité de la commande publique. *Notes du conseil d'analyse économique*, *22*(3), 1. https://doi.org/10.3917/ncae.022.0001

Schapper, P. R., Malta, J. N. V., & Gilbert, D. L. (2006). An analytical framework for the management and reform of public procurement. *Journal of Public Procurement*, *6*(1/2), 1.

Schedler, K., & Proeller, I. (2011). *New public management* (5., korrigierte Aufl.). *UTB: Vol. 2132*. Stuttgart: Haupt.

Schmidt, M. (2015). Price Determination in Public Procurement: A Game Theory Approach. *European Financial and Accounting Journal*, *2015*(1). https://doi.org/10.18267/j.efaj.137

Schnabel, M. (2016). *Electronic Reverse Auctions - Zielorientierte Gestaltung auktionsintegrierter Beschaffungsprozesse.* https://doi.org/10.18419/OPUS-8762

Schotanus, F., & Telgen, J. (2007). Developing a typology of organisational forms of cooperative purchasing. *Journal of Purchasing and Supply Management, 13*(1), 53–68. https://doi.org/10.1016/j.pursup.2007.03.002

Schwartz, J. I. (Ed.) 2010. *Procurement as a Tool for Economic Stimulus: The United States' Experience, 2008-2010.*

Schweinsberg, M., Ku, G., Wang, C. S., & Pillutla, M. M. (2012). Starting high and ending with nothing: The role of anchors and power in negotiations. *Journal of Experimental Social Psychology, 48*(1), 226–231. https://doi.org/10.1016/j.jesp.2011.07.005

Shalvi, S., Moran, S., & Ritov, I. (2010). Overcoming Initial Anchors: The Effect of Negotiators' Dispositional Control Beliefs. *Negotiation and Conflict Management Research, 3*(3), 232–248. https://doi.org/10.1111/j.1750-4716.2010.00059.x

Shepherd, W. G., & Shepherd, J. M. (2004). *The economics of industrial organization* (5th ed.). Long Grove Ill.: Waveland Press.

Sheppard, S. (1999). Hedonic analysis of housing markets. In *Handbook of Regional and Urban Economics. Applied Urban Economics* (Vol. 3, pp. 1595–1635). Elsevier. https://doi.org/10.1016/S1574-0080(99)80010-8

Silberston, A. (1972). Economies of Scale in Theory and Practice. *The Economic Journal, 82*(325), 369. https://doi.org/10.2307/2229943

Silva, D. G. de, Dunne, T., Kankanamge, A., & Kosmopoulou, G. (2008). The impact of public information on bidding in highway procurement auctions. *European Economic Review, 52*(1), 150–181. https://doi.org/10.1016/j.euroecorev.2007.07.003

Silva, D. G. de, Kosmopoulou, G., & Lamarche, C. (2009). The effect of information on the bidding and survival of entrants in procurement auctions. *Journal of Public Economics, 93*(1-2), 56–72. https://doi.org/10.1016/j.jpubeco.2008.05.001

Søreide, T. (2004). Corruption in international business transactions: The perspective of Norwegian firms. Retrieved from https://brage.bibsys.no/xmlui/bitstream/11250/2436108/2/Report%20R%202004-10.pdf

Soudek, J., & Skuhro, J. (2013). *Public procurement of homogeneous goods: The Czech Republic case study* (IES Working Paper No. 05/2013).

Spagnolo, G. (2012). Reputation, competition, and entry in procurement. *International Journal of Industrial Organization, 30*(3), 291–296. https://doi.org/10.1016/j.ijindorg.2012.01.001

Spina, G., Caniato, F., Luzzini, D., & Ronchi, S. (2013). Past, present and future trends of purchasing and supply management: An extensive literature review. *Industrial Marketing Management, 42*(8), 1202–1212. https://doi.org/10.1016/j.indmarman.2013.04.001

Strack, F., & Mussweiler, T. (1997). Explaining the enigmatic anchoring effect: Mechanisms of selective accessibility. *Journal of Personality and Social Psychology, 73*(3), 437–446. https://doi.org/10.1037/0022-3514.73.3.437

Subramanian, G. (2009). Negotiation? Auction? A Deal Maker's Guide. *Harvard business review, 87*(12), 101–107.

Tadelis, S. (2012). Public procurement design: Lessons from the private sector. *International Journal of Industrial Organization, 30*(3), 297–302. https://doi.org/10.1016/j.ijindorg.2012.02.002

Tas, B. K. O. (2014). *How to Achieve Efficiency in Public Procurement Auctions.*

Tassabehji, R., & Moorhouse, A. (2008). The changing role of procurement: Developing professional effectiveness. *Journal of Purchasing and Supply Management, 14*(1), 55–68. https://doi.org/10.1016/j.pursup.2008.01.005

Telgen, J., Harland, C., & Knight, L. (2007). Public procurement in perspective. In L. Knight (Ed.), *Public procurement: International cases and commentary / edited by Louise Knight ... [et al.]* (pp. 16–24). London: Routledge.

Telles, P., & Butler, L. (2014). Public Procurement Award Procedures in Directive 2014/24/EU.

Thai, K. V. (2001). Public procurement re-examined. *Journal of Public Procurement, 1*(1), 9.

Thai, K. V. (Ed.). (2008). *International handbook of public procurement*: CRC Press.

Thai, K. V. (Ed.). (2017a). *Global Public Procurement Theories and Practices*. Cham: Springer International Publishing. https://doi.org/10.1007/978-3-319-49280-3

Thai, K. V. (2017b). Global Public Procurement Theories and Practices: An Introduction. In K. V. Thai (Ed.), *Global Public Procurement Theories and Practices* (pp. 1–14). Cham: Springer International Publishing. https://doi.org/10.1007/978-3-319-49280-3_1

Thomas, M., & Park, J. (2013). The Precision Effect: How Numerical Precision Influences Everyday Judgments. *SSRN Electronic Journal*. Advance online publication. https://doi.org/10.2139/ssrn.2229833

Thomas, M., Simon, D. H., & Kadiyali, V. (2010). The Price Precision Effect: Evidence from Laboratory and Market Data. *Marketing Science*, *29*(1), 175–190. https://doi.org/10.1287/mksc.1090.0512

Thompson, L. L. (2015). *The mind and heart of the negotiator*. Boston: Pearson.

Tirole, J. (2009). Cognition and Incomplete Contracts. *American Economic Review*, *99*(1), 265–294. https://doi.org/10.1257/aer.99.1.265

Topp-Blatt, B. (2008). *Die Verfahren zur Vergabe öffentlicher Aufträge: Unter besonderer Berücksichtigung des wettbewerblichen Dialogs* (1., Auflage). *Praxis und Theorie des Bau- und Immobilienrechts: Vol. 9*. Berlin: Lexxion Verlagsgesellschaft.

Tran, A. (2010). Which regulations reduce corruption? Evidence from the internal records of a bribe-paying firm. *Journal of Development Economics*.

Trautmann, S. T., & Traxler, C. (2010). Reserve prices as reference points – Evidence from auctions for football players at Hattrick.org. *Journal of Economic Psychology*, *31*(2), 230–240. https://doi.org/10.1016/j.joep.2009.08.004

Tversky, A., & Kahneman, D. (1974). Judgment under Uncertainty: Heuristics and Biases. *Science (New York, N.Y.)*, *185*(4157), 1124–1131. https://doi.org/10.1126/science.185.4157.1124

Uyarra, E., & Flanagan, K. (2010). Understanding the Innovation Impacts of Public Procurement. *European Planning Studies*, *18*(1), 123–143. https://doi.org/10.1080/09654310903343567

Vaidya, K., Sajeev, A. S. M., & Callender, G. (2006). Critical factors that influence e-procurement implementation success in the public sector. *Journal of Public Procurement*, *6*(1/2), 70–99. https://doi.org/10.1108/JOPP-06-01-02-2006-B004

Van Poucke, D., & Buelens, M. (2002). Predicting the outcome of a two-party price negotiation: Contribution of reservation price, aspiration price and opening offer. *Journal of Economic Psychology*, *23*(1), 67–76. https://doi.org/10.1016/S0167-4870(01)00068-X

Van Weele, A. J. (2014). *Purchasing & supply chain management: Analysis, strategy, planning and practice / Arjan J. van Weele* (6th edition). Andover: Cengage Learning.

Van Weele, A. J., & Eßig, M. (2017). *Strategische Beschaffung: Grundlagen, Planung und Umsetzung eines integrierten Supply Management.* https://doi.org/10.1007/978-3-658-08491-2

Voeth, M., & Herbst, U. (2015). Preisverhandlungen. In K. Backhaus & M. Voeth (Eds.), *Handbuch Business-to-Business-Marketing: Grundlagen, Geschäftsmodelle, Instrumente des Industriegütermarketing* (2nd ed., pp. 537–556). Wiesbaden: Springer Gabler. https://doi.org/10.1007/978-3-8349-4681-2_26

Waara, F., & Bröchner, J. (2006). Price and Nonprice Criteria for Contractor Selection. *Journal of Construction Engineering and Management*, *132*(8), 797–804. https://doi.org/10.1061/(ASCE)0733-9364(2006)132:8(797)

Wang, S., & Bunn, M. D. (2004). Government/business relationships: Insights into contract implementation. *Journal of Public Procurement*, *4*(1), 84.

Wilson, T. D., Houston, C. E., Etling, K. M., & Brekke, N. (1996). A new look at anchoring effects: Basic anchoring and its antecedents. *Journal of Experimental Psychology: General*, *125*(4), 387–402. https://doi.org/10.1037/0096-3445.125.4.387

Wong, C. H., Holt, G. D., & Harris, P. (2001). Multi-criteria selection or lowest price?: Investigation of UK construction clients' tender evaluation preferences. *Engineering, Construction and Architectural Management*, *8*(4), 257–271. https://doi.org/10.1108/eb021187

World Bank Group. (2016). *Benchmarking Public Procurement 2016: Assessing Public Procurement Systems in 77 Economies*. Washington, DC. https://doi.org/10.1596/978-4648-0276-8

Yan, D., & Pena-Marin, J. (2017). Round Off the Bargaining: The Effects of Offer Roundness on Willingness to Accept. *Journal of Consumer Research*, *44*(2), 381–395. https://doi.org/10.1093/jcr/ucx046

Yip, J. A., & Schweinsberg, M. (2017). Infuriating Impasses. *Social Psychological and Personality Science*, *8*(6), 706–714. https://doi.org/10.1177/1948550616683021

Printed by Printforce, the Netherlands